The Sense of Music

THE SENSE OF MUSIC

BY VICTOR ZUCKERKANDL

PRINCETON UNIVERSITY PRESS

PRINCETON, NEW JERSEY

Publication of this book has been aided
by the Ford Foundation program to support publication,
through university presses,
of works in the humanities and social sciences.

The Library of Congress Catalog Card Number 57-8670
ISBN 0-691-02700-5 (paperback edn.)
ISBN 0-691-09102-1 (hardcover edn.)

Corrected Edition, with index, 1971

Preface

The approach to music set forth in this book was originally developed in response to the demands of a concrete environment. St. John's College in Annapolis, the Great Books College, as it is also called, conceives of a liberally educated person as one who is clearly aware of the continuity of Western tradition and conscious of the spiritual forces that over a period of two and a half millenia have created and shaped this tradition and, ultimately, himself. Liberal education today, in the view of this college, consists of the study and intelligent discussion of the books in which this spirit has found its principal embodiment. Most of these books, an unbroken chain reaching from the early Greeks down to our own day, have been written in words; some, in numbers and figures; some, in tones. With music so essential and characteristic an element of Western tradition, it follows that among the books read and discussed there should be musical scores.

No intelligent discussion of a musical score is possible without some knowledge of music. Most liberal arts students do not possess this knowledge. So they must acquire it. Where will they find it?

Experience has shown what could have been anticipated: the academic disciplines of music theory and music history are not the answer. They provide the prerequisites for the making of music and for scholarly research; they lead to a discussion that is technical and professional. They are not geared to encourage a discussion of music among those for whose sake music ultimately exists: the nonprofessionals, the listeners.

The liberal arts student, at St. John's as anywhere else, is in this category. His fundamental relationship to music is that of the listener. He has little use for knowledge that would enable him to discuss music professionally. The alternative offered occasionally, under the name of music appreciation, a mixture of diluted professional discipline, factual information, and informal talk on many things connected in many ways with music, will not satisfy him either. What he needs is a study of music equally apart from the professionalism of the academic disciplines and the superficiality of music appreciation, oriented directly and exclusively at the intellectual requirements of his situation.

The classroom problem is a reflection on a smaller scale of a problem of the community as a whole. We all have become listeners today: the long-playing record, radio, and television have transformed the whole community into one vast musical audience. Most people want to think about, to talk about their significant new experiences. So they are in need of some basic knowledge that would provide the necessary framework for thought and communication. Many books have been written for that purpose. Insofar as they follow—as most of them do—the lines of the professional disciplines or of music appreciation they do not have the real answers. A void is created, an active void that wants to be filled.

The present book sets out to move right into that void. It addresses itself to the alert mind that is not satisfied with musical experience in the raw—blind experience, as it were—that wants to see clearer, to understand better; to music students who feel that their studies do not really answer, do not fully measure up to the questions the contact with music has stirred up in their minds; to music teachers in search of new approaches to their subject. Although it is certainly not a textbook, a course could easily be organized using it as a basis. Each of its main sections could serve as a starting point for further development; nowhere is it finished. If it has merit, it should prove itself by setting things in motion rather than by bringing them to rest.

The relation of this study to the traditional disciplines is both positive and negative. Insofar as it shares with them certain basic concepts and makes use of their terminology, they provide its foundation. But the course it pursues from the outset turns away quite radically from any of the directions they follow. References to and discussions of specific works from the fields of musical theory and history seemed out of place in this context. The reader who is told at the beginning that these disciplines cannot do justice to the problems of his situation might even find such references illogical.

Yet one name must be cited. The doctrine of *Heinrich Schenker,* whose understanding of the inner workings of a tonal organism and of the laws that govern it marks an epoch in musical history, has been a guiding light throughout this investigation. It is an active presence everywhere, mostly under the surface, occasionally—as in the distinction of "foreground" and "background" or in the symbols for dynamic tone qualities (though not in the concept of dynamic tone quality itself)—also above the surface. The ultimate authority, however, remains music itself. Whatever is said in this book will be proved right or wrong not by agreement or disagreement with one theory or another but by agreement or disagreement with the facts of the musical experience.

What the reader ought to bring to this book, apart from intellectual curiosity, is some acquaintance with musical notation and a little practice with an instrument so that the printed symbols of the simpler examples can be transformed more or less faithfully into sound. Throughout the book the closest connection is maintained between words and tones; there is hardly a sentence that does not refer to some sound, that does not need some representation of the sound to make sense. People with a little practice in choral singing may be capable of imagining the sounds, which should work just as well. Some of the examples in the later sections are more complex and extensive; the sound in these instances, except when the reader is an expert pianist and score reader, will have to be provided by records. The works from which these examples are taken have all been recorded. The scores are included in the book.

Contents

The Sense of Music

Introduction

A meeting of man and music such as has never occurred before is taking place among us. Hitherto music, except for its popular branch, has always been considered a kind of restricted domain, accessible to those few only who by special talent or education were privileged to understand its message. Suddenly Mozart, Bach, Beethoven, Vivaldi, Stravinsky are everywhere—and not just because someone did not care to turn off a knob. The sale of so-called classical records has assumed proportions nobody would have believed possible a few years ago. This is not to say that now workers are rushing home in masses from the factories, and farmers from the fields, to catch a broadcast of the *Art of the Fugue*. It is to say that the fence around music is dissolving, that music reaches out everywhere for minds open and eager to listen, and that it finds such minds everywhere, not just among the members of a privileged elite dwelling in a secluded area.

For the meeting with music on a broad front people are on the whole utterly unprepared. What they meet is one of the most highly developed, most intricately organized, must subtly constructed creations of the human mind, the result of centuries of work carried on with utmost devotion by men of highest genius. And it comes to them all at once, one accumulated mass, in one shock. Nothing in their background and schooling has prepared them for the experience. They are dumped without warning, as it were, out of the void into the midst of a bewildering world of sounds, and supposed to find their way in it.

3

One might well ask: Why is preparation necessary? The very response we are talking about seems to indicate it is not. If music can take hold of minds whether they are prepared for it or not, why worry about preparation?

One cannot insist too strongly on the truth of the assertion that the experience of great music does not presuppose a special gift or special learning. This is precisely the unique thing about music: it speaks a language that is understood without learning, understood by everyone, not just by the so-called musical people. If this were not so, folk music would not be the universal phenomenon it is. Fundamentally, Bach and Beethoven speak no other language than the folk song. The recent developments should once and for all prove wrong the old contention that acted as a main brace for the fence, namely, that in the absence of a particular and rare inborn talent the *study* of music is a prerequisite of the understanding of music. Many a person has felt the full impact of a great work of the tonal art and been moved by it from bottom to top at the first meeting. If there had not been some understanding, some communication, he would not have felt the impact, he would not have been so moved.

This does not dispose of preparation, though. An experience is an isolated moment, life is a continuity. For music to come to life in a mind, experience must somehow connect with experience, one musical experience with another, musical experiences with experiences of different kinds, the whole thing must develop, must grow in scope and in depth. Exposing oneself again and again to musical sounds just is not enough. Perhaps the proper place for preparation in this case is *after* the experience; perhaps preparation is the wrong word, and one should rather call it a cultivation, a taking care of seeds planted. The seeds *are* planted; one has to attend to the growing.

The more alive mentally a person is, the less will he have to be told these things. He does not forget music every time the last tone of a composition has sounded; the excitement of the experience continues to reverberate, there is something completely out of the ordinary about it, reminiscent of nothing, in fact, incomprehensible. It moves the mind to wonder, to think, to question. To assign a definite meaning to music is as impossible as to deny that it is supremely meaningful. With time and repetition the sense of its importance grows, and with it the desire to come closer to it in a rational, a communicable way, to understand it better, in short, to *know*.

In the case of music the desire to know meets a curious obstacle. There is current among people an opinion, or rather a superstition, that a deadly antagonism exists between music and knowledge, that the light of thought turned on the musical experience must destroy it or at least so severely damage it that it could no longer be enjoyed as before. As if music were some sort of plant that flourishes in the dark only. Music, they say, is something to be felt, not known. Now music is neither something to be felt nor something to be known but something to be heard. Clearly, the more I hear the more will I feel; and the more I know the better will I hear. It is, of course, true that knowing cannot substitute for hearing, and that if I am not capable of forgetting about knowing the moment I begin to hear, I will not hear much and consequently not feel much either. But the right kind of knowledge, rightly applied, cannot but strengthen and deepen musical experience.

Still that superstition is not totally without foundation. What is the right kind of knowledge?

The whole of our knowledge of music is today contained in two large bodies, one concerned with the theoretical, the other with the historical aspect. The first consists mainly of the old and venerable discipline of counterpoint and the less old and less venerable doctrine of harmony; its purpose is the demonstration of the rules that must be observed in the handling of tonal material, and the development of the necessary skills of the art. The other, the history, deals with music as an event in time and place, emerging and changing; it investigates the nature and significance of these changes. Apart from establishing factual correctness in regard to the place and time of musical events its main problem is that of style. All this is strictly professional knowledge, assembled over the centuries by the music scholars of Europe and applied to the training of successive generations of professional musicians and music scholars, who as students absorbed it in the professional environment of the European universities and conservatories of music. The whole of Europe, until recent years, knew of no other music education than the professional; it needed no other. With music the exclusive concern of an elite whose members grew up with it as a part of their social environment and got to know it thoroughly in the course of the routine of their lives, education had no other task than the training of the professionals. Obviously the knowledge assembled in the traditional academic disciplines was the right kind of knowledge for the purpose. Can one expect it to be at the same time the right kind of knowledge for the very different purpose outlined above; namely, to build a bridge of understanding between music and its new audience?

A hundred years ago Harvard became the first American university to include the study of music in its curriculum. From the outset the new department was planned for the purpose not of training musicians but rather of getting nonmusicians, liberal arts students, intellectually in close contact with music. This was an entirely new venture in the academic field, and decidedly an American venture, prompted by the different relationship between music and society in this country. Not that a cultural elite similar to the European and capable of sustaining

6

musical life did not exist here; but while in Europe the situation was temporarily stable, here it was not. It seems that in the American democracy music, like any other manifestation of cultural life, can really take root and prosper only if it is ultimately supported by the community as a whole. With considerable foresight the new music department at Harvard was warned very early not to copy its European counterparts: rather than focus its work on the interests of those who later would be the actors on the stage of musical life it should recognize its paramount responsibility towards those who later would make up the musical audiences.

Of course, it was much easier to give such advice than to follow it. To teach means to impart the knowledge available at the time. The only knowledge available was that assembled by the European scholars in the course of their professional pursuits. If this was the right kind of knowledge for the people on the stage, it could hardly also be the right kind of knowledge for the people on the other side of the curtain. The questions that preoccupy the actors who perform a play are not the questions the play performed raises in the spectator's mind. One answer cannot possibly be meaningful to both actor and spectator. Still, education cannot wait for some new kind of knowledge to be discovered. It must go on, working as best it can with what is at hand. This is what it did, trying first the theoretical approach, then the historical, then the dead-end road of appreciation, returning to the former approaches, restricting here, modifying there, compromising, changing emphases, hoping with all this to accomplish the impossible: to bend strict disciplines, shaped to satisfy specific demands, so as to make them serve entirely different needs.

The hundred years since the beginning at Harvard have seen unparalleled expansion of music in the nation, music in the schools and colleges, music in adult education. If one surveys the pertinent literature of that period one is struck by the uniform recurrence through this whole development of the same refrain: do not train professionals, educate listeners. The note that was sounded at the beginning has never abated—a sure sign that what it called for was not accomplished. Today, as ever, the only knowledge of music available, and worth the name, is that incorporated in the professional disciplines. Gradually the attitude has been adopted that there just is no other way to know music. So even today, whether as teachers in classrooms, as lecturers on platforms, as authors of books "for the layman" —the very word smacks of the old fence—we still take our stand among the people on the stage, talking to the spectators of the things that concern the actors, giving them as much professional information as we think they can absorb, mixing in some incidental intelligence, taking for granted all the while that this is what they want to get: a look behind the curtain, a glimpse of the goings on on the stage—discarding the possibility that their problems may be of an altogether different nature, that by doing what we are doing we answer questions they would not ask and leave unanswered those they would ask. If they are dissatisfied and insist that all this knowledge seems marginal and even extraneous to music as they know it from their experience, they may in return be lectured on the virtue of intellectual humility: Precisely because music is what it is, the miracle, knowledge can never do more than touch its surface. The rest must always remain a mystery. One cannot explain a miracle or rationalize a mystery. There just are no answers to questions that would probe beyond the surface—not because our knowledge is deficient but because the questions are not legitimate. This is supposed to close the chapter.

Such are the foundations supporting the superstition mentioned before, namely, that experience of music and knowledge of music are essentially in conflict with one another and lead in opposite directions.

The present book wants to reopen the whole case. It denies emphatically that the way musicians and music scholars *know* music today, the way of the traditional disciplines of music theory and music history, is the *only* way or the *best* way to know music. It believes in the complete validity and legitimacy of the listener's questions, inarticulate though they may mostly be: it is difficult to articulate questions in the state of ignorance. If our knowledge so far has failed even to articulate, much less to answer these questions, one must not blame the questioner but go out and search for more and better knowledge. The result may even prove useful on the other side of the superficial division separating professionals and laymen: after all, before music we are all listeners first—a truth that musicians and music scholars are only too apt sometimes to forget.

It is in a search, then, the search for a listener's knowledge of music, that this book will engage the reader. It takes its stand definitely among the audience, not on the stage. Its starting point is the point where tones meet a listener's mind. Here the first and decisive problems arise: How do tones come to life in a listener's mind? What is it that binds tones together and us to them, what gives them significance? What are the forces by which they act on each other and all together on the listener, forming ever more complex wholes from elementary particles and involving the listener in an ever more intense participation? The only way to answer such questions responsibly is by a careful investigation of the tonal events themselves. No one need fear that such an investigation will violate the mystery and do away with the miracle. Music is not a fata morgana and not a fake that it should dissolve before knowledge. On the contrary, the true miracle will appear the more miraculous the closer our knowledge can approach it. There is no doubt that we *can* come closer than we do now, that between the known surface of music and the central mystery there lies a vast area of potential knowledge as yet largely unexplored, a great chal-

9

lenge to thought, a promise of high reward. Our elementary inquiry will certainly not penetrate very far into this area. But if an opening can be made, and a few sound steps taken, proof will have been given that there *is* solid ground to tread on paths other than the traditional ones, and that it is not necessarily futile to push the search for a knowledge of music beyond its rather narrow present day limitations.

I ✦ Melody

I play Beethoven's Bagatelle in A minor, Opus 112, No. 9. Instead of ending as I should

with 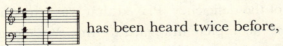, I play and stop.

The first instinctive reaction of the listeners will be: Why did you not finish? This is not the end. Something is missing here.

I would ask: How do you know I did not finish? Probably you do not know the piece, have not heard it before? Those who have picked up some knowledge of harmony may try the answer: You have suppressed the tonic chord—using a technical term to cover a genuine problem. Those who lack the vocabulary will try to find some kind of pattern established by the piece itself and which my way to end it would have left unfinished. They may actually find one:

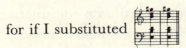 has been heard twice before,

and my failure to restate this correctly at the end might possibly have caused the feeling of incompleteness. This argument cannot be valid, however;

for if I substituted

for the correct version all the way through, no pattern would be broken at the end, yet the feeling of incompleteness would

11

remain the same. At this point it does not seem possible to say more than that it just sounds incomplete.

We can say more, though. A person who knows no German cannot possibly tell whether the words "Heute habe ich mit zwei Freunden" represent a complete or incomplete statement. In order to make the distinction one must understand the language. A sentence is complete or incomplete not with reference to its sound but with reference to its meaning. Accordingly, if in our response to a musical statement (a sequence of tones) we distinguish completeness or incompleteness, this demonstrates two things: one, that the tones must have some sort of meaning, some meaningful context in reference to which their sequence may appear complete or incomplete; and, two, that in some instinctive way we understand the tonal language—that is, all of us, not just those that have learned it from a teacher.

Next, the conditions of the little experiment are changed;

I play this ending: 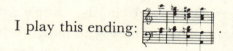 .

The reaction will again be: incomplete, something is missing. This time, however, it will be possible to be more specific about the nature of the deficiency. Played that way, the thing appears *too short*. It is incomplete in regard to time. We recognize a certain time pattern, a pattern of beats, set up in the course of the piece and which my playing left incomplete at the end. The correct ending shows the pattern completed.

In these two experiments we have met the two factors, elements, or forces whose intimate conjunction generates music: tone and time. We have met them in action, and we have noted a certain kinship in their actions insofar as both make themselves felt in a similar manner, through experiences of completeness and incompleteness. In music, the two are practically never separated. In this study, however, we make an artificial separation and investigate them one at a time. We begin with tone.

Tone and Pitch

Al - le - lu - jah, Al - le - lu - jah, Praise be to God, Sing out with heart and voice all people living, For God's dear Son Salvation's won, For evermore to him be praise unceas - ing.

This is an old hymn tune: a melody—a sequence of tones arranged in a certain order.

Every important word in this statement stands for a problem. What is a melody? What is this order of successive tones? What is a tone itself?

We take up the last question first. If someone asks, for instance, What is a circle?—we can tell him in so many words; we can produce an exact verbal equivalent for the thing "circle," and he who understands our words *knows* what a circle is. In other words, we can *define* circle. But we cannot define tone. To the question, What is a tone?—there is no answer except to produce one. There is no verbal equivalent for the thing "tone"; and the only way to know what a tone is, is to hear one.

If we cannot define a tone, we can still define the physical cause of a tone sensation. It is the vibration of air, which stimulates the auditory organs. The vibration is in turn caused by some vibrating body—a string, a glass, a metal plate—or by the vibrating air column inside a pipe, as with wind instruments.

We can furthermore distinguish a number of different qualities that belong to every tone sensation. Psychology identifies five such qualities. They are: pitch, loudness, duration, tone color, and volume. Loudness and duration require no explanation. Tone color, or timbre, is the quality that distinguishes a tone played on a flute from the same tone played on a trumpet. Volume is the quality by virtue of which a tone seems to fill up space. It is not an independent variable but rather a function of pitch and loudness; a loud, low tone seems more voluminous than a high and soft one.

By far the most important of these five qualities is pitch. In everyday language, "two different tones" means two tones of different pitch.

Like tone itself, pitch cannot be defined. The only way to know what it is, is to hear two different tones. Pitch is the quality to which we refer when we call one of the tones higher, the other lower. Pitch difference is the difference that we express in the words "higher" and "lower."

Taken literally, these two words indicate a spatial relation. Do we mean to say that there is actually a spatial element involved in the difference of pitches, comparable to the steps of a ladder; or are we using the words "high" and "low" here merely in a metaphorical sense, as when we talk about high and low temperatures, although no temperature is actually higher or lower than another, only the marks on the ordinary thermometer scale are?

At first sight it seems that the terms are used in the latter sense, metaphorically. No tone is actually higher or lower than another tone; only the symbols of our musical notation are placed higher or lower on the staff. Also, different languages do not agree in their choice of terms denoting pitch difference. The Greeks, for instance, used the words "sharp" and "heavy." In English, too, the words "sharp" and "flat" are sometimes used as synonyms for high and low. If we were taught from childhood to distinguish between "light" and "dark" tones we would accept it without feeling any discrepancy between these words and the tone qualities indicated. (But we could not possibly say that the eleventh step of a ladder is "sharper" or "lighter" than the tenth.)

On the other hand, there is something very real about the "ascending" and "descending" movement of a melody, about the "high" and "low" location of tones, particularly at the extreme range. The psychologist Géza Révesz, who studied the nature of the enjoyment deaf people get from exposing themselves to music, found it to be based on delicate sensations of vibration, which are felt to be located in higher or lower parts of the body according to the pitch differences between the tones played. There is enough evidence to support the thesis that an element of actual spatiality is involved in the relation between pitches.

The books and scientific papers dealing with this question would fill a good-sized library shelf. We mention the matter here to indicate the presence of a significant problem. In our conventional classification of the arts as spatial or temporal, music always figures as the foremost instance of a nonspatial, purely temporal art. This distinction may be in need of drastic revision.

If we cannot define pitch, we can again, as in the case of tone, define its physical cause. The pitch of a tone depends on the frequency of the vibrations, that is, the number of vibrations per second. The greater that number, the higher the tone. The upper limit, beyond which the human ear does not respond, lies at a frequency of about 20,000; the lower limit is roughly 16 vibrations per second.

Other circumstances being equal, the frequency in turn depends on the length of the vibrating body or air column. The longer the vibrating body (e.g. a string) or air column, the slower the vibration and the lower the tone.

Here, then, we see how tones get related to numbers: either by counting frequencies or by measuring string lengths. The latter was the practice with the Ancients, the former is our practice. The results, however, are the same in either case. Nature has conveniently arranged things in such a way that, for instance, if a string measures exactly one third of another, the frequency of its vibration will be exactly three times that of the other. The ratio in either case is 1:3, with the only difference that if the numbers stand for frequencies the greater number represents the higher tone, while if they stand for string lengths it is the other way around: the greater number indicates the longer string, the lower tone. We shall deal with the problem of tone and number more extensively in a later context.

Selection of Tones

So much about tones as such. What about their order as exhibited in the hymn tune?

We observe what goes on. At first there is an ascending sequence that touches three different tones. After this, the direction is reversed. The 4th and 5th tones, which are touched on the way down, are the same as the 2nd and 1st, respectively. (It is by no means self-evident that this should be so.)

The 6th tone is new; so is the 7th. The 8th is the same as the 3rd, and for the rest of the tune no other new tones will appear.

Theoretically the number of possible tones within the limits of our perceptive faculty is infinite. From an infinite number of possible tones our hymn tune has selected precisely five to serve as its tonal material.

The way of this hymn tune is the way of music in general. From a theoretical infinity of possible choices music selects a strictly limited number of tones to serve as the material for all its structures. The validity of this sweeping generalization will appear as we proceed.

As it stands here, this statement seems open to immediate challenge. Suppose we sing the hymn tune twice, the second time beginning a little higher or a little lower. The tones will then all be different; yet it will still be the same old hymn tune. Strictly speaking it cannot be true that this tune selects five tones that make up its material, as it is possible to build the same tune from a different set of five tones. It is not at all easy to understand how this can happen: how the whole—the tune —can be the same although all of its parts have been changed. (A new psychological theory, the so-called *Gestalt* theory, has sprung precisely from the observation of this musical phenomenon.) There seems only one way to explain it: What matters in a tune is not the tones as such but the relations between tone and tone. Whatever the tones are, as long as these relations remain the same, the tune itself will be the same. It was therefore not quite correct to say that a tune selects a number of tones; what it actually selects are tone relations. Its order is an order of tone relations rather than of tones.

The same is true of music in general. When we say that music selects a definite set of tones for its material, this selection does not fix the exact pitch of the tones; but it does fix the relations between the tones. It selects not tones but an *order* of tones.

The term "music" as used in the last paragraph stands for a concept, an abstract thing. Concretely, "music" exists no more than "language." What actually exists is not "language" but specific languages, not "music" but specific musics. By and large, language boundaries follow national boundaries, music boundaries follow the boundaries of civilizations. We have Western music, Chinese music, East Indian music, Islamic music, and so on.

The basic feature that distinguishes one music from another is the selection of its tonal material. Each music makes its own selection of tones or, to be precise, of tone relations; it selects a specific order of tones. This selection constitutes the tonal system of that particular music. Some civilizations have more than one tonal system, more than one kind of music. Western music for the last 2,500 years has been thriving on one selection, one tonal system. Lately (that is, during the last 100 years or so) a new

17

selection is gradually emerging. Whether this indicates growth or decay is still a matter for debate. In any event, it is an unavoidable development, and it unavoidably creates strife, perplexity, and dismay.

The barriers between music and music are far more impassable than language barriers. We can translate from any language into any other language; yet the mere idea of translating, say, Chinese music into the Western tonal idiom is obvious nonsense. We can take a course and learn the Chinese language; but we must actually live with Chinese music and to a certain extent become Chinese if we want to understand the Chinese tonal language. The favorite quotation about music as the universal language of mankind only betrays a naive tendency on our part to think of ourselves, the representatives of Western civilization, as representing all of mankind.

Dynamic Quality

In talking of our hymn we have used the words *tune, melody.* What is a tune, or melody? What distinguishes a melody from a random succession of tones? Is it the fact of selection, of order? Is it correct to define melody as a succession of tones belonging to a certain order?

There is no composition of Western music, no matter for what instruments or voices it has been written, that cannot be played on a piano. In the white and black keys of the piano keyboard we have at our disposal the full set of tones from which the musical compositions of our civilization have been constructed. Yet a cat walking across a keyboard does not necessarily produce a melody. The fact that the successively sounding tones all belong to the tonal order of our music does not guarantee that the tone sequence is a melody.

We experiment with our hymn tune. We play or sing the tune from the beginning, but instead of ending ♪ we try this: ♪.

This reminds us of our first experiment with the Beethoven Bagatelle. The normal reaction of the listener will be: No! This is no ending. It is incomplete. It sounds like an unfinished sentence. It leaves us with an acute expectancy of something more to come, something that would complete the statement.

This time we look closer to see what makes us react that way. It is a certain quality or property of the tone ♪, the last tone of the melody in the changed version: something we sense in the tone, a state of unrest, a tension, an urge, almost a will to move on, as if a force were acting on the tone and pulling it in a certain direction. We shall call this quality of the tone its *dynamic quality*.

If we compare this to the behavior of our original closing tone, ♪, as it appeared at the end of the tune, we shall notice a marked difference. While the other tone, ♪, seemed to point towards something beyond itself, this one, ♪, seems exactly the thing towards which the other was pointing. While the first created expectancy, this one satisfies it; while the first appeared in a state of unrest, of tension, lacking balance, this one appears fully at rest, self-satisfied, perfectly balanced. It is this difference of dynamic quality that makes ♪ fit, ♪ unfit, to serve as the closing tone of our tune.

The dynamic quality of a tone is part of the immediate tone sensation. We *hear* it just as we hear pitch or tone color—but not under all circumstances. A tone must belong to a musical context in order to have dynamic quality. Within a musical context no tone will be without its proper dynamic quality. Outside the musical context, however—for instance, in the laboratory—tones have no dynamic qualities. Thus, the dynamic quality of a tone is its musical quality proper. It distinguishes the musical from the physical phenomenon.

$$\hat{1} \quad \hat{2} \quad \hat{3} \quad \hat{4} \quad \hat{5}$$

We proceed to experiment with the dynamic qualities of the five tones appearing in our tune. To do this, we bring each tone in a position where it has a chance to reveal its dynamic quality clearly and fully to the ear. Best suited to this purpose is always the position at the end of a melodic phrase. We change the ending of the tune accordingly, trying this ♪, or this ♪, or this ♪. (It is essential in these experiments that the tune always be played from the beginning; if the whole is not heard, the result may be inconclusive.) What do we hear? What does the tone at the end tell us about its dynamic state, its tendency?

What we hear is this: The tone ♪ is very much like ♪ in its lack of balance, its tendency to move on, except that the tone towards which it is leaning and where it wants to move to is not ♪ but ♪. (This we find out by comparing the two endings ♪ and ♪.) The tone ♪ shows a sort of mixed state. Compared to ♪ or ♪ it appears better balanced, more at rest; yet if we compare it to ♪, we immediately realize that its balance is by no means perfect; there is, so to speak, an inner tension left in the tone, and if we try other tones to find out where this tension is directed, ♪ will again emerge in this preferred function. The same description applies to the tone ♪, although the character of its tension, of its pointing towards ♪, is clearly different from that of the tone ♪; the difference is immediately manifest to the ear, but it cannot be described in words.

Thus, each of the five tones investigated so far ♪, has its own distinctive dynamic quality. We shall identify the dynamic qualities of the tones of this series by the symbols $\hat{1}$, $\hat{2}$, $\hat{3}$, $\hat{4}$, $\hat{5}$. They can be classified according to dynamic state: perfectly balanced, $\hat{1}$; comparatively balanced, $\hat{3}$ and $\hat{5}$; unbalanced, $\hat{2}$ and $\hat{4}$. The following diagram is an attempt to translate the results of these observations into graphic symbols:

*

The Oscilloscope

We know now a little more about the order of tones and about melody. Tonal order in music is a dynamic order; a succession of tones is a melody when the tones exhibit definite dynamic qualities and, in their succession, reveal a dynamic order.

In our hymn the dynamic qualities $\hat{1}$, $\hat{2}$, $\hat{3}$, $\hat{4}$, and $\hat{5}$ were associated with the pitches 🎵. They are not tied to these pitches, though; they are not attributes of them. To show this, we sing or play the tune, beginning on 🎵 instead of 🎵. It appears that the tone 🎵, which in the former context exhibited the perfect balance of $\hat{1}$, now conveys the opposite dynamic state of $\hat{2}$; that the tone 🎵, which before carried the quality $\hat{4}$, now carries the quality $\hat{5}$, while $\hat{4}$ has been moved to the tone 🎵, the former carrier of $\hat{3}$—and so on. These experiments can be multiplied. The conclusion: a given pitch can assume any dynamic quality, and a given dynamic quality can associate itself with any pitch.

The dynamic tone qualities are not a new discovery turned up in the course of this study. They form the basis of most of our conventional ear training; but they are never explicitly mentioned, nor are they recognized for what they are: namely, not just another acoustical property but *the* musical property of tones, the property that makes music possible.

With the help of an ingenious instrument, the oscilloscope, tones can be made visible. If a tone is sounded in front of the instrument, a picture of a wave line lights up on a little screen. To every acoustical property of the tone there corresponds a certain feature of the wave line: to pitch, the horizontal distance from crest to crest; to loudness, the vertical distance from crest to trough; to tone color, certain characteristics in the profile of the wave. An experienced observer can read from the picture everything pertaining to the tone—with one exception. The one thing he cannot read from it is the dynamic quality of the tone, its musical quality. Nothing in the picture corresponds to it. The wave line will be exactly the same whether the dynamic quality of a given tone be $\widehat{1}$, or $\widehat{2}$, or any other. The slightest change in pitch, loudness, or tone color will immediately produce a corresponding change in the wave line; but the extremest dynamic change, from perfect balance to acutest tension, will produce no effect whatsoever.

Actually the wave line is a picture not of a tone but of a vibration, the physical event that causes a tone sensation. There is a one-to-one correspondence between the acoustical properties of the tone on one hand and the physical event on the other. But there is no correspondence between the musical event and the physical event. The musical event seems to slip through the net of the physical world like light rays through a window pane.

If the origin of the dynamic qualities cannot be physical it must be psychological—it must be habit. This is the conclusion usually drawn. We have heard certain typical tone sequences so often that by now, when we hear music, we necessarily associate certain expectations with the tones; we feel satisfaction or dissatisfaction according as the expectations are or are not fulfilled; these feelings we project into the tones and call them dynamic qualities. A rash conclusion this is indeed. If there is no music without dynamic qualities, the dynamic qualities cannot arise from our getting habituated to music. The fact that we develop habits when listening to music does not prove that music originates from habits. There is no evidence to support this thesis—except habit again, an old habit of thought, namely, to assume that if an event has no physical cause it must have a psychological cause; in other words, if it is not objective it must be subjective.

Music is neither. The conventional distinction between physical and psychological, objective and subjective reality does not apply to it. How a thing can be neither the one nor the other and yet still exist—in other words, how music is possible —remains a major problem for philosophy to clarify.[1]

The Octave

The beginning of another hymn will acquaint us with some more tones:

Seven different tones supply the material for this tune. Lined up according to pitch, they are . Our ear tells us that the tone towards which the others are directed and which appears perfectly balanced, the tone $\hat{1}$, is . correspond to $\hat{1}, \hat{2}, \hat{3}, \hat{4}, \hat{5}$ of the former example: and are new.

The first thing we notice is the difference in the tone $\hat{3}$, compared to the corresponding tone of the former tune. If we listen to $\hat{1}$–$\hat{2}$–$\hat{3}$ as it sounds here, , and as it sounded there, , the difference stands out most clearly. The characteriza-

---

[1] This problem is the topic of a separate study by the author (*Sound and Symbol*, Bollingen Series XLIV. New York: Pantheon Books, 1956).

tion of the dynamic quality of $\widehat{3}$ given before would fit either case; the difference is of another order. It is what is called a difference of *mode;* the mode of the first tune is *minor,* of the second, *major.* We merely mention the phenomenon here and postpone its discussion for a later chapter.

The two new tones prove to the ear that they belong dynamically to the unbalanced type. ♭♪ , which we identify as $\widehat{6}$, seems to lean towards $\widehat{5}$; this tendency stands out particularly when we hear the sequence $\widehat{1}$–$\widehat{6}$, which sounds somehow like an overshooting of the mark $\widehat{5}$. (There is a certain ambiguity about the dynamic meaning of $\widehat{6}$ which will be explained shortly.) The other tone, ♭♪ , or $\widehat{7}$, points most sharply to the neighboring $\widehat{1}$, voices the most urgent desire to move on to this tone.

What happens if we look for more new tones above $\widehat{6}$ or below $\widehat{7}$? The beginning of the following hymn tune has the answer.

E - ter-ni-ty, tremendous word, a soul and body piercing sword, beginning without ending.

The tune begins on $\widehat{1}$, ascends through the intervening tones to $\widehat{5}$, takes a new start on $\widehat{5}$ repeated, continuing the ascending motion through $\widehat{6}$ and beyond. The first tone after $\widehat{6}$ is not a new tone; we recognize its dynamic quality: it is the same as $\widehat{7}$. We hear its desire to move on to the next higher tone, and the tune complies with this desire. The tone that follows turns out to be $\widehat{1}$ again, another $\widehat{1}$, the same tone on a higher pitch level. ($\widehat{1}$ above $\widehat{7}$, as in the move ♯♪♪ , is often designated $\widehat{8}$, and the move, $\widehat{7}$–$\widehat{8}$—with the understanding that $\widehat{1}$ and $\widehat{8}$ are two different symbols for the same dynamic quality.) If the ascending motion were continued further, beyond this higher $\widehat{1}$, another $\widehat{2}$ would appear, then another $\widehat{3}$, and so on. If we look in the other direction, below ♯♪ , $\widehat{7}$, we obviously get another $\widehat{6}$, then $\widehat{5}$, and so on.

This shows that after a certain pitch distance has been traversed, upward or downward, no more new tones appear; the old ones keep returning. The pitch distance at which this happens is called the *octave*. Thus, the tonal material of our music must be contained within the limits of an octave.

We have reached this limit. Seven tones, dynamically interrelated: one of them functioning, audibly functioning, as the center of action; the others directed, audibly directed, towards that center, each one in its own, almost personal way; some immediately, as $\hat{2}$ to $\hat{1}$, or $\hat{3}$ to $\hat{1}$, others via a mediating tone, as $\hat{4}$ to $\hat{3}$ and through $\hat{3}$ to $\hat{1}$, $\hat{6}$ to $\hat{5}$ and through $\hat{5}$ to $\hat{1}$. This is the stuff all our music is made of—at least all our music up to the end of the last century, when the transition from seven tone music to twelve tone music began.

The Scale

The series of seven tones, beginning with $\hat{1}$, plus the return of $\hat{1}$ as $\hat{8}$, is called a *scale*. The seven tone scale represents the tone selection, the tonal system of Western music.

The scale is not the beginning of music. Figuring out a scale first, then building melodies from the material of the scale: this is not the way music develops. People sing. Melodies appear. Scales are later theoretical abstractions, the result of reflection about the tonal material used in melodies.

We take a scale, e.g. , and consider the dynamic aspect of this tone sequence.

The dynamic situation between the first two tones, represented graphically, is this: . Accordingly the first move in the scale, the move $\hat{1}$–$\hat{2}$, is a move *against* the acting force, a move *away from* the center of action.

The dynamic situation between the last two tones of the series is this: . Accordingly the last move in the scale, the move

$\hat{7}$–$\hat{8}$, is a move *with* the acting force, a move *towards* the center of action. In the course of the movement along the scale the relation of the movement to the acting force has been reversed. Thus, the relation of the movement to the acting force at the end has turned into the opposite of what it was at the beginning. Where is the turning point?

We know that all tones between $\hat{1}$ and $\hat{5}$ look back towards $\hat{1}$. Up to $\hat{5}$, the relation of the movement to the acting force remains unchanged; it proceeds *against* the direction of the force, *away from* the center. $\hat{5}$ itself, however, seems to look not only back to $\hat{1}$ but also ahead to $\hat{8}$: the move $\hat{5}$–$\hat{8}$ satisfies the will of the tone $\hat{5}$ just as well as the move $\hat{5}$–$\hat{1}$. This indicates that beyond $\hat{5}$ we move *towards* $\hat{8}$, the center, *with* the acting force. $\hat{5}$ is the turning point.

This explains the ambiguity of the tone $\hat{6}$ mentioned before. In one sense, $\hat{6}$ appears to lean towards $\hat{5}$, the next better balanced tone; in another sense, it is an intermediate station in the larger movement from $\hat{5}$ to $\hat{8}$, directing us onward through $\hat{7}$ to the destination.

The exceptional position of $\hat{5}$ among the tones dependent on $\hat{1}$ becomes now apparent. It is a sort of counter-pole to $\hat{1}$: it marks the greatest possible distance, dynamically, from the center. If we go beyond $\hat{5}$ we approach again the center—on the other side of $\hat{5}$. All tonal action can be said to take place between the extremes $\hat{1}$ and $\hat{5}$; the relationship between these two tones establishes the over-all framework for our tonal language.

The spiral line, ascending continually and returning after every turn to points exactly above those passed before, has often been suggested as a graphic symbolization of the octave structure of the pitch series. As a representation of the acoustical phenomena, this is satisfactory; as a representation of the dynamic, that is, the musical phenomena, it is not. It fails to express the sense of arriving at a destination that we experience when the movement along the scale reaches $\hat{8}$. Something clicks here; but no sign of any clicking shows in the even course of the spiral.

The following diagram of a curve seems better suited to express graphically the movement through the seven tone scale—considered dynamically—as a musical phenomenon:

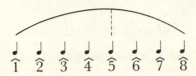

The strange fact of the octave—some authors have rightly spoken of "the miracle of the octave"—is responsible for the paradoxical situation that the movement along the scale brings into the open. It is a unique situation, one which has no parallel anywhere. Where else would we, by moving on continuously in a given direction, *return* to our starting point?—by increasing the distance from the starting point, *approach* that point again? For dynamically, and that is musically, $\hat{8}$ *is* $\hat{1}$, there is no mistaking the testimony of our ear regarding the sameness of start and goal of this movement. Going away means coming back; advancing is returning; movement ahead leads to the origin of the movement: these are statements of concrete fact in music.

It is true that there exist spatial parallels to this situation. If I move in a circle I shall always return to my starting point. If I walk out of the front door of my house and continue walking straight ahead in the same direction I shall in due course enter my house by the back door. But there is no need to move in space that way; we can do it, we are not constrained to do it. In music, however, there is no escaping the octave structure of the tonal world. Here every movement which is not prematurely interrupted must with inevitable necessity return to its starting point; either it turns back and so returns of its own will, as it were, or it goes on in the same direction and runs into the octave. There is no way of escaping the dynamic center by moving away from it in pitch. After a while it will have caught up with us, and we shall discover that what we thought we had left behind is already there, ahead, waiting for us.

There is perhaps no other single factor that more deeply influences the ways of our music than the octave and all it stands for.

Whole and Half Tones

Do we hear the scale sequence ♫ as an even or uneven movement—"even" in the sense that the pitch distances of the successive steps are equal? Which line represents this movement more truly, this   or this ?

Most people whose reaction is not influenced by knowledge will have the impression that the scale movement proceeds evenly, by equal steps. They will reject the jagged line as a proper symbol. How could we test the correctness of this impression?

We know that a given pitch can assume any dynamic quality. Let us take the second tone of our scale, ♪ , and imagine it as having the quality $\hat{1}$. Using a piano keyboard, we look for the tone which, if ♪ were taken as the first tone of a new scale, would appear in the position of $\hat{2}$. We find this to be ♪ , which is the same tone as the tone $\hat{3}$ of our original scale. This shows that the two tones $\hat{2}$ and $\hat{3}$ can equally function as $\hat{1}$ and $\hat{2}$; in other words, that the pitch distances $\hat{1}$–$\hat{2}$ and $\hat{2}$–$\hat{3}$ are the same. Expressed in a diagram:

We go on and imagine the third tone of the original scale, as
$\hat{1}$. We try whether the original $\hat{4}$ can serve as $\hat{2}$ to the new $\hat{1}$.
It cannot. The tone is too low. The pitch distance $\hat{3}$–$\hat{4}$ is not
the same as $\hat{1}$–$\hat{2}$ or $\hat{2}$–$\hat{3}$, it is smaller. The tone $\hat{2}$ we are looking
for now lies beyond the original $\hat{4}$. In the symbols of the
diagram:

$$
\begin{array}{cccc}
\downarrow & \downarrow & \downarrow & \downarrow \\
\hat{1} & \hat{2} & \hat{3} & \hat{4} \\
& & & \\
& \downarrow & \downarrow & \\
& \hat{1} & \hat{2} & \\
& & & \\
& & \downarrow & \downarrow \\
& & \hat{1} & \hat{2}
\end{array}
$$

If we continue in this manner we shall find that $\hat{4}$–$\hat{5}$, $\hat{5}$–$\hat{6}$,
and $\hat{6}$–$\hat{7}$ are all the same as $\hat{1}$–$\hat{2}$ or $\hat{2}$–$\hat{3}$, but that $\hat{7}$–$\hat{8}$ is again
smaller, the same as $\hat{3}$–$\hat{4}$. We realize that the steps of the scale,
in terms of pitch distance, are of two different sizes.

By how much is the larger size larger than the smaller? If we
attribute to the tone $\hat{1}$ of the original scale the dynamic quality
$\hat{7}$, the corresponding $\hat{8}$ will lie between the original $\hat{1}$ and $\hat{2}$. If
we repeat this, and give to that $\hat{8}$ the quality $\hat{7}$, the new $\hat{8}$
which corresponds to the new $\hat{7}$ will be the same tone as the
original $\hat{2}$.

$$
\begin{array}{cc}
\downarrow & \downarrow \\
\hat{1} & \hat{2} \\
& \\
\downarrow & \downarrow \\
\hat{7} & \hat{8} \\
& \\
\downarrow & \downarrow \\
\hat{7} & \hat{8}
\end{array}
$$

Two $\hat{7}$–$\hat{8}$ steps in succession add up to one $\hat{1}$–$\hat{2}$ step. The smaller
pitch distance in the scale seems to divide the larger in two
equal parts.

The larger pitch distance is called *whole tone,* the smaller *half tone.* This gives us the following formula for the pitch pattern of our scale: two wholes, one half, three wholes, one half; or, translated into a spatial pattern:

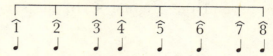

The word "tone" in the terms *whole tone* and *half tone* does not stand for what it usually means, namely, an auditory sensation of a definite pitch. Here it refers not to one pitch but to a distance between pitches. This is in line with the original meaning of the Greek word "tonos," which is translated "tension." If we apply this meaning to certain commonplace statements and instead of "tones" read "tensions"—"tensions" are the material of music; music speaks a language of "tensions"—the sentences seem to express more of the true nature of music. It has indeed been said that our hearing of melody is not a hearing *of* tones but *between* tones—that music occurs not in the tones but between them.

The Diatonic Order. The Modes

The pattern of our scale as shown in the last diagram—two whole tones, one half tone, three whole tones, one half tone—does not strike the mind's eye as distinguished in any easily discernible way. Still, this selection and distribution of seven tones has the unique distinction of representing the tonal order from which the music of Western civilization has grown, the *diatonic order.*

There is only one diatonic order, but there are different diatonic scales, each one having its peculiar pattern and producing its peculiar tonal expression. The differences are called differences of *mode.*

30

We have mentioned in passing one such difference, that of major and minor. The scale that we have analyzed is the diatonic scale, major mode, or more briefly, the major scale. The pattern we have extracted from it is the pattern of the major scale. What is the pattern of the minor scale?

When we compared the tones $\hat{1}$–$\hat{2}$–$\hat{3}$–$\hat{4}$–$\hat{5}$ as they appeared in the tunes of our first two examples ( in the first, which we called minor, in the second, which we called major), we could pin the difference to the change in character of the tone $\hat{3}$. No change was observed in the other tones. We see now that the tone $\hat{3}$ of the minor series, , is lower, and closer in pitch to $\hat{2}$, than the tone $\hat{3}$ of the major series, . From the pitch pattern of the major series, which we know, we can infer that of the minor series. The following diagram shows the two patterns:

major: $\hat{1}$ $\hat{2}$ $\hat{3}$ $\hat{4}$ $\hat{5}$

minor: $\hat{1}$ $\hat{2}$ $\hat{3}$ $\hat{4}$ $\hat{5}$

We see that the whole difference between major and minor hinges on a small change of pitch of the one tone $\hat{3}$. A whole tone between $\hat{2}$ and $\hat{3}$ makes the mode major, a half tone, minor. Consequently $\hat{3}$–$\hat{4}$, the half tone in major, must become a whole tone in minor. Strangely enough the shift in pitch does not affect the dynamic quality of the tone $\hat{3}$; in minor as in major it shows the characteristic half-balanced state with a slight but marked inner tension pointing towards $\hat{1}$.

What about the rest of the minor scale?

There is a Reaper men call Death And God has given him Pow'r. The blade he is whetting, sharp,
sharper it's growing, soon will he be mowing, all must fall before him. Beware, o lovely Flower.

31

This is the tune of an old German folk song, "Reaper Death." At this point we consider only its first and last phrases. Taken together, they give us the complete seven tone series of the minor scale in descending direction. For clarity's sake we transpose the beginning one octave up:

In ascending direction:

We know the pattern from $\hat{1}$ to $\hat{5}$. What about $\hat{6}$ and $\hat{7}$?

The difference of the sequence $\hat{5}$–$\hat{6}$–$\hat{7}$–$\hat{8}$ here, , and in major, , is striking to the ear. Both $\hat{6}$ and $\hat{7}$ are lower in pitch; the half tone between $\hat{7}$ and $\hat{8}$ in major has disappeared and is replaced by a whole tone; and the pushing down of $\hat{6}$ produces a half tone between $\hat{5}$ and $\hat{6}$ where there was a whole tone in major. These are the two patterns:

The disturbance of the dynamic picture created by this change of pitch will be discussed later. Here we mention only that in minor as in major $\hat{6}$ and $\hat{7}$ are both unbalanced tones. Here, finally, are the complete patterns of both scales:

Two diatonic scales, each having its own distinctive pattern. How can we reconcile this with the statement that there is only one diatonic order of tones?

We picture the diatonic pattern—two wholes, one half, three wholes, one half—extending from octave to octave through the tonal expanse:

We see immediately that both scales are part of this picture. They are merely two different cuts, so to speak, from the basic pattern—different as a consequence of their starting (that is, fixing their tone $\widehat{1}$) at different points of the order. The minor scale has its tone $\widehat{1}$ at the point of the tone $\widehat{6}$ of the major scale; the major has its $\widehat{1}$ where the $\widehat{3}$ of the minor is situated. It is not the major pattern which contains the minor pattern, or vice versa; it is the diatonic pattern which contains both in its framework.

It contains still other scales. The scale could begin at any point. Starting, for instance, at the point corresponding to $\widehat{2}$ of major ($\widehat{4}$ of minor), we get the following scale pattern:

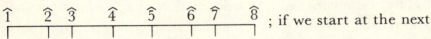 ; if we start at the next

point, corresponding to $\widehat{3}$ or $\widehat{5}$ respectively, the result is this:

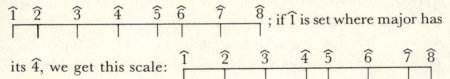 ; if $\widehat{1}$ is set where major has

its $\widehat{4}$, we get this scale:

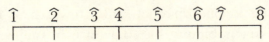

beginning at the next point, it is this:

These four scale patterns are not mere theoretical possibilities. They represent four distinctive modes of tonal expression, the Dorian, the Phrygian, the Lydian, and the Mixolydian—modes that dominated the music of the Middle Ages and that went out of existence with the advent of the major and minor modes (originally called the Ionian and the Aeolian) during the early seventeenth century. To a certain extent they have for some time now been in the ascendancy again, while the turn has come for major and minor to go out of existence.

As the main body of our musical heritage belongs to the major-minor period, we restrict our study to these two scales as representatives of the diatonic order.

Minor

Taking the major scale as our example, we have read the meaning of its movement as: going away from the center, drawing closer to it again, and finally reaching it (in the guise of its octave replica) as the goal, with a sense of finality.

In the minor scale, , we do not hear any of this. To be sure, we hear the going away from the center between $\hat{1}$ and $\hat{5}$; but as the movement proceeds beyond $\hat{5}$ there is no feeling of drawing closer to a destination, of approaching a goal, and particularly no sense of having reached a goal, no sense of finality as we arrive at $\hat{8}$. Why?

If we hear $\hat{8}$–$\hat{7}$ in major and stop at $\hat{7}$, the tone pulls back quite sharply to $\hat{8}$, audibly voices its desire to return there. If we listen to $\hat{8}$–$\hat{7}$ in minor, we hear nothing of that sort. The tone $\hat{7}$ seems here to have been pushed away from $\hat{8}$ so strongly that this impulse outweighs the attraction of $\hat{8}$. $\hat{7}$ in minor does not point towards $\hat{8}$ but rather away from it. As to $\hat{6}$, it sounds as if it were leaning in one direction only, towards $\hat{5}$; there is no indication of an ambiguity like that of $\hat{6}$ in major, no feeling whatever of being a station on the road, the downward incline, from $\hat{5}$ to $\hat{8}$. Since nothing in these two tones, $\hat{6}$ and $\hat{7}$, points to $\hat{8}$, it is clear that the sequence $\hat{5}$–$\hat{6}$–$\hat{7}$–$\hat{8}$ cannot convey the meaning of drawing closer to the destination $\hat{8}$, cannot stress $\hat{8}$ as the goal of the motion.

In order to impart to the movement through the minor scale the same kind of conclusiveness it has in major, something must be done to the stretch between $\hat{5}$ and $\hat{8}$. The main obstacle seems to be the lowered pitch of $\hat{7}$, its greater distance from $\hat{8}$. If $\hat{7}$ is a whole tone distant from $\hat{8}$, the step $\hat{7}$–$\hat{8}$ cannot have the affirmative character, the conclusiveness and finality character- istic of the satisfaction of a clear and strong desire, and the power to stress $\hat{8}$ as the point of destination—all of which it has in major. Therefore, to produce these effects in minor, too, it is necessary to raise the pitch of $\hat{7}$ to the half tone distance from $\hat{8}$:

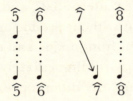

As we see—and hear—this creates an oversized pitch distance and an awkward step from $\hat{6}$ to $\hat{7}$. To equalize the unevenness, $\hat{6}$ must follow suit and pull up closer to the new $\hat{7}$:

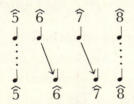

With this distribution of tones the movement from $\hat{5}$ to $\hat{8}$ will have the same effect, the same meaning it has in major; in fact, it *is* the same movement, the pitch pattern is the same. To state it briefly, then: If the minor scale in ascending direction is ex- pected to express the same sense of conclusiveness manifested by the major scale, it must borrow the tones $\hat{6}$ and $\hat{7}$ from major. (In descending direction there is no problem as the last move, $\hat{2}$–$\hat{1}$, is the same in both scales.)

This gives us two alternate positions of the tones $\hat{6}$ and $\hat{7}$ in minor, and two alternate scale patterns: (1) the normal, or diatonic, usually associated with the descending direction, and (2) another, with elements from major mixed in, which usually appears in connection with the ascending direction. Here they are:

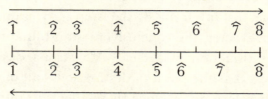

To sum up: The difference of major and minor appears at three points of the scale pattern: $\widehat{3}$, $\widehat{6}$, and $\widehat{7}$. Yet while the position of $\widehat{6}$ and $\widehat{7}$ can shift without producing a change of mode—minor can borrow them from major and still remain minor—a shift in the position of $\widehat{3}$ will immediately produce the change. This is the decisive tone; the difference of major and minor is concentrated in it. The moment one hears $\widehat{3}$ one knows which of these two modes prevails.

Declaring the Center

We have tentatively defined melody as a sequence of dynamically interrelated tones. This does not mean that, first, dynamic qualities are given as a sort of material, and second, melodies are built from this material. The relation of melody to dynamic quality is of a more intricate type. The tones themselves by their movement call into action the forces which then shape the movement, create context, meaning, structure, unity: a melody.

Dynamic qualities are audible relations of tones to other tones and ultimately to one central tone. Without a dynamic center there would be no dynamic qualities. So first there must be a center. How does it come into being? How do we know a certain tone is $\widehat{1}$? How does a tone tell us that it is the center?

Obviously not just by sounding. If we hear a single tone we

may feel inclined to take it for $\hat{1}$; but as long as nothing else happens this is mere presumption. The fact that the sun is the center of our planetary system is not established at the place of the sun itself but way out in space where the planets through their movements confirm the sun's ruling power. Similarly the central position of a tone will be established not by that tone itself, its mere presence, but by the events occurring around it.

The way the tones move—the steps they choose, the paths they follow up and down, the turns they take—spells out to the ear which tone is $\hat{1}$. To every dynamic center there belongs a dynamic field of which it is the center. Music is movement of tones in dynamic fields. From the movement of the tones the ear gathers the configuration of the field; we hear in what direction the tones are oriented, where they point. By the other tones' pointing at it, the tone $\hat{1}$ is revealed to the ear as the center of action.

There are many ways for a melody to state the dynamic center, some obvious and conventional, others more remote and intricate. Most complete and unequivocal is the one chosen by the "Eternity" hymn: 𝄞 ♪♩ ♩ ♩ ♩ ♩ 𝄐 . Here we have all the seven tones of the system, arrayed in scale pattern, beginning and ending with $\hat{1}$: we cannot want more. The "Allelujah" hymn gets along with a briefer statement 𝄞 ♩ ♩ ♩ 𝄐 , $\hat{1}$–$\hat{2}$–$\hat{3}$–$\hat{2}$–$\hat{1}$. It has to be repeated, though, for stronger confirmation. The hymn tune 𝄞 ♩♩♩♩♩𝄐 does not begin with $\hat{1}$, but chooses to declare its center by a $\hat{3}$–$\hat{2}$–$\hat{1}$–$\hat{2}$–$\hat{3}$–$\hat{4}$–$\hat{5}$ motion. Brief formulas—like half tone down and up again, which the ear interprets as $\hat{8}$–$\hat{7}$–$\hat{8}$, or whole tone up and back, $\hat{1}$–$\hat{2}$–$\hat{1}$—may be used; but they are not unambiguous. The half tone move could well be $\hat{3}$–$\hat{2}$–$\hat{3}$ in minor, the whole tone move $\hat{5}$–$\hat{6}$–$\hat{5}$ in major, or what not. However, this very ambiguity may occasionally be exploited for the sake of a special effect: the ear is allowed to incline towards a certain dynamic interpretation that a subsequent event proves wrong, thereby retroactively changing the meaning of the preceding moves. If this happens on a larger scale, the effect can be quite shattering (the beginning of Beethoven's Ninth Symphony is a famous example). Ordinarily a piece will declare its center right away; but sometimes a definite center will emerge only after a long search that keeps the hearer in a prolonged suspense. The first movement of Schumann's Piano Fantasia finds its center only at the very end.

The Making of Melody

A close study of the tune of the "Allelujah" hymn will demonstrate concretely the making of a melody through the action of the tonal forces.

The first move, ♪♫♩, ascending and descending, away-from-and-back-to- ♩ , makes that tone appear as $\hat{1}$. The repeating of the move confirms ♩ as center. What next?

♩ , $\hat{5}$: the counter-pole. We hear the direction of the tone towards ♩ , the tendency to return there.

The melody complies with this will: ♪♫♩ . Not all the way, though. Just at the point where the tension is most acute, where the will to make one more move is most outspoken—at $\hat{2}$, ♩ —the movement comes to a halt. Accumulated suspense. What will happen now?

What happens is the very opposite of what the last tone wanted to happen. The movement turns around, draws away from $\hat{1}$, goes up, through $\hat{3}$ and $\hat{4}$, to reach $\hat{5}$ again: ♪♫♩ . The going is slower now than on the downward stretch, the movement seems to take a new breath before each step, ♪♫♩ , we almost feel how it works against the pressure of the acting force.

With the reaching of $\hat{5}$ the opposition to the acting force is spent, the movement once more conforms to the will of the tone

$\widehat{5}$, and the second try succeeds:  . The way is completed, the goal reached:

Through the whole second half of this melody, from the moment the movement came to a stop at $\widehat{2}$, we are waiting for the fulfillment of the expectation aroused by that tone. Its tension underlies and ties together everything that follows and is released only at the end, with the entry of $\widehat{1}$.

The second part of the tune is on the whole a repetition of the first, but it does not begin as the first did. There is no need now for the repetition of a short phrase whose main function it was to establish $\widehat{1}$. Still, the beginning should again be the repetition of a short phrase. So we begin with the second phrase, ♪ , and repeat this.

This means that now we have *two* unsuccessful tries; twice the movement is stopped at $\widehat{2}$. As a consequence, the tension of this tone is greatly enhanced. What follows is therefore more than a mere repetition of the second half of the first part: the ascending phrase works against a stronger force, carries greater weight. Finally, the entry of $\widehat{1}$ brings a more emphatic release, makes a stronger punctuation than at the midway mark—which is as it should be:

We see two things here. First, the action of the tonal forces organizes the tune, holds it together, gives it its meaning. Second, the tones in their movements are not simply subjected to the acting forces, as inanimate bodies are subjected to the force of gravity; they are free to move with or against the acting forces, as the animate body of the dancer is free to move with or against the force of gravity.

The tonal forces do not determine the tonal movement, but they do determine another thing, and this in the strictest sense: the *musical meaning* of that movement. In our tune the movement was free any time to proceed from $\hat{2}$ to $\hat{1}$ or to any other tone it chose; but once it did take the step $\widehat{2-1}$, nothing on earth could give that move another meaning than "in conformity with the acting force, reaching the center," and make us hear in it anything but a move from an unbalanced to a perfectly balanced state. Just as strictly and unequivocally will the meaning of any other move be determined by the prevailing dynamic situation.

(Mendelssohn once said that the tonal language is too precise to be translated into words. We see the truth of this statement. An author has a certain margin of freedom to change the meaning of his material, words; a composer has none.)

The forces that we have observed in action, which are responsible for the making of this simple tune (a very beautiful, an excellent tune in all its simplicity), are the same ones that form and unite the most complex musical organism. In this respect the difference between a folk song and a Beethoven symphony is only one of degree. The increase in complexity may be comparable to that from grade school arithmetic to calculus; the principle is the same.

Background and Foreground

In the "Allelujah" tune every single tone represented, as it were, a station on the main road of the melodic movement. For instance, when the melody moved from $\hat{5}$ through $\hat{4}$ and $\hat{3}$ to $\hat{2}$, it did so in the most simple, straightforward way, using one tone for every station, .

This is by no means the only way, nor is it the most usual way, for a melody to move. We could call it the naive way, characteristic of music in the state of nature, of folk music. Rarely will it be met with in art music, which develops more complex types of movement. Occasionally a folk tune, too, will show a higher degree of complexity. The "Reaper Death" melody is an example.

Its first phrase, $\hat{1}\,\hat{1}\,\hat{3}\,\hat{2}\,\hat{1}\,\hat{7}\,\hat{6}\,\hat{5}$, takes us after a little tour indicating the center, $\hat{1}$–$\hat{3}$–$\hat{2}$–$\hat{1}$, down through $\hat{7}$ and $\hat{6}$ to $\hat{5}$ and stops there; the counter-pole is stated. This is done in the simple manner with which we are familiar.

The second phrase begins by taking up $\hat{5}$ to the higher octave: ; the tone is thereby put into strong relief, and rightly so since all that follows hinges on it. Next, the tones are released on their downward journey, towards $\hat{1}$; they get no farther than $\hat{3}$: . The sum of this is a movement from $\hat{5}$ to $\hat{3}$. Not a simple $\hat{5}$–$\hat{4}$–$\hat{3}$, though. If we spelled it out tone by tone it would read $\hat{5}$–$\hat{4}$–$\hat{3}$–$\hat{4}$–$\hat{3}$–$\hat{2}$–$\hat{3}$. This, however, is not a true representation of what we hear. For instance, nobody will hear in the tone of the second measure the dynamic quality $\hat{3}$. What we do hear is better represented this way: . It *is* a $\hat{5}$–$\hat{4}$–$\hat{3}$ movement; but the individual links of the movement are no longer single tones: they are small groups of tones. It is a movement not from tone to tone but from group to group, with each group comprising three tones and representing one station on the main road. (Obviously the rhythm contributes much to this understanding, but we do not consider the time factor here.)

Nothing conclusive has been achieved so far. The melody returns to $\hat{5}$ for another start. This time we get farther; but the movement is even slower and, one might say, more massive than before: the groups have grown to twice their former size:

41

When the movement arrives at $\hat{2}$ it seems not ready to take the final step. It skips $\hat{1}$ and drops down to the lower $\hat{5}$.

Once more, $\hat{5}$ is lifted to the higher level; and now only, returning to the simple manner of the beginning, the melody takes us all the way from $\hat{5}$ to $\hat{1}$.

With this we can give a reasonable account of the tonal story of this tune:

On the whole, it is a movement through the full octave, descending from $\hat{8}$ to $\hat{1}$. The first stretch, from $\hat{8}$ to $\hat{5}$, is traversed quickly and directly. The remaining part of the tune consists in repeated attempts to complete the journey. More roundabout ways are now chosen, first through groups of three notes, which gets us to $\hat{3}$, then through groups of six notes—this comes to a halt on $\hat{2}$. The last attempt again strips the movement to its bare essentials, one tone to one station, and succeeds.

We see from this example that a melody does not simply string tones together, one after another, as in a single file. In the middle section of the tune a kind of organic partition develops, the movement proceeds on two planes simultaneously. In the background, as it were, the succession of main stations; in the foreground the detours, the subordinate patterns by which station is linked to station.

The succession of main stations shall be called the *skeleton* of a melody. Its function in the life of the melody is exactly that of the skeleton in a living organism. Beauty, individuality, distinction do not reside in the skeleton but rather in that which the skeleton supports. Yet it is the skeleton that does all the supporting; without it, the whole thing would immediately collapse.

The normal listener will follow the thread of the "Reaper Death" tune without difficulty. It will make sense to him, connected sense. Since it is the skeleton that creates the connection, the ear must instinctively be aware of its existence and of the corresponding background-foreground structure of the melody. Since the beauty and the interest and in fact the very meaning of this tune, as of every tune, rests precisely in the relation between the flesh and blood of the musical foreground and the supporting skeleton of the background, the ear of any person who finds any interest or beauty or sense in this melody must somehow have understood that relation.

Listening to a melody we intuitively distinguish between the main road of the movement and the sideroads and detours that take us from one station on the main road to the next, elaborating, expanding, enriching the movement. The ear is constantly engaged in forming smaller and larger sums of tones, according to the structure of the movement, grouping together what belongs together, keeping apart what should be kept apart. It does not simply register tone after tone, taking every tone at its face value; it evaluates every tone according to its function in the context of the melodic movement. In measure 14 of our tune, for example, the tone ♪ is identical in pitch with $\hat{1}$; but it will not be heard as $\hat{1}$. The tone at this point is a link in the subordinate movement into which the tone $\hat{2}$ has expanded, a part of the group that as a whole represents the station $\hat{2}$ of the background movement; it does not function as $\hat{1}$ here. This the ear understands, and it evaluates the tone accordingly. If the ear were not capable of making these distinctions and judgments, the tune would not make sense.

What happens in this simple folk tune happens similarly, on an ever larger and more complex scale, in elaborate compositions. To the intellect, intent on laying bare the skeleton, on demonstrating the background-foreground structure, such compositions present increasingly difficult tasks. But it is not so with the ear, which will all along perform the proper operations with the same instinctive certainty, gathering tones into smaller and larger groups, groups and sequences into units of a higher order, separating and uniting in line with the organization of the tonal movement. This synthetic power of the human ear goes far beyond a mere reaction to a series of stimuli; it can be greatly developed by training, but in an elementary way it will function even without any training. If it were not for this power, there would be no music.

The Center Moves

We can look at a piano keyboard as a fair visualization of the diatonic order. The white keys represent the tones of that order. The alternating groups of two and three black keys, separated by one empty space, mark the places of the alternating two-whole-tone and three-whole-tone groups; the location of the half tones is indicated by the absence of a black key between two white keys.

We identify the white keys by simple letter names—a, b, c, d, e, f, g—and represent them by the successive positions of the plain symbols on the staff, .

If the white keys correspond to the tones of the diatonic order, they must form a major scale. As we know the pattern of that scale we can locate its tone $\hat{1}$: it is the first of the three tones forming the two-whole-tone group (the 4th white key from the left on the sketch above). This tone is called c, the white keys give us the C major scale. The same keys must give us a minor scale, too. Its $\hat{1}$ will be located at the tone $\hat{6}$ of the major scale, the tone a; it is the A minor scale.

If our music is seven tone music, why do we need the addi-

44

tional tones, the black keys—five of them to every octave? The raising and lowering of the pitch of a piece, like the transposing of a melody to a higher or lower pitch level, could be taken care of by a mechanism, like that on a harp, that in one move changes the pitch level of the whole series. The following tune exemplifies the crucial event that necessitates the introduction of new tones without basically changing the nature of the seven tone system:

We have listened to the first part of the tune before. The center is ♮. The movement proceeds without disturbance up to the point marked x. Here the ear feels a light shock. Something has happened.

We listen to the dynamic quality of the tone ♮ in the measure following that event. The phrase comes to a completely satisfactory ending on it, the tone is perfectly balanced. We compare this to the dynamic quality of the same tone as it appeared shortly before, in the measure ♮: we realize the difference. There, it was $\hat{5}$; now it is $\hat{1}$. This is the crucial happening: in the course of the movement of the melody the dynamic center has changed place, has moved from one tone to another.

How has this been brought about? Among the typical short ways by which the tonal movement may establish a tone as the dynamic center we have mentioned the move $\hat{7}$–$\hat{8}$, a half tone step upward. If the melody chooses this method to make $\hat{5}$ appear as $\hat{1}$, it must approach and reach this tone through an ascending half tone step. The lower scale neighbor of $\hat{5}$ in the original pattern, the tone $\hat{4}$, is a whole tone distant. Accordingly a new tone, half way between $\hat{4}$ and $\hat{5}$, must be introduced in order to achieve the desired result. This is the tone that caused the light shock to the hearer, ♮. It breaks the prevailing seven

45

tone pattern, or rather, it breaks the pattern loose from its mooring to the prevailing tone $\hat{1}$ and shifts it over to a new anchorage.

In a delicate way the movement itself has prepared us for that event. When it occurs we have not heard ♪, the original tone $\hat{1}$, for almost 5 measures. In the measure immediately preceding it, ♪, the failure of the movement to touch $\hat{1}$ was quite conspicuous. It seems as if the grip of the center on the movement were loosening; and immediately another tone takes advantage of the situation and attracts the movement towards itself, pushes itself in the position of $\hat{1}$. Shaken from its complacency by this event, the original center returns to active life and smoothly directs the movement back where it belongs, into *its* own orbit, by simply annulling in the following phrase the raised tone, returning it to its original pitch position: ♪. The original order is duly restored.

As a tone is $\hat{1}$ not by itself but in relation to the other tones of the seven tone pattern, a shift in the position of $\hat{1}$ implies a shift of the whole pattern. The following diagram shows that such a shift will necessarily call forth new tones, that is, tones that were not parts of the original seven tone set. What the problem practically amounts to is the construction of new scales beginning at other tones than the original $\hat{1}$. (In the diagram we consider major only.)

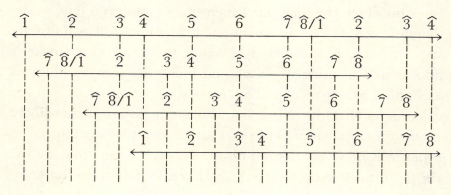

First, the tone $\hat{2}$ of the original set should become $\hat{1}$. We know from an earlier observation that the tone $\hat{3}$ of the original scale can be used as second tone of the new scale. What about the new $\hat{3}$? It must lie a whole tone above the new $\hat{2}$, or the original $\hat{3}$; but the original $\hat{4}$ lies a half tone above $\hat{3}$. It cannot be used, it is too low to function as $\hat{3}$ in the new scale; a new tone, half way between the original $\hat{4}$ and $\hat{5}$ must be produced for the purpose. For the following tones the new scale can use pitches of the original scale; except for $\hat{7}$. Here again a new tone has to be created. Similarly, if the original tone $\hat{3}$ is made $\hat{1}$ of a new scale, it will be necessary to introduce new tones for the functions $\hat{3}$ and $\hat{7}$. If the original $\hat{4}$ becomes $\hat{1}$, a new tone is needed for $\hat{4}$ of the new scale.

There is no need to carry this further. The five whole tones of the diatonic order from which we started are now all filled up, the tonal expanse is evenly divided into equal pitch distances, the tones are evenly distributed at half tone intervals, twelve of them to the octave. Consequently the major scale pattern—or the minor scale pattern, or any diatonic pattern—can now be applied beginning from any tone; there are tones available for any position of the pattern.

The series of twelve tones is called the *chromatic scale*. When we hear it we notice a striking difference from the seven tone, the diatonic, scale. The dynamic qualities have disappeared. One tone is as good as another; no tone is audibly related to any other tone; all that remains is difference of pitch. The organization, the musical order has gone.

Looked at quantitatively, the chromatic scale with its even distribution of tones seems a much better order than the arbitrary diatonic arrangement. Musically, however, the even distribution spells the end of order. The chromatic scale is the musical equivalent of chaos.

The expansion of the tonal material from seven to twelve

tones does not replace the seven tone order with a twelve tone order. The twelve tones are no more than a kind of storehouse,[2] a reservoir where music finds the material needed to establish a diatonic order with any tone as center. Thus, the tonal movement wins an additional freedom, a momentous freedom: that of moving its own center at will. It is not only movement about a center but movement of a center. The latent tendency of every tone to establish itself as the center of dynamic action can make itself felt; the competition among tones for the central position in the dynamic field becomes one of the major topics of music.

Sharps and Flats

What should the new tones be called, and how should they be represented on the staff?

We take the C major scale as the starting point, as the zero series, so to speak: c, d, e, f, g, a, b, c. For every position of the center other than c—the mode remaining the same—one or more tones of this series will prove out of line with the requirements of the seven tone pattern.

Assume that the tone d has become $\hat{1}$. The tone e will then be $\hat{2}$; but f cannot serve as $\hat{3}$, since it is too low (e–f is a half tone, whereas $\hat{2}$–$\hat{3}$ in major is a whole tone). In order to get a tone that will function as $\hat{3}$ in the new context, the pitch of f must be raised—sharpened—by a half tone. The new tone we get that way is called f sharp. Symbol: 🎼.

Assume that f becomes $\hat{1}$. Tones g and a can be used as $\hat{2}$ and $\hat{3}$, respectively; but b cannot serve as $\hat{4}$, it is too high (a–b is a whole tone, $\hat{3}$–$\hat{4}$ in major a half tone). In order to get the tone that will function as $\hat{4}$ in the new context, the pitch of b must be lowered—flattened—by a half tone. The new tone is called b flat. Symbol: 🎼.

---

[2] In modern twelve-tone music, too, the chromatic scale represents an assembly of materials rather than an underlying order—materials needed for the building of tone rows.

We generalize: Whenever one of the tones of the zero series, c, d, e, etc., proves too low and must be raised in order to fit the requirements of the pattern in a new position, the tones thus introduced are called c sharp, d sharp, e sharp, etc.; whenever for the same reasons these tones must be lowered, they are called c flat, d flat, e flat, etc. Symbols:

This seems to give us altogether 3 times 7, that is, 21 names, 21 symbols. Twelve pitches only are available. How are we to reconcile this?

Let us consider, for instance, the situation between c and d. If d is too high and must be lowered by a half tone, we get d flat. If c is too low and must be raised by a half tone, we get c sharp. Both c sharp and d flat are supposed to lie half way between c and d; they will coincide in pitch. One pitch can take care of both eventualities. If c is too high and must be lowered by a half tone, the tone b, which is a half tone below c, can take care of that. If e is too low and must be raised by a half tone, the tone f can supply the needed pitch. (A little cheating is involved in all this. The pitch distance we call a half tone is not exactly one half of a whole tone; c sharp is not exactly the same as d flat, c flat is not exactly b, and so on; but the difference is small enough to be neglected in practice. We shall hear more of this later.)

The following diagram shows the distribution of the 21 tones over the 12 pitches:

	a♯		b♯	c♯		d♯		e♯	f♯		g♯		a♯		b♯	c♯
a		b	c		d		e	f		g		a		b	c	
	b♭	c♭		d♭		e♭	f♭		g♭		a♭		b♭	c♭		d♭

This looks disconcertingly confused. However, we have only to connect what belongs together, and the inherent order of the whole system will immediately emerge.

```
   |   |   |   |   |   |   |   |   |   |   |   |   |   |   |   |   |   |   |
   |  a♯ |  b♯  c♯ |  d♯ |  e♯  f♯ |  g♯ |  a♯ |  b♯  c♯ |
   | / | | / | / | | / | / | / | | / | | / | | / | / |
   a |  b   c |  d |  e   f |  g |  a |  b   c |
 / | | / | / | | / | / | / | | / | | / | | / | / |  /
   |  b♭  c♭ |  d♭ |  e♭  f♭ |  g♭ |  a♭ |  b♭  c♭ |  d♭
```

EXAMPLES

A major: 1̂   2̂   3̂ 4̂   5̂   6̂   7̂ 8̂

B♭ major: 1̂   2̂   3̂ 4̂   5̂   6̂   7̂ 8̂

B minor: 1̂   2̂ 3̂   4̂   5̂ 6̂   7̂   8̂

C minor: 1̂   2̂ 3̂   4̂   5̂ 6̂   7̂   8̂

From this table we can read the names of the tones of any seven tone set—the set belonging to any given tone 1̂; in other words, we can read from it any scale, beginning with any tone, in any mode. The principle is this: Every letter station—the three "appearances" of the letter connected by diagonal lines— must be represented by one tone in the scale. No station shall be skipped, none used twice. Accordingly, for example, the A major scale spells as follows: a, b (not c flat, as this would skip the b station), c sharp (not d flat, because then the c station would not be represented), d, e, f sharp, g sharp, a. The B flat major scale: b flat, c, d, e flat (not d sharp, because then the d sta- tion would be used twice), f, g, a, b flat. The B flat minor scale (not shown in the diagram) would spell: b flat, c, d flat (one half tone above c, but not c sharp, because c has already been used), e flat, f, g flat (not f sharp, for the same reason), a flat, b flat. And so on.

Key and Signature

We open a volume of music and read on the title page: Symphony No. 4 in B flat major, opus 60, by Ludwig van Beethoven. What does this mean, "in B flat major"? The answer is: It indicates the *key* of this particular piece. What is a key?

Key, as a technical term in music, signifies the organization of the twelve tone material with reference to a particular tone as the dynamic center. A key is the selection of seven tones in accordance with the requirements of the pattern—major or minor mode, as the case may be—which puts one particular tone in the position of $\hat{1}$. Selecting seven tones out of twelve means at the same time rejecting five. Thus, every key draws a dividing line across the twelve tone reservoir, separating the seven tones that belong to it from those that do not belong. The seven chosen tones are called *diatonic,* the rejected, *chromatic* tones. The dividing line between diatonic and chromatic tones is not fixed but changes with the key; different tones are diatonic or chromatic for different keys.

(In one respect this statement is not quite accurate. A key rejects not five tones but five pitches. If we consider the 21 tones of our last diagram as the material from which a key selects its seven diatonic tones, there will be 14 rejects. However, some of them will practically coincide in pitch, while others will share the same pitch with diatonic tones; for instance, in the key of C major the tone c is a diatonic tone while b sharp, practically identical in pitch with c, would be a chromatic tone.)

The key is B flat major: this means that the tone b flat is the center, and the diatonic tones are the seven tones that make up the pattern, major mode, for b flat as $\hat{1}$; in other words, the tones of the B flat major scale. With one exception, to be mentioned later, no two keys have the same set of diatonic tones; each key makes its own selection. This selection, as we have seen in the scales, takes the form of replacing the tones of the zero series by their sharpened or flattened versions. The B flat major scale, for instance, came into being by replacing the tones b and e of the zero series by b flat and e flat. The A major scale changed the tones c, f, and g of the zero series into c sharp, f sharp, and g sharp.

The sharps or flats that belong to the diatonic tones of a key are called its *signature*. In our system of notation they are always put ahead of the text, at the beginning of every line. If a piece is in B flat major, every line will begin with 𝄢. This says literally: As long as this signature stands here, every b symbol of the text means b flat, every e symbol e flat. In A major the signature is 𝄢, the three sharps that we know the A major scale contains. (It will be explained later why they appear in this particular arrangement.) Actually the signature spells out all seven diatonic tones of a key: the tones of the zero series which are not flattened or sharpened will appear in the key in their unflattened-unsharpened, their natural version. In this sense the signature identifies the key.

Tonality

Musical thoughts may occur to a composer in a kind of abstract form, not fixed to particular pitches. As soon as he wants to express them in writing or playing, he will have to choose definite tones. He can think a melody in the major mode; he can write or play a melody only in a major key, that is, definitely localized in the tonal area, centered about a definite tone.

What determines the choice of key, apart from technical considerations such as the pitch range of instruments or the difficulty of execution, is a highly interesting and puzzling question for musical psychology and esthetics. A definite coordination seems to exist in many instances between the character of a piece and its key. Sometimes, as in certain typical arias of 18th century opera, the choice is rooted in tradition. In other cases it appears as a distinctly personal factor. One can find a community of character among many D major pieces, of another character among many E major pieces, of Mozart, or Beethoven, or Bach; but Mozart's D major character is very different from Beethoven's, which is again different from Bach's. The problem is further obscured by the change of the pitch standard over the centuries, and in the case of Bach and his contemporaries and predecessors, by the different tunings of keyboard instruments (a piece to be played on a certain organ would have to be written in C major if one wanted it to sound in D major). However, on the whole and particularly from the middle of the 18th century on, one can assume that normally a musical idea would occur to a composer from the outset as located in a definite key, idea and key belonging intrinsically together.

The music that was to become his Fourth Symphony occurred to Beethoven as centered about the tone b flat, embodied in the key of B flat major. Are we to assume that no tones except the seven tones of the B flat major scale will appear throughout the piece?

We can expect the music of this symphony, as of any larger composition, to make ample use of the freedom of moving the center. This implies the introduction of new tones, tones that do not belong to the diatonic set of this key: chromatic tones.

In the tune quoted before (p. 45) as an example of shifting center, the tone 🎵, which brought about the shift, was a chromatic tone; it replaced the diatonic g, the tone $\hat{4}$ of D major, the key of the tune. Whenever the center changes, one or more tones of the original seven tone set of the key will be too high or too low and will have to be flattened or sharpened. New sharps and flats, in addition to those that belong to the signature, will then appear in the text. If a tone that is sharpened by the signature should prove too high and must be lowered, the sharp will be cancelled for the moment; for the opposite reason a flat of the signature will be momentarily cancelled. The symbol for cancellation of either sharp or flat is ♮, the *natural*. Occasionally a sharpened tone must be further sharpened, a flattened tone further flattened; this brings in double sharps, ✕ , and double flats ♭♭. Together these symbols —sharps, flats, naturals, double sharps, double flats—are called accidentals. Between the sharps and flats that belong to diatonic tones and make up the signature, and the accidentals that mark chromatic tones, there is this distinction: the former are set apart, at the beginning of the line, and are valid as long as the key is in force, while the latter are written immediately before the symbol to which they refer and are valid for one measure only.

If in the course of a piece of music the center can move, what sense does it make to talk of key, which means that one definite tone is the center?

The notion of key does not imply that a certain tone will be $\hat{1}$ all through the piece. What it does imply is that the movements of the center will not be arbitrary, that in some way they will manifest the presence of a power behind the stage, as it were, a center of centers: this is the tone $\hat{1}$ of the key. Whatever power any other tone may hold in the course of the piece is only temporary, delegated power that in due time will return to the true sovereign. In order to understand how this happens one has to observe in detail the movements of the center throughout a piece: a task for a later chapter.

This is not all. Key itself is not the ultimate of stability either. In the course of a larger composition the key may change, too. However, the changes of key will only repeat on a larger scale the story of the movements of the center. There will be nothing arbitrary about them; from the ways of the changing keys a definite pattern will emerge and clearly point at one of them as the key of keys, the ultimate ruler. This, then, is *the* key of the piece, the one named in the title.

The following is a graphic summary of these relations:

Tones

Centers (moving)

Keys (changing)

The key

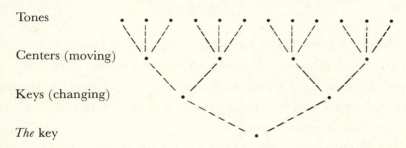

(In actual music these levels are not strictly separated. Some changes of center are so swift that they can hardly be counted as such; sometimes a new center will entrench itself so strongly that it practically amounts to a change of key.)

All this together, the relation of tones to centers, of centers to keys, of keys to a super-key, is implied in the term *tonality*. In a superficial sense tonal music simply means music built on audible relations of tones to a central tone, on the dynamic qualities as we have observed them. In a truer sense tonality means what the last diagram shows: the manifestation of the power of one tone through all the levels of a complex musical organism. Tonal music in this sense culminates in the works of the great masters of the 18th and 19th centuries. Towards the end of the 19th century the disintegration of tonality begins. The first link to be cut is that between the changing keys and the super-key: music is written in keys but not in a key. The foundation is no longer stability; it is change. Later, key dissolves, the moving centers cut themselves loose from the common point of reference. Finally, the ever more rapid succession of changes of center put the notion of center itself in doubt; the diatonic order disappears, and with it all tonal relations as we have known them. This is *atonal* music, the product of our century; in the perspective of tonality the purest negation; in its own perspective a search for new kinds of tone relations.

Key Relations

Different keys do not meet each other, so to speak, as absolute strangers. Delicately shaded degrees of kinship exist between them and make themselves felt to the ear. Stated in the most general terms, the relationship of two keys is determined by the things they have in common.

We have mentioned that there is one exception to the rule that every key has its own set of seven diatonic tones. We know that the diatonic pattern furnishes the framework for various scale patterns, each beginning at a different point of the diatonic order, each corresponding to a particular mode. Thus a given seven tone set provides the tonal material for more than one scale—specifically, for one major and one minor scale—as we saw the zero series provide the material for the C major and A minor scales, with the tone $\hat{6}$ of major supplying the pitch for $\hat{1}$ of minor, and $\hat{3}$ of minor coinciding in pitch with $\hat{1}$ of major. In the same way every seven tone set can give birth to one major and one minor scale, beginning with different tones; this means that one seven tone set can provide the tonal basis for two different keys, one major, one minor. This particular pair of keys of different mode that have one seven tone set in common is called the *relative major and minor* or, briefly, the *relatives*. Since the seven tone selection of a key is determined by the signature, relative major and minor will always have the same signature. The statement that the signature defines the key is to be understood with this restriction: actually the signature defines one pair of keys, one major, one minor. In order to tell which of the two is the key of a piece we must hear or see a little of the music itself.

Another distinguished pair of keys is the major and the minor that have their *center* in common, as, for instance, C major and C minor. These two keys have of course different seven tone sets, different signatures (C minor replaces the tones e, a, and b of C major, $\hat{3}$, $\hat{6}$, and $\hat{7}$, by e flat, a flat, and b flat). But the sameness of center ties them together so closely that a change from one to the other, involving a change of mode only, is often not felt as an actual move. In practice they are frequently treated as two versions of the same key rather than two different keys.

Most important of all key relations is that of two keys having all but one tone in common.

We approach the problem through the question: Are there any two such keys, two keys that have six tones in common? We state the question in terms of an arrangement of points in space: Given a series of points arranged in the pattern of the diatonic order, is it possible to change the position of just one point (including of course its "octave replicas") and get the same pattern again? We number the points in a "major scale" succession:

$$1 \quad 2 \quad 3 \ 4 \quad 5 \quad 6 \quad 7 \ 8$$

Using the trial and error method, we find easily that any shift in the position of points 2, 5, or 6 would immediately destroy the pattern by creating an oversize distance on the side opposite the shift. For the same reason, $\hat{3}$ or $\hat{7}$ cannot be shifted to the right, nor 1 or 4 to the left; but 3 cannot be moved to the left either, nor 1 (8) to the right, because this would produce four consecutive 'whole tones' on the opposite side of the move. Only two possibilities remain, the shift of 4 to the right and of 7 to the left. The following diagram shows that either of these shifts actually produces the desired result: after the shift the pattern reappears, moved into another position. 4 after the shift is 7 in the new position; 7 after the shift is 4 in the new position. One move is the reverse of the other, the two possibilities are at the bottom only one

Substituting tones for points, extending the pattern over two octaves, and starting from the C major scale as the middle, or zero, position, we get the following picture:

$\hat{4}$ $\hat{5}$ $\hat{6}$ $\hat{7}$ $8/\hat{1}$ $\hat{2}$ $\hat{3}$ $\hat{4}$ $\hat{5}$ $\hat{6}$ $\hat{7}$ $8/\hat{1}$ $\hat{2}$ $\hat{3}$ $\hat{4}$
c   d   e   f♯ g   a   b   c   d   e   f♯ g   a   b   c

$\hat{1}$ $\hat{2}$ $\hat{3}$ $\hat{4}$ $\hat{5}$ $\hat{6}$ $\hat{7}$ $8/\hat{1}$ $\hat{2}$ $\hat{3}$ $\hat{4}$ $\hat{5}$ $\hat{6}$ $\hat{7}$ $\hat{8}$
c   d   e   f   g   a   b   c   d   e   f   g   a   b   c

$\hat{5}$ $\hat{6}$ $\hat{7}$ $8/\hat{1}$ $\hat{2}$ $\hat{3}$ $\hat{4}$ $\hat{5}$ $\hat{6}$ $\hat{7}$ $8/\hat{1}$ $\hat{2}$ $\hat{3}$ $\hat{4}$ $\hat{5}$
c   d   e   f   g   a   b♭ c   d   e   f   g   a   b♭ c

This diagram makes it plain that there are two keys, major mode, that have six tones common with C major, one on either side, as it were. It also shows us which keys they are. One is the result of the raising of f, $\hat{4}$ in C major, to f sharp, $\hat{7}$ in the new context; $\hat{8}$ is g, the new key is G major (signature: one sharp, 🎼). The tone g was $\hat{5}$ in C major: $\hat{5}$ has become $\hat{1}$. The other key results from the change of b, $\hat{7}$ in C major, to b flat, $\hat{4}$ in the new context. The key is F major (signature: one flat, 🎼). In F major the tone c is $\hat{5}$: $\hat{1}$ has become $\hat{5}$.

It is clear that the process can be continued with the same result in either direction. There are again two keys that have six tones in common with G major. One of them is C major. The other will be the result of G major's $\hat{4}$, the tone c, being raised to c sharp, which will be $\hat{7}$ in the new context, making d = $\hat{8}$. The key is D major (signature: one more sharp, two altogether, 🎼). In the same way there are two keys that have six tones in common with F major. One of them is C major. The other will result from F major's $\hat{7}$, e, being lowered to e flat, the new $\hat{4}$. $\hat{1}$ will be b flat (the key: B flat major; signature: one more flat, two of them altogether, 🎼. And so on. Every new step will add one more sharp or flat to the signature.

58

Every step is a transformation of $\hat{5}$ into $\hat{1}$ or $\hat{1}$ into $\hat{5}$. The same kind of relation exists of course between the minor keys. The only difference is in the numbers of the two tones whose change effects the key changes: in minor they are not $\hat{4}$ and $\hat{7}$ but $\hat{6}$ and $\hat{2}$.

If we call the pitch distance between the tones $\hat{1}$ and $\hat{5}$ a *fifth*, we can formulate the following law of key relations: Apart from the pair of relatives, those keys are closely related whose centers are a fifth distant of each other. This binds two keys to any given key in close relationship, one whose center lies a fifth above, the other with its center a fifth below, that of the given key—as in ♮. In the chain of these relations every step "upward" from a given key will be expressed in the signature by the addition of one sharp or the taking away of one flat; every step "downward" by the addition of one flat or the taking away of one sharp. This explains the arrangement of sharps and flats in the signature, and also why no diatonic signature can contain sharps *and* flats: on the way from sharps to flats—and vice versa—the zero point of no sharps no flats—C major or A minor—must be passed.

The following is the so-called *Circle of Fifths*, the systematic tabulation, with their signatures, of all the keys of our music:

Three Types of Chromatic Tones

So far we have considered chromatic tones as a means of changing the center. This is not their only function, however; nor is the change of center always a necessary consequence of the appearance of chromatic tones. It depends entirely upon the way the tones move whether or not chromatic tones and chromatic steps affect the center. Here is an example where they do not:

This is the theme of the D minor fugue from Bach's *Well-Tempered Clavichord, II*. The line starts from $\hat{1}$, ascends in a kind of rolling motion to $\hat{5}$, then jumps from $\hat{5}$ directly to $\hat{8}$, without touching any intervening tones. On $\hat{8}$ it turns around and descends again, through $\hat{5}$ to $\hat{1}$. It is the descending stretch between $\hat{8}$ and $\hat{5}$ that catches our interest. We hear a succession of chromatic steps. They do not change the audible direction of the movement towards the tone d—d remains the goal, $\hat{1}$. The chromatic tones have had no effect on the center. What are they needed for, then?

They allow more moves to be squeezed into a given pitch distance than the diatonic pattern would provide! We need only hear the theme with a diatonic ♪♪♪♪ replacing the chromatic ♪♪♪♪ to realize the gain. It seems that the rolling motion from $\hat{1}$ up to $\hat{5}$, followed by the skip $\hat{5}$–$\hat{8}$, accumulates an impulse that the diatonic $\hat{8}$–$\hat{7}$–$\hat{6}$–$\hat{5}$ would allow to peter out much too quickly and ineffectually; in the chromatic sequence, on the other hand, the movement seems almost to force its way against a counter-pressure that constrains the tones to take smaller steps than they normally would. Thus, these chromatic tones do not affect the center, but they greatly affect the character of the *movement.*

Since this example is in D minor one could argue that the tones involved in the chromatic motion were not chromatic tones in a strict sense; the chromatic motion resulted from the successive touching of the two alternative positions of the tones $\hat{7}$ and $\hat{6}$—the sharpened first, then the diatonic—so that actually no tones foreign to the key were introduced. However, the story is the same in major, as shown by the following melody from the minuet of Mozart's String Quartet in G major, K. 387:

The same tone g which is $\hat{1}$ at the beginning is heard as $\hat{1}$ immediately after the chromatic sequence, which therefore cannot have affected the center.

Another typical use of chromatic tones occurs in this theme from the finale of Mozart's *Haffner* Symphony, K. 335: . The g sharp is certainly a chromatic tone in D major, the key of the piece; however, the dynamic quality of the that concludes each of the two short phrases is exactly the same after the second as after the first, the chromatic tone does not disturb the center at all. It is a sort of private excursion of the tone a, $\hat{5}$: instead of merely repeating that tone as in the first phrase, , the movement allows it a margin of freedom just big enough to accomplish a swift away-and-back move, touching the tone that *would be* its $\hat{7}$ if it were to become $\hat{1}$, the tone g sharp. Music is full of such would-be $\hat{7}$–$\hat{8}$ moves involving chromatic tones, which never have a chance to transform the tone at which they aim into a center; they leave the dynamic quality of that tone unaffected —as in our example the move from g sharp to a did not alter the dynamic quality of a = $\hat{5}$. Yet whenever they appear they attract the attention to that point; they distribute a series of lights of varying intensity over the line that ventures into such excursions, producing all sorts of subordinate tensions and releases—as for instance in this melody from Mozart's E flat major String Quartet, K. 428:

This kind of indirect language—the replacing of the diatonic tones actually meant by the chromatic tones most sharply pointing at them—which is used with light touch here, can be intensified to produce the highest degree of emphasis, the strongest inner accents of which tonal expression is capable.

The three types of chromatic tones, those that change the center, those that change the character of the motion, and those that stress individual tones, are not strictly separated in actual music. All sorts of mixtures and combinations of these types occur all the time: strong emphasis on a particular tone may be carried to the point of suggesting for a passing moment that this tone has become $\hat{1}$; chromatic motion may include a stressing of particular tones; and so on.

Move of Center Without Chromatic Tones

Ordinarily a shift of center carries with it the appearance of chromatic tones; but just as on the one hand chromatic tones appear that do not change the center, so on the other a change of center may occur without the appearance of chromatic tones. Merely by the way they move, without expressedly breaking the pattern, the tones can communicate to the ear that their center of attraction has shifted to another place. The following hymn tune shows how this happens.

The key is G minor (the f sharp in the first measure is not a chromatic tone but a tone which belongs: raised $\hat{7}$). After the initial $\widehat{8}$–$\widehat{7}$–$\widehat{5}$–$\widehat{8}$ motion that fixes the center, the line ascends to c, $\widehat{4}$, and turns back again, coming to a halt on the tone a, $\widehat{2}$. The next phrase begins with a move away from $\widehat{1}$, 2–3; when the phrase comes to a conclusion in measure 6, with 𝄞 , this last tone, b flat, is clearly heard as $\widehat{1}$. So in the course of this phrase the center has changed place. How?

The tones involved in this phrase form a pitch pattern that can be interpreted in two ways:

$$a \quad b\flat \quad c \quad d \quad e\flat$$

G minor $\quad \widehat{2} \quad \widehat{3} \quad \widehat{4} \quad \widehat{5} \quad \widehat{6}$

B♭ major $\quad \widehat{7} \quad 8/\widehat{1} \quad \widehat{2} \quad \widehat{3} \quad \widehat{4}$

As the movement fails to reassert g and instead turns repeatedly to the tone b flat, the ear somehow loses sight of the original center and accepts b flat as $\widehat{1}$. It is as if a slight loosening of the grip of center g on the movement had given the other tone the chance to establish itself in the position of center. Only for a short time, though. The following phrase, after moving away from b flat, $\widehat{8}$–$\widehat{7}$–$\widehat{6}$–$\widehat{5}$, in its turn fails to reaffirm the new center; it seems as if the original center, awakened from its inactivity, would not allow this to happen. Very delicately it draws the movement back into the original orbit, first, by leaving the situation somewhat in doubt at the phrase ending 𝄞 (second measure from the last)—is this $\widehat{4}$–$\widehat{3}$ or $\widehat{6}$–$\widehat{5}$?—then, by lifting the tone d up an octave and attracting the motion definitively toward itself: so that d *was* $\widehat{5}$, and the end is $\widehat{5}$–$\widehat{4}$–$\widehat{3}$–$\widehat{2}$–$\widehat{1}$.

The shift in this case involved G minor and B flat major, the relatives that have all seven diatonic tones in common. Another tune shows a similar development, a shift from e flat = $\widehat{1}$ to b flat = $\widehat{1}$ and back again, all in major. The diatonic sets involved have six tones in common.

moving toward.....b♭=$\widehat{1}$ return to.......................c=$\widehat{1}$

The original center loses its hold on the motion when in measure 6 the melody fails to move from $\hat{7}$, d, to $\hat{8}$, e flat, ♪♪♪ , and instead turns around and comes to a halt on b flat, ♪♪♪. The return to the original center is accomplished in one moment, with the appearance of the tone a flat in the ♪♪♪ move that follows immediately upon the assertion of b flat as $\hat{1}$. Had the melody wished to maintain the new center in power, it would have moved ♪♪♪ .

It is obvious that the fewer tones two seven tone sets have in common, the less likely it will be for the shift of center to occur without chromatic tones.

Intervals

One tone is not yet music. One might say it is only a promise of music. The promise is fulfilled, and music comes into being, only when tone follows upon tone. Strictly speaking, therefore, the basic elements of music are not the individual tones but the individual tone-to-tone moves.

Each one of these moves spans a certain pitch distance. The pitch distance between two tones is called an *interval*. If the basic elements of a melody are the individual moves, melody is a succession of intervals rather than of tones.

There are two types of moves according to the intervals spanned; the following theme from Bach's Two-part Invention in F major shows them neatly side by side: ♪♪♪ . In the second half of this theme the motion, upward or downward, proceeds throughout from tone to neighboring tone on the scale. This is called *stepwise* motion. In the first half, on the contrary, every move skips one or more intervening scale tones. Compared to the homogeneity of the stepwise motion the motion by skips shows great variety. It is clear that the combination of stepwise and skipwise motion will be a major factor in determining the profile, the personal character of a melody. In the hymn tunes we have quoted, the motion was mostly stepwise. In a way, stepwise motion can be considered normal motion, in the sense that it involves the least effort in the move from tone to tone; while every skip goes beyond the norm in that it expresses a greater effort by taking us to a more distant tone more rapidly than the normal succession of intervening steps would permit.

Intervals are identified and named according to the number of successive scale tones that go into the pitch distance. The interval between any two successive scale tones is called a *second* (♮, or ♮, or ♮, and so on); the interval between any tone of the scale and the third tone from it is called a *third* (♮, or ♮, or ♮, etc.). Next comes the *fourth,* ♮ etc., then the *fifth,* ♮ etc., the *sixth,* ♮ etc., the *seventh,* ♮ etc., the *octave,* ♮. Intervals larger than the octave—the *ninth,* the *tenth,* and so on—are rarely used, except in some 20th century music.

Any two intervals that taken together make up an octave are called *complementary.* Such pairs are:

second	+ seventh	= octave
third	+ sixth	= octave
fourth	+ fifth	= octave

These relationships are important because they give the tones the freedom to perform, for instance, the move $\widehat{1}$–$\widehat{2}$ either as a second up ♮ or as a seventh down ♮, the move $\widehat{5}$–$\widehat{1}$ either as a fourth up (where we call it $\widehat{5}$–$\widehat{8}$) ♮ or as a fifth down ♮. (In current terminology this relationship of intervals is called *inversion.* This creates confusion, as the same term is used also for another, entirely different interval relation: namely, between, for example, a second up and a second down, a third up and a third down.)

The complementary interval of the octave is the *prime:* an

interval by name only, as here the pitch distance between the two tones is zero.

We realize that the number of successive scale steps is not a very reliable means of measuring pitch distances since the distance between successive scale tones is not always the same; sometimes it is a whole tone, sometimes a half tone. Accordingly intervals called by the same name will not always measure the same pitch distance. In the major scale, for instance, the second between the 1st and 2nd, and between the 2nd and 3rd tones measures one whole tone; but the second between the 3rd and 4th tones measures one half tone. Consequently the third between the 1st and 3rd tones will measure two whole tones, the third between the 2nd and 4th tones one whole plus one half tone. A corresponding difference will appear in the complementary intervals: the seventh that complements the larger second will be smaller than the seventh that complements the smaller second; the same will be true for the sixth.

We have therefore to distinguish between two kinds of seconds, thirds, sixths, and sevenths, which are called *major* and *minor* second, third, sixth, and seventh. The difference in every case is one half tone. ("Major" and "minor" in this context must not be confused with "major" and "minor" as a distinction of mode; minor intervals occur in the major mode—e.g. the minor second between the 3rd and 4th tones, the minor third between the 2nd and 4th tones—and vice versa.)

The situation is somewhat different for the remaining pair of intervals, the fourth and the fifth. As we can see from the scale pattern, all the fourths, except one, are alike—each measuring two whole plus one half tones; so all the fifths, except one, must be alike, measuring three whole plus one half tones each. These fourths and fifths are called *perfect* and distinguished from the two exceptions, the *augmented* fourth which is one half tone too large, and the *diminished* fifth which is one half tone too small.

The striking contrast between the "good" sound of the perfect and the "bad" sound of the augmented and diminished intervals will justify the use of this special terminology.

The augmented fourth occurs between the tones $\hat{4}$ and $\hat{7}$ of the major scale (for instance, in C major,); it measures three whole tones. The diminished fifth occurs between the tones $\hat{7}$ and $\hat{4}$ (above), ; it measures two whole and two half tones. The two pitch distances are the same; thus, these intervals may be said to divide the octave exactly in half. We have noted once before, in the case of the chromatic scale, that the quantitatively most satisfactory distribution produces the most unsatisfactory musical result.

The octaves are all alike, all *perfect*.

Two pairs of odd-sized intervals are occasionally created as a consequence of the raising of $\hat{7}$ in minor. They are: (1) the *diminished seventh* (e.g. in A minor,) with its complement, the *augmented second*, ; and (2) the *augmented fifth* with its complement, the *diminished fourth*, .

Chromatic tones may produce other distortions of intervals, like augmented and diminished octaves; and so on.

Tone and Number

These intervals of the diatonic order possess an extraordinary property, which has caused amazement and wonder ever since it was discovered by the ancient Greeks, reputedly by Pythagoras.

We take two strings, stretched with the same tension over a sounding board, the second more than twice as long as the first. If plucked, string 2 will produce a much lower tone than string 1.

It is clear that in order to produce the higher tone on string 2 I must reduce the length of the vibrating stretch to exactly the size of string 1. This I do by pressing it down, against the board, at the proper place:

String 1 ├───────────────────────┤

String 2 ├─────────────────────●--------------------------┤

(the broken line indicates the nonvibrating section of the string.)

If I lengthen the vibrating section of string 2, I get different tones that will form different intervals with the tone of string 1. The question is this: How much must I add to the vibrating length in order to get, one after the other, the intervals of the octave, the fifth, the fourth, the major third, the minor third? The following table gives the answer. (The length of string 1 is taken as the unit of measurement.)

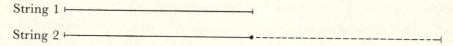

Interval		Ratio
	1	
octave	+1	1:2
fifth	$+\frac{1}{2}$	2:3
fourth	$+\frac{1}{3}$	3:4
major third	$+\frac{1}{4}$	4:5
minor third	$+\frac{1}{5}$	5:6

It appears that in order to get the octave I must add the full length of string 1, so that of the two lengths forming the interval one will be twice as long as the other; in other words, the lengths of the two strings will have the ratio of 1:2. In order to get the fifth I have to add one half of string 1, so that the ratio corresponding to the interval will be $1:1\frac{1}{2}$, or in whole numbers, 2:3. For the fourth I must add one third of the unit length, which gives a corresponding ratio of 3:4. And so on, as the table shows: 4:5 for the major third, 5:6 for the minor third.

The rest is simple calculation. We know that the pitch difference between a fourth and a fifth is one whole tone; the ratio of the two vibrating lengths is $1\frac{1}{3}$ to $1\frac{1}{2}$, or 4/3 to 3/2, or 8/6 to 9/6, or 8:9. So this will be the ratio corresponding to the interval of the major second. To its complementary interval, the minor seventh, will correspond the ratio 9:16 (as 8:16 gives the octave). Similarly we find the following correspondences between intervals and ratios:

Interval	Ratio
Minor second (pitch difference between major third and fourth)	15:16
Major seventh (complement of minor second)	8:15 (16:30)
Minor sixth (complement of major third)	5:8
Major sixth (complement of minor third)	3:5 (6:10)

This was the great discovery: A link exists between music and mathematics; the intervals of the diatonic order can be expressed in terms of simple ratios. As no ancient Mathematician-King is known to have constructed the diatonic scale according to a mathematical order and to have imposed it by decree on the peoples of the Western world, we must conclude that these people, when choosing to adhere in their melodies to the intervals of the diatonic order, unconsciously followed the Law of Number. Their singing, certainly one of their most spontaneous activities, appears secretly governed by mathematical necessity. The philosophical faith of the Greeks in the divine power of Number and in the mathematical order of the universe (kosmos) must have been immensely strengthened by this discovery.[3]

[3] The way the mathematics of the diatonic scale has been presented here is not the way in which it presented itself to the Greeks. The so-called Pythagorean scale uses one ratio only, 2:3, and constructs the diatonic system as a succession of 2:3 ratios:

Transposed into the limits of one octave:

The problems engendered by this construction of the diatonic scale will be discussed presently.

Acoustics—Greek and Modern

We have already noted in passing that number in reference to tones means something else to us than it did to the Ancients. To them, it meant string length; to us, frequency, number of vibrations per second. We have also mentioned the law of acoustics, which establishes a fixed connection between the two: they are inversely proportional; that is to say, if the ratio of two string lengths is $1:2$, the ratio of frequencies will be $2:1$; if the ratio of string lengths is $2:3$, that of frequencies will be $3:2$. For instance, if a string 12 inches long vibrates with frequency 300, a string 24 inches long (ratio $1:2$) will vibrate with frequency 150 ($2:1$); to a string length of 18 inches ($2:3$) a frequency of 200 ($3:2$) will correspond, to a string length of 8 inches ($3:2$) a frequency of 450 ($2:3$), and so on.

The difference between the two interpretations will therefore not show in the ratios that characterize the intervals. $1:2$ identifies the octave here as there, $2:3$ the fifth, $3:4$ the fourth, and so on for all the intervals; but the numbers point in different directions, as it were. To the Greeks the greater number, referring to the longer string, indicates the *lower* tone; to us, because it refers to the higher frequency, it indicates the *higher* tone. If a Greek speaks of the octave $1:2$ he means the interval between a tone and its *lower* octave; to us it means the *higher* octave. For the Greeks the fifth, $2:3$, meant the interval between a tone and the tone a fifth below, e.g. ♮, a–d; for us, it means the opposite, ♮, a–e. Generally speaking, when we name the intervals, "a third, a fourth, a fifth," we always mean it as counted from the bottom up; the other direction would have to be expressly indicated: "a fifth down, a fifth below." With the Greeks, it was the opposite way; they always counted intervals from the top down. So the fifth of the tone a, for instance, is for us the tone e; for the Greeks it is the tone d.

This difference of approach is not restricted to acoustics. To us, the normal, the natural direction of music, if one may say so, is the direction upward. Ask anyone to play a scale: not one in a hundred will do it downward, except if he is explicitly asked to do so. In all our music textbooks scales are presented and discussed in ascending direction; it is taken for granted that this should be so. The letter sequence that name the tones is that of the ascending scale. The Greeks took the opposite for granted. In their texts the scales are as a matter of course presented in downward direction. The tones of the scales are numbered in downward sequence. They seem to have felt that the natural direction of music was downward. The change of attitude must have taken place during the early centuries of the Christian era. With the modes of the Gregorian Chant the upward direction emerges as normal.

For several reasons the modern method of acoustical measurement, the counting of frequencies, is preferable to that of the Greeks, the measuring of vibrating bodies. The frequency number fully defines the pitch; the length of the vibrating body by itself does not, since tension, material, diameter must also be considered. Most important, however, the modern way can claim to have the support of nature itself, in the phenomenon of the so-called *overtones,* or *harmonics.*

Overtones are caused by a certain physical property of vibrating bodies. Normally a string or whatever body produces the sound will not vibrate as one whole only; it will divide itself into sections of exactly one half, one third, one fourth, one fifth, etc., of its length and vibrate in all these divisions simultaneously. Besides the wave with the frequency corresponding to its full length it will emit subordinate waves of twice, three times, four times, five times, etc., that frequency. These subordinate waves are the overtones. Too weak in comparison with the main wave to be heard as distinct tones, they make their presence felt in another way. The different *color* or *timbre* of the sound of different instruments is the result of a difference in relative strength of the individual overtones. An artificial muting of the overtones produces 'pure' tones, tones without color. They sound strangely dead, vacuous.

Normally, if a tone sounds, the frequencies of the overtones, which are twice, three times, four times, etc., its own frequency, will be in the air, too. The ratio of the main wave to these subordinate waves is as $1:2:3:4:5:6$, etc. That is to say, the intervals between the main tone and the first overtone, between the first and second, second and third overtones, and so on, are successively the octave, fifth, fourth, major third, minor third. The sixth overtone is not a part of the diatonic order. The interval between the seventh and eighth overtones is the major second, that between the fourteenth and fifteenth overtones the minor second.

Thus, all the intervals of the diatonic order are actually contained, in their correct ratios, in the acoustical appearance of a single tone. In a very real sense they are part of every tone— but only if we interpret the numbers as referring to frequencies, as indicating intervals in *ascending* direction. The octave, fifth, fourth, etc., *below* a given tone—which is what the Greeks meant by their $1:2:3:4:5$ series—are *not* contained in the tone. For instance, if the tone 🎵 is taken, the ratios $1:2:3$ referring to frequencies represent the intervals 🎵 ; if the ratios refer to string lengths, the intervals they indicate are 🎵 ; but only 🎵 and 🎵 are contained in, are overtones of, the tone 🎵 (or 🎵); 🎵 and 🎵 are not.

The Greek interpretation established the fundamental two-term relation between music and number. The modern interpretation brings in a third term: nature. It reveals the natural phenomenon "tone" as the mediating term between music and number.

In the following paragraphs all numbers should be understood as referring to frequencies, not string lengths.

The Irreconcilables

We now propose to tune a piano the strings of which have all been loosened. The only tools we need are a key for the tightening of the strings and an instrument that indicates frequency numbers. For the time being we forget about the black keys and work on the white keys only; in other words, we tune the seven tones of the C major scale.

To make the mathematics simple we decree that the tone c, 𝄞 , with which we begin shall have the frequency 240. For the rest we need only to apply the proper ratios to the various intervals, as shown in the following table:

	Interval	Ratio	Tone	Frequency
	octave	1:2 or 240:480	c	480
	fifth	2:3 or 240:360	g	360
	fourth	3:4 or 240:320	f	320
	major third	4:5 or 240:300	e	300
	major second	8:9 or 240:270	d	270
	major sixth	3:5 or 240:400	a	400
	major seventh	8:15 or 240:450		450

This gives us the frequencies of the successive tones of the C major scale as follows:

$$\begin{array}{cccccccc} c & d & e & f & g & a & b & c \\ 240 & 270 & 300 & 320 & 360 & 400 & 450 & 480 \end{array}$$

From this we get all the other octaves, higher and lower, by simply doubling and halving the frequency numbers.

One thing we might notice here—a warning of trouble to come—is that the whole tone steps are not all alike: d–e, 270:300, is not as 8:9 but as 9:10; and so is g–a. Still we can accept this as a fact of observation which merely introduces another simple ratio but otherwise does not disturb the order.

At this point a violinist comes along and wants to tune his instrument in preparation for a duo with the piano. The violin has four strings, tuned in intervals of fifths to the pitches 𝄞. Let the violinist get the pitch of his lowest string, the g-string, from the piano, and go on from there by applying the 2:3 ratio to the successive fifths. When he has done this we discover to our surprise that he is out of tune with the piano.

This is what happened:

Working with the 2:3 ratio on the first fifth, g–d, the violinist gets 270 for the tone d. This is in agreement with the piano. But the next step, d–a, will create the discrepancy: the frequency that is in the ratio of 2:3 to 270 is 405, not 400. The tone a will be higher on the violin than on the piano. The last step, a–e, will necessarily carry the discrepancy along: e will turn out to be $607\frac{1}{2}$ instead of 600.

We could try to adjust the piano to the violin in order to keep the two instruments in tune and the fifths all pure, that is, all in the 2:3 ratio. To accomplish this we have to change several pitches. If one tone a of the series becomes 405, its octaves must be changed accordingly; so 𝄞 becomes $202\frac{1}{2}$. The same is true of the tone e; 𝄞 must become $303\frac{3}{4}$. In consequence of this the tone b, a fifth above this e, in order to satisfy the 2:3 ratio, must be changed to $455\frac{5}{8}$, and its lower octave, 𝄞, to $227\frac{13}{16}$. After this adjustment our series looks like this:

180   $202\frac{1}{2}$ $227\frac{13}{16}$ 240   270 $303\frac{3}{4}$ 320   360   405 $455\frac{5}{8}$ 480   540 $607\frac{1}{2}$

The beautiful whole number ratios are for the most part gone; and in the process of adjusting the fifths we have ruined all the thirds.

It appears that the order of the ratios cannot at the same time do justice to the successive scale tones and the successive fifths. Different sets of intervals make equally justified, but incompatible demands on the mathematical order, and every attempt to reconcile the discrepancies seems to make things only worse. An element of conflict is revealed at the core of the beautiful harmony of Tone and Number.

Equal Temperament

This state of things has created two set of problems: one for the philosopher-mathematician, another for the musician. The former cannot reconcile himself to this picture of irreconcilability. To do so would be tantamount to conceding defeat—defeat for reason, which fails to discover order when it is hidden, defeat for the faith in the ultimate mathematical order of the world. From the mythical Pythagoras down, the search for the Perfect Scale has continued through the ages.

The musician's problems are of a different sort. He worries less about number than about sound. He might reconcile himself to the way we tuned the white keys; he might accept the fact that the whole tones between the tones $\hat{2}$ and $\hat{3}$, and the tones $\hat{5}$ and $\hat{6}$, are slightly smaller than the others; he might even accept the slightly impure sound of the fifth between the tones $\hat{2}$ and $\hat{6}$ of the system. In fact, the problem might never have bothered him seriously if it had not been for the development of his art that introduced the new element of the movement of center and the change of key.

Let us assume a key change from C major to D major. Now the impure fifth, d–a, involves the tones $\hat{1}$ and $\hat{5}$, the two pillars of the system; and the step $\hat{1}$–$\hat{2}$, 8 : 9 in our original scale, is now 9 : 10. The whole order appears somehow shaken. In addition, new tones have to be introduced, chromatic tones in reference to C major, black keys in terms of the keyboard; and it is here that things get really bad.

We have not yet considered the black keys at all. How should they be tuned? The slight discrepancies that occurred in the case of the white keys multiply with the introduction of chromatic tones. If we want to provide for all possible keys, for any change of center, the conflicting demands on the pitch of each black key will be so wide apart that no matter how we tune them to satisfy one set of conditions we will fail by a wide margin to satisfy other sets of conditions. Consequently music involving many sharps and flats will simply sound badly off-pitch if played on such a keyboard instrument.

What we have described here was approximately the state of affairs up to Bach's time. That is to say, in music for keyboard instruments the choice of keys was limited, the movement of the center sharply restricted. The situation imposed a severe check on the composer. Finally, relief came with the introduction of the so-called *equal temperament*.

Equal temperament is a very crude solution of the problem; yet it works. It simply takes the octave, 1 : 2, and divides it into twelve proportionally equal parts. On this keyboard all the half tones, whole tones, major and minor thirds, fourths, fifths, etc., are exactly alike; but they are all wrong. Not one interval, with the exception of the octaves, is pure, not one conforms to the correct whole number ratio. Yet by distributing the mistakes evenly over all the twelve tones the discrepancy at each individual point has become so small that it can be practically disregarded. It is noticeable to a trained ear; but it is never large enough, disturbing enough, to keep the dynamic quality of the tone from emerging clearly and cleanly. And this, after all, is what matters in music. The fact that Bach came out as a strong supporter of the new system by writing a series of keyboard compositions *in all keys*—a thing unheard of before—and calling it *The Well-Tempered Clavichord,* is sufficient proof that equal temperament well serves the art of music. Nobody's ear need be more sensitive than Bach's.

The beautiful whole number ratios, however, the holy numbers, are gone. In their stead we get a series of seven digit decimals.

Meanings of Intervals

When we called the interval between two successive tones in a melody a third, a fourth, a fifth, or whatever, we were in a sense using very inaccurate language. By definition an interval is the pitch distance between two tones. Yet in music there is no pitch pure and simple; pitch enters the musical picture as bearer of dynamic qualities. The move that connects two successive tones of a melody does not just bridge a pitch distance; it ties together two dynamic qualities into the unity of one statement.

♪, for instance. What is it? A perfect fourth. In acoustical terms this is a correct and complete answer. In musical terms, it is not. As a statement involving the relation of two dynamic qualities it may have any one of many possible meanings. We know that there is a perfect fourth, $\hat{1}$–$\hat{4}$, another, $\hat{2}$–$\hat{5}$, still others, $\hat{3}$–$\hat{6}$ major, $\hat{3}$–$\hat{6}$ minor, $\hat{4}$–$\hat{7}$ minor (not major where $\hat{4}$–$\hat{7}$ is the augmented fourth), $\hat{5}$–$\hat{8}$, and so on. The meaning will of course be determined by the position of the center. When g is $\hat{1}$, as in the following example from a Bach Cello Suite*, ♪, the move d—g says $\hat{5}$–$\hat{8}$; the same move in this

---

* Many examples in the following two paragraphs are transposed so as to bring them in the position best suited to a clear demonstration of the change of meaning in the intervals.

Bach theme (Fugue 20, WTC II) where b is $\hat{1}$, ♪♪ , says something entirely different; namely, $\hat{3}-\hat{6}$ in minor. The two statements have no more in common than the noun "bear" and the verb "bear." $\hat{5}-\hat{8}$ is a precise and determined move that takes us exactly to the point where we belong. $\hat{3}-\hat{6}$ expresses an effort to lift us higher than necessary, as it were, to the tone "beyond" $\hat{5}$, which pulls sharply back to $\hat{5}$ and in this sense is "too high." In the tune of the "Marseillaise" (center c), ♪♪ , the d–g move expresses the upward sweep of $\hat{2}-\hat{5}$.

To consider other intervals: In the last Bach example the first move, ♪♪ , a major third, said $\hat{5}-\hat{3}$ minor; the center was b; if d is $\hat{1}$, as in the following melody, ♪♪ , the same major third says $\hat{3}-\hat{1}$ major. This example is from Bach's Second Cello Suite. The first move of this theme (Fugue 8, WCT II), ♪♪ , is the fifth $\hat{1}-\hat{5}$; if d is the center, the fifth becomes $\hat{5}-\hat{2}$—as in the theme of the Chaconne for violin (last movement of Partita II): ♪♪ . The tremendous energy of that theme which alone supports ten pages of music rests principally in the extraordinary character of its first move. In this fugue theme (center c), ♪♪ , the major sixth has the meaning $\hat{1}-\hat{6}$; in another fugue theme (center b flat), ♪♪ , from Fugue 23, WTC II, the same interval has the meaning $\hat{2}-\hat{7}$. The difference, in this case, is particularly striking. The examples can be multiplied at will.

The different meanings of one and the same interval are not equivalent possibilities. It appears that every interval has a kind of preference for one particular meaning; if heard by itself, without any previous or simultaneous declaration of a center, it will suggest to the ear that preferred meaning. When we hear a fifth, ♪♪ —nothing but that—like a signal, we will always hear $\hat{1}-\hat{5}$; a fourth, under the same conditions, will be $\hat{5}-\hat{8}$; a major

78

third, $\hat{1}$–$\hat{3}$ major; a minor third, $\hat{1}$–$\hat{3}$ minor; a major second, $\hat{1}$–$\hat{2}$; a minor second, $\hat{7}$–$\hat{8}$. (With the larger intervals the situation is not as clear, as other factors enter the picture, harmonic factors.) In this way every interval seems to place itself by its own weight, as it were, into a definite position in the dynamic field. This might be called its natural position, and the corresponding dynamic meaning its natural or normal meaning. In relation to it the other possible meanings of the interval assume the character of deviations, significant deviations, from a norm. The possibility not only of saying different things with the same move but also of exhibiting in this difference the presence of a norm and of the freedom to depart from it, is one of the chief means of expression of the tonal language.

Sometimes a melody will take an interval through a series of different meanings in straight succession; e.g., this Bach theme, [musical notation], where the successive fourths say $\hat{1}$–$\hat{4}$, $\hat{2}$–$\hat{5}$, $\hat{3}$–$\hat{6}$; or, a similar case, this Beethoven theme, [musical notation], from the piano sonata, op. 110; this theme, after three ascending fourths, ends with a descending fourth, *traversed stepwise*. In the following melody, also by Beethoven (last movement, Eroica Symphony), the third is prominent: [musical notation]. We end with a Bach theme (Fugue 1, WTC I) that shows how an interval becomes the main structural factor of a melody; here it is again the fourth that dominates the picture in surface and depth:

[musical notation]

In this kind of integrated structure one recognizes the mark of genius; only in a superior mind will an elementary tonal idea, such as an interval, unfold like a germ and produce an organic form.[4]

[4] In an earlier version of this fugue the theme read: [musical notation]. The later correction, which lengthened the tone f by adding the dot, has the purpose of clarifying the idea: the brief stop on [musical notation] has the effect of pulling together precisely the first four tones that mark off the interval of the fourth.

II • *Texture and Structure*

From the study of melody we turn to the study of the wholes of which melody is a part. In two ways can melody be said to be a part of wholes, namely, in regard to *texture* and *structure*.

Texture refers to the composition of the musical fabric. Our music knows two fundamental types of texture, which we distinguish by the terms *polyphonic* and *homophonic*.

The fabric of polyphonic—translated: many-voiced—music is the result of an interweaving of a number of individual melodic threads. The single thread is called *voice* or *part*. Usually the composer decides at the outset the number of threads to be woven into the fabric of the piece he is about to write, and he does not change that number during the piece. In this sense he will not write a fugue, a mass, a madrigal, but a 3-part fugue, a mass for four voices, a 5-part madrigal. Taken individually each voice is a consistent melodic movement in its own right, makes sense by itself; the whole combines, or rather integrates, the several individual voices into one collective movement. This makes for a homogeneous fabric in polyphonic music: no part is subordinated to any other part, the voices move in the compound as equals.

The literal translation of the word homophonic is "same-voiced." Obviously the musical term does not have this meaning: in homophonic music all do not sing or play the same thing (when this happens we call it unison singing or playing). In homophonic as in polyphonic music different tones sound together all the time. Here, however, this is not the result of a combination of melodies, or precisely, of equivalent melodies going on at the same time; here the fabric consists of *one leading* melody or voice combined with a supporting body of sound. This body of sound is essentially *harmony*. The texture of homophonic music is therefore not homogeneous. Individuality, personality, that which identifies a piece is concentrated in the leading voice; leave that out, and the piece becomes nameless. Heard by itself the supporting sound body, however interesting it may be as such, is like a pedestal without a statue. In polyphonic music, on the contrary, any voice heard by itself will identify the piece. In other words, if in a homophonic piece the leading voice is left out, that which remains will be of a different nature from that which has been left out, while in a polyphonic piece, whatever is left out, the remainder will be of the same nature with it.

If tones of different pitch sound together the attention of the ear will quite naturally focus on the highest. Accordingly the natural place for the leading voice in homophonic music is the top layer of the tonal compound: the treble. While this condition of nature sets the norm, music does not feel constrained to stick to it at all times. In Chopin's C minor Polonaise, for instance, the leading voice is in the bass, at the bottom of the tonal compound. In the same piece we hear the leading voice change place, too, and move from the bottom to the top and back again. Towards the end there even occurs an overlapping: the treble, instead of handing over the leadership to the bass which enters carrying the leading melody, insists on continuing its own leading melody for a while: the leading voice is split in two, as it were; treble and bass compete for leadership. In this and similar ways the pattern of homophonic texture is capable of subtle variations.

Actually our music knows a third type of texture, if it can be called that, namely, one in which the single thread is already the whole fabric. The great representative of this type, of music that is whole in one line—of *monophonic* music—is the Gregorian Chant. We often fail to realize that what is to us the exceptional case—not more than one tone sounding at a time—is the normal state of music for all nations except those of Western civilization, just as it was the normal state of our music up to the time nine centuries ago when people in the small geographical area on both sides of the English Channel made the momentous discovery that more than one tone could sound at a time *and make sense*.

As to the historical development: The first fruit of this discovery was polyphony; harmony, and with it homophonic music, came only much later. It is interesting that the birth of polyphony, properly so called, coincided with the building of the great Gothic cathedrals, and the birth of harmony with the culmination of the Renaissance and the beginning of modern science and mathematics: that is, the two great changes in our understanding of the tonal world coincide with two great changes in our understanding of *space*. However, the two types of musical texture are not characteristics of historical periods in the sense that the old goes when the new comes in. If we express polyphonic texture by the formula "melody plus melody," and homophonic by "melody plus harmony," we shall find many instances that call for a combined formula, "melody plus melody plus harmony." In fact, such a synthesis marks two culminating points of musical development: harmony asserting itself within the framework of polyphony marks J. S. Bach's art; and the reappearance of polyphony, in a new guise, within the framework of homophonic-harmonic music characterizes the art of the great symphonic composers of the late 18th and 19th century, Haydn, Mozart, Beethoven, Brahms, Wagner, and Bruckner.

The characteristics of the two textural types will be discussed in more detail later, in the sections on polyphony and harmony.

Arrow and Circle

Structure in music, understood in the most general sense, means relationship of *successive* parts of the temporal whole. Music unfolds in time; musical structures are *time structures*.

Insofar as our study of melody had as its object the relation of tones or intervals—that is, of successive parts of the melodic whole—to one another and to the whole of the melody, it was a study of melodic structure. The basic principle of this structure we found to be the action of the tonal forces. Ultimately all musical structures, the smallest as well as the largest, will appear to be based on tonal dynamics. However, even in a simple and short melody we can discover the manifestation of a structural principle of a different order:

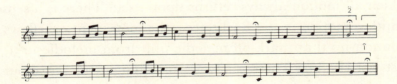

The new principle referred to is the repetition of larger sections of the tonal movement. What has been heard before is heard again. In the first tune the repetition produces a binary structure; its dynamic function is expressed by the ending of the first section on $\widehat{2}$, of the second on $\widehat{1}$.

In the present chapter we are dealing with structure on the larger scale where an individual melody is not the whole but the part, the unit, whose repetition produces structure; or, to put it more precisely, with structure insofar as it is based on the repetition of smaller or larger melodic units.

To get a first glimpse of fundamental structural differences we listen to the second of Bach's Twelve Little Preludes, in C minor, and to the theme of Schubert's B flat major Impromptu.[1] Repetition of melodic units is prominent in both instances, but the structural results are radically different. In the Bach piece the repeated melodic units are like successive waves of a continuous flow: each repetition is an advance. In the Schubert, on the contrary, the accent in the repetitions is on recurrence: they take us *back*. The same thing, repetition, seems to serve two different masters, to lend itself to the expression of two different desires, the desire to move on and on and on, and the desire to return again and again to the origin. Proper symbols are the straight line with the arrow, ⟶ , the line along which the movement can go on endlessly, and the circle, ◯ , along which all motion always returns upon itself. There is a sense of limitless motion in the Bach piece, the movement overflows the boundaries that mark off melodic unit from melodic unit, the last word is flux. There is always something arbitrary about the close of such a piece; in truth it should never end (in practice a composer, after having finished the work, would quite often decide that it was not long enough and attach a few more moves). In the Schubert piece, on the other hand, the individual melodic units are sharply set off against one another; the accent is on their mutual complementing and balancing rather than on flux, continuous advance; no sense of the unlimited here, everything happens within well defined limits, everything spells out the triumph of the finite, symmetry.

The two tendencies—arrow and circle, one open, the other closed, one cumulative, the other symmetrical—underlie all

[1] See Section of Scores, p. *2*.

musical structures, either separately or, more often, in all sorts of combinations and crossings. According to which of them dominates the structure we shall talk of chain forms and circle forms (chain forms, because the successive structural units follow one another without breaks like links in a chain). We shall see later that both tendencies have a common source in the phenomenon of meter.

A–B–A

We investigate the structure of Schubert's Impromptu in A flat major, Opus 142, No. 2.[2] First, we look at the piece from a distance, as it were, where only the major structural distinctions stand out to the observer, the minor ones do not count.

From this vantage point, three sections can be easily distinguished; of these, the first and third are identical (except for a brief extension at the end of the third), the second is different. This is a standard structural pattern of 18th and 19th century music; it is called three-part or A–B–A form.

Now we move closer and focus on the next lower level of structural distinctions.[3] We observe that the pattern of the higher level is reproduced here: each of the major sections shows the same kind of three-part structure in itself. A structural division appears after the first 16 measures of the large A section; after this, the music goes on in a somewhat different way, coming to a halt on a note of expectation in measure 30 (dynamically: $\widehat{5}$), whereafter the first section—we call it "small a"—is repeated. In the large B section the first subsection, "small c," occupies 12 measures; this is followed by 20 measures similar in character but different in content, leading to a repetition of "small c." A

---

[2] See Section of Scores, p. 4.

[3] We disregard in this analysis all repeat signs. Their observance is optional, and they do not affect the essential structural pattern.

short extension prepares for the recurrence of the large *A* section.

We can once more move closer and observe the structure of the subsections. We find "small *a*" divided into two halves: the melody of the first 8 measures is repeated, with slight changes, an octave higher. "Small *c*" is also divided, but not into equal parts; only the first four measures are repeated.

Taken together, this gives us the following three-level diagram of the structure:

A			B			A		
a	b	a	c	d	c	a	b	a
α α			α α γ γ′		γ γ′ α α			α α	

The first question that arises here is: What is the sense of doing such a thing? What is the meaning of a formal pattern that carries repetition to such an extreme degree? This is not a space pattern where repetition of this type might be quite normal— for instance in architecture, or in ornamental design—because there the individual sections are given all at once. This is a *time pattern,* and repetition in time means saying or hearing again what has been said or heard before. Of the 148 measures of this piece only 58 contain music that has not been heard before— and heard more than once: counting all the repeats called for by the double bars, we hear the first melody at the end for the twelfth time! We must imagine the same procedure in another medium to realize how extraordinary it is. What would we think if we should read a poem consisting of thirty stanzas, of which the 2nd stanza repeated the 1st; the 3rd and 4th repeated the 1st and 2nd; the 7th and 8th did the same; stanzas 9–12 repeated stanzas 5–8; 14 repeated 13; 15 and 16 repeated 13 and 14; 19 and 20 did the same; 21–24 repeated 15–18; and finally, 25–30 repeated 1–2–5–6–7–8! This would make nonsense of the poetry long before we reached the end. How can it make sense in music?

The answer is: Nowhere in music is repetition a mere saying again of what has been said before. In our example every repetition fulfills a need for symmetric complementation. This appears most clearly in the *b* section, which our ear recognizes as a *bridge:* that is, as leading from somewhere to somewhere; and what it leads to, the point towards which the bridge directs our attention, the event whose entry we are tensely awaiting at the end of *b,* turns out to be the recurrence of the beginning. At this moment we realize that the *a* section—which in itself seemed complete, a closed circle—in the larger perspective appears incomplete, a semicircle in need of being closed, and actually now being closed by the return of *a:* the process was merely delayed, and the tension heightened, by the intervening of the *b* section. Thus, our satisfaction is not only that of hearing a lovely melody again but rather of experiencing the incomplete becoming complete, and the universal law of symmetry fulfilled.

Similar considerations apply to the repetitions on the higher level. It is interesting to observe that the degree of otherness— if such an expression be permitted—in the middle sections, *B,* *b,* and *d,* is adjusted to the structural level. *B* is other than *A* in a rather striking manner: the key is different, the rhythm is different; the texture in *A* makes a clear distinction between the leading melody and the supporting harmony, while in *B* it is hard to tell the two apart, the melody is hidden: who could *sing* *B?* Small *b,* on the other hand, has the more noticeable features in common with *a:* key, rhythm, texture; just the melody itself is not the same. Similarly, *d* shares these features with *c,* otherness is confined here to the change from major to minor and a striking movement of the tonal center.

Within the *a* subsection symmetry is operating in the simplest manner, in a two-part structure, without a middle section separating the two complementary halves. Thus, the same tendency, the tendency towards return to the origin, towards symmetry and balance, operates on all structural levels. The movement is everywhere circular; this is a clear-cut circle form.

A–B–A–B–A

In Schubert's Moment Musical, No. 2,[4] in A flat major, we observe an interesting development of three-part symmetry. Considering the major structural divisions we find an *A* section 17 measures long, followed by a *B* section of 18 measures and repeated after this, with slight changes and an extension at the end, in the normal *A–B–A* manner. Yet after the law of symmetry has thus been fulfilled we find ourselves suddenly and with a shock thrown into a repeat of *B*, which in turn necessitates a third appearance of *A*. This gives us altogether five sections, *A–B–A–B–A*.

Is this still a symmetrical pattern? It is—but not in the way it looks. To the eye, and as an arrangement in space, the second *A* appears as the middle, the axis, about which the rest is symmetrically arranged. To the ear, however, this section cannot possibly mean "middle." Musically, it is the function of a middle or *B* section not merely to separate two corresponding sections but to keep alive and unfulfilled a latent desire for symmetrical complementation of something gone by, by something to come; and this seems the only way for symmetry to be realized *in time*. Now the music of that second *A* section cannot possibly be heard as a middle in this sense. It does not delay the fulfillment of a desire for symmetry, it does the very opposite, it satisfies such a desire, namely in relation to the first *A* section. At its end a circle seems closed. If it were a middle it should leave us waiting for something to come, and we should be satisfied if

[4] See Section of Scores, p. 7.

this turned out to be the repetition of the preceding, the B section. Yet the last thing we expect here is a return of B; when it happens, it comes as a great surprise. It does not satisfy a need for symmetry, it creates rather a new one; now the second A is in need of symmetrical complementation by a third repeat. Thus A_2 is not middle but both end and beginning at the same time—end in relation to A_1, beginning in relation to A_3: $A–B–A–B–A$.

In a delicate manner the music of A_2 gives us an indication that it cannot really be the last word, that something remains to be said. The main melody is heard twice in A_1 but only once in A_2 and A_3. In this sense A_2 balances only half of A_1, and only A_2 and A_3 together balance A_1 fully. The music plays deliberately with the contradiction between this and the extension of the melody in the last 9 measures of A_2, which seem to bring everything to a real end and so make the new B a real surprise.

The following diagram shows in what sense this five-part structure can be understood as an outgrowth of the basic three-part pattern:

Another version of three-part structure is represented by the slow movement of Beethoven's Piano Sonata, Opus 13.[5] The pattern here is $A–B–A–C–A$.[6] The decisive factor is the different degree of "otherness" in B and C. While B is just "other than A," C is "in contrast to A." In the perspective of the contrasting C section everything that came before is pulled together, as it were, and appears as comparatively "same." $A–B–A$ taken

[5] See Section of Scores, p. *10*.

[6] A: measures 1–16; B: 17–29; A: 29–36; C: 37–51; A: 51–66. Closing phrase: 66–end.

together, a "beginning-middle-end" structure in itself, acts as "beginning" in relation to C as "middle" and the third A as "end": $A\overset{\frown}{-B-}A-C-A$. Differences in the three A sections support the differences of structural meaning: A_2 is lightened by being only half as long as A_1; and the intensification of the rhythm in A_3 helps this section in its task of counterbalancing all the music "on the other side" of C.

Fast-Slow-Fast

In each of the Schubert pieces, we were dealing with a complete composition. The Beethoven piece, though complete in itself, is not meant as a complete composition; it is a part of a still larger whole, a *sonata*.

Literally, sonata means "piece to be played" as distinguished from cantata, "piece to be sung."[7] As a musical form sonata is a whole of wholes, as it were, a combination of several structures, each of which is complete in itself, into one large superstructure. The individual structures are called *movements*.

The meaning of such a superstructure can be grasped when the Beethoven piece is heard in the context of the Sonata as a whole. The second of three movements, it is preceded and followed by music of very different character. The wonderful repose of its melodic line appears doubly precious when it is wrested, as it were, from the excitement of the first movement and lost again to the restlessness of the last. The first and third movements, although they are different pieces of music, have certain traits in common: both move at a rapid pace, and in both the dramatic impact is stressed by sudden changes from swift to halting motion. In the first movement, speed of flow and weight of content combine to produce the effect; while the last movement balances the lighter weight by the still greater

[7] *Sonare* (Italian), to play; *cantare*, to sing.

drive of its onrush. In these most general terms the three movements together, the slow one flanked by the two fast ones, represent a three-part structure symmetrical in intent: "same-other-same."

For almost 150 years, from the middle of the 18th to the end of the 19th century, the pattern "fast-slow-fast" dominated musical thought. Sonatas, symphonies, concertos, chamber music pieces were all cast in this mold. Established as a convention and mechanically repeated by generations of mediocre composers it nevertheless constituted the greatest challenge to the superior minds who understood its implications: the possibility to create, on the largest scale, intangible symmetries out of tangible diversities. There are innumerable ways for the first and last movements to balance each other across the "otherness" of the middle movement or movements—for very often a second middle movement, dance-like in character, called Menuetto or Scherzo, is added to the structure. Each of the great composers had his personal ideas about the problem; each composition represents one possible solution. Of particular interest are occasional departures from the basic pattern, such as two-movement or five-movement structures, or structures with transitions between the movements. In the course of time the idea of symmetrical balance entered into a combination with the idea of progress: the last movement should not merely balance the first but also represent a development, an advance, a "more." This problem was particularly Beethoven's preoccupation. His whole career as a symphonic composer exhibits the struggle for a synthesis of balance and progress—the limited and the unlimited, the circle and the arrow. He succeeded not by compromising but by driving both principles to their extremes.

The great compositions of Beethoven, Schubert, Brahms, and Bruckner mark the culmination of the circle as a principle of musical form.

Repetition without Symmetry

For examples of structures definitely not of the circular type we turn to Bach's *Well-Tempered Clavichord*. We listen to the Prelude and Fugue in C minor of Volume I.[8]

After the Schubert and Beethoven pieces the absence of divisions is striking. No sections or subsections are formed, consequently no symmetries, no balances can emerge. Continuous forward motion dominates the picture. This does not imply, however, that nothing is repeated. On the contrary, repetition seems to be everywhere. But as mentioned before, repetition has a different meaning in a different context; here it means advance, not return.

What is the thing repeated if there are no sections? In the case of the Prelude it is a sharply drawn tone line, , one half measure long, a formula rather than an explicit statement, not meant to be taken by itself, meaningful only as an element of the continuous flow. The formula is duplicated within every measure (in this sense the principle of symmetry can be said to operate here on the lowest level only) and restated with constant modification from measure to measure, until towards the end it gradually disintegrates. The whole is like one long melody—not of tone after tone but of block after block, with each block representing the content of one formula, thus:

In the Fugue, this is different. The thing to be repeated is here a *theme:* a little tonal organism in its own right, a statement well capable of standing on its own feet and one which taken by itself makes good sense. It is clear, however, that the

8 See Section of Scores, p. *13.*

statement of the theme does not close the case, as it were; it is rather like presenting a thought for further discussion. The discussion takes the form of repeating the theme in an ever changing tonal environment, of showing it in different situations. In this Fugue we hear the theme eight times: in measures 1, 3, 7 (in the bass), 11 (treble), 15 (middle voice), 20 (treble), 26 (bass), and 29 (treble). Certain things in these statements of the theme, particularly at the beginning, are standard procedure and identify a polyphonic piece as a fugue; namely, that the voices, whatever their number—in our case it is three—should enter successively, each beginning with a full statement of the theme, and that these entries should be so arranged that the first states the theme centered about $\hat{1}$, the second centered about $\hat{5}$, the third at $\hat{1}$ again, and so on, till all the voices have had their turn.

The theme of this Fugue is 2 measures long, its eight repetitions fill 16 measures. As the Fugue is 31 measures long it is clear that not all in it can be repetition of the theme. We observe what happens. The first repetition of the theme, in measure 3, follows immediately upon the completion of the first statement; but between the end of the second statement, at the beginning of measure 5, and the third entry, at the beginning of measure 7 in the bass, the theme is withheld from us. We get small bits of it, in the treble, combined with a scalewise motion in the other voice, but not until measure 7 do we hear the theme again, complete and in its true form. Similar things happen in measures 9 and 10; in measures 13 and 14 not even those small bits—the technical term is *motifs*—remind us of the existence of the theme. From now on the intervals between the statements of the theme get longer: there are 3 measures between the fifth and the sixth statements, $4\frac{1}{2}$ measures between the sixth and the seventh; only the last two statements are again drawn close to each other, separated only by one half measure.

If we sum this up we have a movement from "theme" to "no theme" to "theme" to "no theme" to "theme," and so on: $A-B-A-B-A$ . . ., or perhaps $A-B-A-C-A$ . . . . This may look like a circular pattern; but the meaning and the corresponding experience are totally different. There is no real "otherness" in the "no theme" sections, we are never actually taken away from the theme; and most important of all, nowhere will the repetition of A be experienced as closing a circle, answering a need for symmetrical complementations. These repetitions lead us on and on and on, never back. It is clearly a chain form.

If we consider the Prelude and Fugue as a whole and compare it with the structure of a sonata we notice the corresponding difference. The two pieces do not form a symmetrical superstructure; they are not mutually complementary halves of one larger whole. The Prelude, as the word says, is a piece of music preparing for and leading up to the Fugue. Here, too, the sense of the succession is advance, not return.

(One function of every prelude is certainly to establish a definite dynamic center, so that the lonely voice that opens the fugue will be met by an ear prepared to understand the dynamic quality of its first tone.)

Other Chain Forms

We mention briefly other instances of chain forms. Two radically opposed realizations of the chain principle are possible: with all links exactly alike, or with no two links even remotely similar—the form in which nothing new is ever added, and the form in which everything added is new. The first can be found more easily in primitive music, which quite often consists of nothing but an endless repetition of one short melodic line (Ravel's "Bolero" is one of Western music's nearest approximations to this). The second form is in the strictest sense only a theoretical possibility; no music is totally devoid of repetition. What this form amounts to in practice is repetition restricted to the smallest scale, within the individual link only, but no repetition from link to link. Much of the old vocal music is of this type—madrigals and motets—where the music moves with the words, from stanza to stanza or from line to line, with each stanza or line corresponding to one link of the musical chain. In opera we may find it, too, when music parallels larger stretches of dramatic action. In instrumental music it is rather rare; some fantasies and preludes of Bach and the older masters show it, also the so-called tone poems of some late 19th century composers.

The opposite solutions of "nothing new" and "everything new" appear happily combined in a pattern like A–B–A–C–A–D . . . where A acts like a refrain. This is called *rondo form*. (In a different sense it is also, as we have seen, the structure of the fugue.) Here the two possibilities alternate to form one pattern. They can also be in action simultaneously. One segment of the texture, e.g. the bass, may repeat one melodic line over and over again while the other parts set something new upon this foundation whenever it returns. This is the form of the passacaglia and chaconne. The complete integration of the two possibilities produces one of the most interesting and suggestive of all musical forms, the *variation form*. A melody is repeated and transformed at the same time; always the same and always new. Every repetition represents a new stage of the transformation. Some of the deepest musical thoughts have been expressed in terms of the variation form.

There is no real equivalent of the chain type to the sonata or symphony as a superstructure of the circle type. The suite, a sequence of pieces dance-like in character, loosely strung together, might be called a structure of the chain type if one *could* be sure that it *is* a structure and not rather the result of the absence of a large-scale structural design.

Circle and Chain Combined

So far we have discussed structures that are either of the circle or of the chain type; but this is not an either-or proposition. The two principles of musical form are not mutually exclusive. On the contrary, their combination produces most interesting results. We mention Mozart's great Piano Fantasy in C minor, which after moving through a number of large chain links finally returns to the beginning in true circular manner and with striking effect. Some variation movements, e.g. the last movement of Beethoven's Piano Sonata, Opus 109, after having led the melody through a full series of transformations, at the end return it in the original form in which we first met it, and so close a circle. There is also a circular rondo form of the pattern *A–B–A–C–A–B–A;* and so on.

The outstanding example of circle and chain tendencies combined in one structure is the so-called *sonata form*—the term is poorly chosen as it implies a relation to the sonata that does not exist. Sonata form is the standard form of the first movement of such large-scale instrumental compositions as sonatas, symphonies, chamber music works and concertos; other movements than the first may also show it. It is a three-part form. In the first section, called the *exposition,* a number of subsections of different content are linked together in chain-like fashion; the middle section, called the *development,* takes the content of the first section on a kind of dramatic journey through remote regions and complex situations and finally leads into the restatement of the first section, now called the *recapitulation.* The whole is symmetrical: *A–B–A;* but within each section the chain principle is dominant; and the otherness of *B* is restricted to treatment of material, does not extend to material itself.

One important formal difference between exposition and recapitulation is in the ending. One understands why the ending of the recapitulation, which closes not only a section but the whole movement, should be made stronger than the ending of the exposition, which closes only one section. This strengthening of the final close normally takes the form of an extension, called the *coda*. In Beethoven's hands the coda grew to such dimensions that it became a full-fledged fourth section of the sonata form. One would think that such a substantial alteration of the pattern would disturb and even destroy the basic three-part symmetry of the structure. The interesting thing is that it does nothing of the sort. Obviously what counts here is not duration but function; and no matter how the coda is extended, functionally it remains a strengthening of the final punctuation. But there is even more to it than this. As we are dealing here with symmetries in time, the *A–B–A* structure of the sonata form does not actually close a circle, does not end where it began. To be precise, it ends with the *last* subsection of the *A* section, not with the first. In the coda Beethoven discovers the possibility of remedying that flaw and of making the circle perfect. He uses the additional section to take us back once more to the very beginning; and the return of the beginning closes the movement. The first movements of his Fifth, Eighth, and Ninth Symphonies are particularly successful in solving this problem.

III ✦ Meter and Rhythm

As a prelude to the discussion of meter and rhythm one might try a little psychological experiment.

Let one of a group of people tap the tabletop with his finger-tip, lightly and regularly, at the rate of about 90 taps per minute. Let the others present concentrate on the incoming sound stimuli, abandon themselves to the experience of their even succession and, after a while, begin to count with them, or associate words with the beats.

Under the primitive conditions of an ordinary room the result will probably not be as clear-cut as in a psychologial laboratory. Still it will appear that only a minority has counted "one-one-one-" or "one-two-three-four-five-" etc., or has associated a long chain of words. The majority will always count "one-two-one-two-" or "one-two-three-one-two-three-" or in some similar manner, or associate one word or a few words only with the beats and repeat these over and over.

The following conclusion can be drawn from this experiment: Identical stimuli in regular succession (identical and regular to immediate observation) are not experienced as a series of single events, or "points," but as *groups*. Nothing can be found in the stimuli themselves that would cause the grouping; still they automatically fall into these groups, irresistibly arrange themselves in such an order. If the speed of the succession increases or decreases beyond certain limits the groups will disappear in a blur or disintegrate into unconnected points. At this point we merely take notice of the facts without going into an inquiry about their causes. One thing must be avoided: namely, pre-judging the case by deciding offhand that the order is a subjective contribution from the listener.[1]

The Beat

Traditional aesthetic doctrine makes a distinction between spatial and temporal arts. To the former belong architecture, painting, sculpture; the outstanding example of the latter is music. Music unfolds in time. Just as a work of the visual arts needs space, and our awareness of space, to come into existence, a work of music needs time, and our awareness of time.

Music is not just *in* time. It does something *with* time. What?

We let Chopin's B flat major Mazurka, Opus 7, No. 1,[2] answer this question.

When we listen to this we hear more than merely successive tones: we hear a definite *regularity* in their succession—regularity in time. They, or at least some of them, appear to follow one another at equal time intervals. It is as if the even flow of time were cut up by the regularly recurrent sounds into short stretches of equal duration: the tones *mark time*. As a consequence the listener becomes immediately aware of the existence of these time marks, of a regular *beat,* and of the fact that the music conforms to the beat as to a measure of its motion.

This is not all. The same tones that divide the time flow into equal parts, units of duration, combine the parts again into small groups, each containing the same number of units; three in the case of our example. In the experience of this particular piece the group stands out even more conspicuously than the beat itself. If the listener were asked to count with the music he

---

[1] Compare the author's *Sound and Symbol,* section "Time."
[2] See Section of Scores, p. *17.*

would fall into the one-two-three-one-two-three count without hesitation.

Meter, the musical term as we understand it today, comprises both the regular time divisions of the beat and the organization of beats into groups. The beat is the primary thing; we shall discuss it first.

Music that adjusts its movement in time to the strict measure of a beat is called *measured music.* To us who are familiar with this type of music only, this seems the normal and natural state. It is not. Where music consists essentially of one melodic line only, as all music does except our own of the last 750 or so years, and where it is not intended as an accompaniment to a dance or some other bodily motion, there is no more reason for it to submit to the rule of a regular beat than, say, for poetry to do so. One does not beat time to the reading of a poem. A Gregorian Chant melody, for instance, proceeds in full freedom to set its pace according to the impulse of the moment, to what it wants to do or to say. It is only when music takes the step into polyphony that this precious freedom must be renounced. If several melodic lines should proceed together, and together make sense, they must submit their movement to some common time measure, to a common pace. This is the beat. Measured music and polyphony have come into existence together. To ears accustomed to the free movement of chant this must at first have sounded as if music had put itself into a strait jacket. Gradually it turned out that the tones, by voluntarily giving up one kind of freedom and putting themselves under a strict rule, made possible the development of an entirely new kind of freedom, the freedom of rhythm under the law of meter.

Rhythm in measured music is time pattern related to a beat. The listener, therefore, in order to catch the sense of the pattern must also catch the beat; somehow the beat must be communicated to him. The tones never fail to achieve this. No one can listen to a piece of measured music without sooner or later being invaded, as it were, by the beat; the beat of the music takes hold of him, inwardly he moves along with the beat, and not always inwardly only; witness the small involuntary motions that are the normal by-product of intense listening: tapping of the feet or the hands, swaying of the head, and what not. The time pattern of the successive sounds is measured by the pulse that the music sets in motion in the listener. Without this involvment there can be no appreciation of rhythm in our music.

The question arises: How do the tones communicate the beat? In the case of the Chopin Mazurka there was no problem; one whole section of the music, the one assigned to the left hand of the player, seemed specifically assigned to the task of spelling out the beat clearly, unambiguously. However, this is by no means the usual situation. More often than not there will be no such direct communication, no straight duplication of the beat by the tones, but rather a succession of tones of very different durations, long and short, in all sorts of irregular arrangements. Still, a beat normally will be communicated all the same. As an example, take the beginning of Schubert's Moment Musical, No. 2, in A flat. We hear the following time sequence of sounds:

In the whole sequence no two consecutive sounds are alike in duration; and only 2 of 27 altogether are equal to what will turn out to be the time value of the beat. Yet by the time that much has been heard the listener will probably have caught the beat, or rather have been caught by the beat.

An indication of how this happens can be gathered from the way time values are represented in our notation. Each musical symbol represents a time value as well as a pitch; with the difference, however, that as a time symbol its meaning is strictly relative. ♮, for instance, tells me exactly what pitch to produce on an instrument; it tells me nothing about the duration of the tone. All it indicates as a time symbol is that the tone should last half as long as another tone symbolized by ♩ , one-fourth as long as ○, twice as long as ♪, four times as long as ♬, and so on.

As indicators of durations our symbols represent a series of relative time values whose successive members are in the ratio of 2:1. ○ stands for what is called the whole, ♩ the half, ♩ the quarter, ♪ the eighth, ♬ sixteenth, ♬ thirty-second, etc. Occasionally we come across the old symbol ╓, whose time value is twice that of the whole. A *dot* attached to any one of these symbols lengthens its value by 50%; a *double dot*, by 75%: ♩.₌₃♩ , ♩.₌₃♩₊♪; a *tie* extends the duration of the first symbol by the value of the second: ♩♪₌♩.♪; the symbol 3 indicates a *triplet*, a subdivision of the next higher value into three equal parts, e.g. ♬♬₌♩ .

Clearly such a system of notation would not have been developed if it did not reflect the actual organization of time values in our music. It demonstrates therefore what measured music means in terms of tone durations. For music to submit its motion to a beat does not imply that all the tones must be equal in duration, equal to the beat; there remains the widest margin for differences of long and short tones. It does imply, though, that no matter what their duration, they must always measure each other, so that one is 3½ times as long as another, or 4/9, or 11/12, or show some similar numerical relationship. In other words, the different durations all conform to a common time measure. If the beat represents the unit, all durations are either simple multiples or simple fractions of the unit.

This explains how tones may communicate the beat even if they do not give it out directly, as in the Chopin Mazurka. There is the possibility of indirect communication: the beat emerges from an irregular succession of long and short tones as a common measure of all their durations.

The Schubert example quoted before may illustrate the process.

There is no immediate trace of a beat here, no direct parceling
out of time units by the tones; we hear a sequence of sounds of
very different duration, the second much shorter than the first,
the third longer than the second but shorter than the first, the
fourth very much longer than any of the preceding, much
longer, in fact, then the three preceding taken together. This
sequence is repeated in the following four sounds. Next, the
time pattern of the first three sounds is stated twice: here the
beat may begin to dawn, from the realization that the three
durations of the ♪♪♪ pattern taken together may form a constant
element. This is supported by what follows: the next sound, ♩,
is exactly equal in duration to the whole of ♪♪♪; and the following two sounds, ♩ ♫ , taken together fill again the same interval
of time (the little grace note is omitted). If we carry this on
through the next sound, the long ♩, we shall find that its duration stretches through exactly twice that time interval. What
follows can only confirm that our choice was right; the duration
equal to the whole of ♪♪♪ is the basic time unit, the beat of this
music:

We have already mentioned that only two of the 27 sounds of
the sequence are equal in duration to the beat. But all of them,
long or short, conform to the measure of the beat, each one in
its way; the long ♩ by lasting for exactly two beats, the three
short ones of the ♪♪♪ pattern by adding up to one beat in the
following manner: the first and second together take up two-
thirds of the beat, the first, ♪., one and one-half of a third, the
second, ♪, one-half; the last of the three tones, ♪, fills the remain-

103

ing third of the beat. Finally, ♩ ♪ amounts to exactly 5/6 of one beat, and the following ♪ to the remaining sixth. In this way the beat, without being directly given, appears as the regulating force behind the whole sequence. The listener who, moving along with the tones, after a while catches the beat has sensed in back of the succession of long and short durations the basic unit, the measure to which the tones have subjected their movement in time.

The Bar

In this piece, too, as in the Chopin Mazurka, it is not simply beats that are communicated but *beats grouped*. The indication of the group, like that of the beat itself, is not as direct here, is much more subtle than in the Chopin example. Still the group will emerge along with the beat, and the listener will become aware of its organization: three beats to the group.

The group of beats is a universal characteristic of almost all the music we hear. So used are we to experiencing the beat as an *organized* sequence—so and so many beats, two, or three, or four, or whatever the case may be, joining to form small groups, the same group always reiterated—that we take this kind of organization and musical meter to be one and the same thing. We shall see later to what extent this opinion is justified. However, we should be aware that measured music is 750 years old, while only during the 17th century did the group begin to dominate the metric picture of our music. Most of the earlier polyphonic music either showed no trace of metric grouping at all or allowed a group to emerge only momentarily, giving it no chance to establish itself as a dominating feature.

The group is called *bar* or *measure* and is marked in our notation by a vertical line across the staff, the *bar line*. There are two basic types of group organization: *duple meter* or *duple time,* with two beats to the bar; and *triple meter,* or *triple time,* with three beats to the bar ("time" as a technical term in this context is a synonym of meter). The term *compound meter* comprises the larger bars formed by combining the basic types: bars with four beats (two times two), six beats (two times three or three times two), occasionally even with eight, nine, or twelve beats; five- or seven-beat measures are rare except in 20th century music. With each type of group there goes an accent pattern corresponding to its metric organization: strong-weak for duple meter, strong-weak-weak for triple time, strong-weak-halfstrong-weak for the four-beat measure, and so on.

The metric organization of a given piece is noted at the beginning of a piece in the *time signature,* such as 3/8, or 2/4. This symbol is a fraction in appearance only, as the two figures refer to totally different things: the "numerator" to the number of beats per measure, the "denominator" to the symbol that in this particular instance represents the time unit, the single beat. The latter symbol is necessary because our notation leaves the composer the choice of one of the basic symbols to represent the beat (usually it will be ♩ or ♪ or ♪). Thus, 3/8 says: three beats to a measure, ♪ represents the beat. We see that what really matters in the time signature is the upper number: it defines the organization of the group, the bar. The lower number has a purely symbolic significance. In other words, no matter whether the time signature is 3/8 or 3/4 or 3/2, we will in every case hear the same one-two-three grouping.

For 4/4 time, also called *common time,* the old symbol ∁ is normally used. This is not capital C for "common," but rather the open circle, symbolizing what was called "tempus imperfectum," meaning subdivision of the beat by two and distinguished from the full circle, ◯, "tempus perfectum," subdivision by three (3 being the "perfect" number). For 2/2 we write ₵ and call it *alla breve.*

There is one situation in which the lower figure of the time signature does not represent the symbol corresponding to the actual unit of the beat: namely, when in duple or triple meter the tones continuously subdivide the beat in three parts. As it would be bothersome to write triplets all the way through, the subdivision is in this case assumed to represent the basic unit; e.g., 2/4 time with triplets in every beat, |♩♪♪♩♪♪|, would be called 6/8 and written |♪♪♪♪♪♪|. The true beat, however, remains the same, one to every three of the eighth notes. (In slow speed, 6/8 may still indicate a true six-beat measure.) In the Schubert Moment Musical discussed before we found a one-two-three grouping of beats, that is, triple time; yet the time signature, for the reason stated here, is 9/8, not 3/4.

Two questions may be asked in connection with the time signature: What is the actual duration of the time unit or beat in a given piece? What determines the choice of the symbol that represents the time unit?

The answer to the first question seems easy. We can construct an instrument consisting of a pendulum with an adjustable weight and a scale with marks for the different positions of the weight. With the weight at point 60 the pendulum would tick off intervals of exactly a second. Such an instrument, called a *metronome,* was built in fact in 1816 by a man named Maelzel, a friend of Beethoven's. All we need, then, is an indication by the composer at what figure the weight should be set in order to give the accurate beat. For instance, if he writes a piece in 3/4 time, he would have to add a metronome mark, say, ♩=84 .

However, certain disturbing things happen in connection with the metronome. Everybody will agree that regularity of the beat is one of the foundations upon which our music rests; and the necessity of strict adherence to a regular beat is one of the first things hammered into every music student's consciousness. Yet to sing or play to the beating of a metronome is a torture for both the performer and the listener. One might think of the metronome mark as indicating an average and allow a certain margin of deviation from it; but the problem is more complex. It appears that a composer's metronome marks vary greatly with time—not only in the sense that the marks may seem all wrong to him ten years after he wrote the piece, but also on the larger scale: some of Beethoven's metronome marks appear absolutely monstrous today, and we cannot do anything with them except regard them as nonexistent. It is the same thing with performing; a pianist or conductor will often reject his own metronome marks of an earlier time; a piece with the same metronome mark that is played by two performers may sound just right in one case, and taken at a wrong speed in the other. As a consequence of all this composers have lately shown an inclination to drop metronome marks altogether and return to the practice of pre-metronome days, the *tempo signatures* —fast, slow, very fast, moderately slow, and so on—which merely hint in general terms at the time value of the beat. Before the middle of the 18th century even tempo signatures were used only sparingly; the composer trusted that the tones themselves would communicate to the performer, better than marks or words could, the speed at which their motion would make good sense. There is always more than one solution to the problem; the one and only right speed of any given piece just does not exist. There is real wisdom in the choice of symbols that refrain from indicating anything except relative duration values and leave the absolute value of the unit undetermined. The whole problem is implied in the term "measured music": how can a living motion be measured?

The second question is not easy to answer either. What determines the choice of the symbol that represents the time unit in a particular instance? Why 3/8 rather than 3/4 or 3/2? Sometimes practical considerations of notation influence the choice;

107

but this is the exception rather than the rule. It seems that each of the symbols that usually represent the time unit, ♩ or ♪ or ♪, has apart from its quantitative meaning of relative duration also a qualitative significance: the composer selects the symbol according to the character of the piece he is writing. Normally a musical thought will occur to the composer in terms of definite time symbols; it would then be as difficult for him to substitute, say, 3/4 for 3/8 as it would be for an artist to execute as a woodcut an idea that had occurred to him in terms of an engraving. To make things worse, these qualitative meanings of the time symbols, whatever they may be, change from epoch to epoch and from composer to composer. Still, a listener who is familiar with the music of a certain composer can make a safe guess at the time signature from the character of a certain piece: that is, if the piece moves in triple time, he can tell whether the time signature is 3/8 or 3/4 or 3/2. (This has nothing to do with speed; the beat represented by ♪ in one case may be much *slower* than the ♩ of another.)

The Forming of Groups

We have observed how the beat emerges from a succession of tones of different lengths. What about the group?

If we think of the Chopin example, the answer seems obvious: the layer of the music that directly gives out the beat does the same thing for the group. The part assigned to the left hand, with its regular stress on every third of three equally long sounds, produces the accent pattern strong-weak-weak that determines the three-beat measure, triple time.

The standard answer to the question of how beats are organized into groups, how bars are formed, takes this particular or a similar case as a paradigm and proceeds to a sweeping generalization: groups are produced by accents; it is the distribution of strong and weak accents that forms the different bars. Care-lessly arrived at, thoughtlessly repeated, and generally accepted, this answer precludes any true understanding of meter and rhythm in music.

One does not have to look very far to find that this opinion has all the evidence of music against it. One of the first things a careful observer will notice is the independence of group from accent. Quite often, as in the Chopin Mazurka, the tones will produce an accent pattern that faithfully duplicates that of the bar; more often, however, this will not be the case. Yet bars will form, and will be communicated, no matter how the tones be-have in regard to accent. There are several sources of accent in music: dynamic stress (strong-weak)—which is what we usually have in mind when we speak of accent—is only one of them; others are duration (long-short), pitch (high-low), phrase (be-ginning and ending of units of tonal context comparable to sen-tences, clauses, word groups in language). We shall hear more about these later. They may duplicate the accent pattern of the bar; usually they will not, but rather will produce accent patterns of their own. There is much music that requires maximum even-ness of sound, complete suppression of any differentiation of dynamic accent, while the other sources give no indication of a reg-ular grouping of time units either; still the beats will fall into groups, the bar will emerge, distinctly, inevitably. If the theory that accent creates bar were right, this would be impossible. In fact, the performer who believes in this theory has no choice but to use stress to make sure that the bar organization is communicated (which it certainly must be). Can we imagine the middle sec-tion of Chopin's Nocturne, Opus 37, No. 1, played with accents set according to the pattern of the 4/4 measure:

or Bach's A minor Fugue presented this way:

We all know this kind of playing—from small children, beginners, or the hopelessly unmusical person. It is certainly the surest way to drive all life out of the music and make nonsense of it.

If it is not accent that creates the bar, what is it? We may look for an answer in the experiment briefly discussed at the beginning of this section. The recurrent beat, the regular marking of time that we sense when we listen to measured music corresponds to the recurrence in the experiment of identical stimuli at equal time intervals. Just as these fell into groups by themselves, the sequence of regular beats cannot but do the same thing. No particular cause is needed for bars to form, over and above what produces the beat; a particular cause is needed, on the contrary, to *prevent* the appearance of groups. In the absence of such a cause the forming of some group is irrepressible. *What* specific group will form in each individual instance—groups of two, or three, or four, or six beats to the measure—will be determined by the actual movement of the tones; they have it in their power to decide this matter one way or the other. However, we observe a sort of natural inclination towards the formation of binary groups, with two, or two times two beats to the measure; so that, all other things being equal, as for instance in the simple beating of a drum, this organization is most likely to emerge. The tones will have to do some special bidding, however discreet, to bring about a grouping by threes. (In the Schubert example it is the recurrence of the duration accent ♩. after three beats that decides the question.)

The tones have it in their power, too, to interfere with the forming of groups altogether and to keep any bar organization from emerging. As mentioned before, this is the situation of most polyphonic music before the 17th century. It is achieved either by frequent and irregular changes from duple to triple meter, and from one unit value to another, as for instance in the following phrase from William Byrd's 3-part Mass:

Ky -ri- e e - - lei - -son, Christe e -lei-- son, Ky-rie e-----lei ----- -son.

or by organizing the different parts at cross purposes metrically, with the same group in all parts, but not occurring at the same time; e.g. in the last verse of Palestrina's Motet "Super flumina":

suspendimus or---gana no------- stra

suspen--dimus or-- gana no --stra

(The bar lines are of course added here; this music was written without bar lines. The modern practice of printing it with bar lines put in uniformly so as to make it look like the music we are familiar with is quite destructive of the sense of its motion. Supposed to make the performance easier, which it does in a purely mechanical sense, it actually necessitates a difficult job of reconstructing the original meaning of the motion from a distorted reproduction.)

When 18th and 19th century music experiments occasionally, very rarely, with bar-less music it is to symbolize an extreme state of freedom, bordering on chaos, preceding the birth of order; or order temporarily breaking down, e.g. in C.P.E. Bach's late Fantasies. Beethoven's free improvisations on the piano, which seem to have excited ear witnesses even more than his written compositions, must have contained music of this type. An echo of it can be found in the introduction to the last movement of the Sonata, Opus 106. An interesting instance of a 19th century melody that deliberately keeps any group order from emerging occurs in the Prelude of Wagner's *Parsifal:*

Written as a time pattern, without bar lines:

Nobody can feel a group here. 20th century music, revolutionary-minded in matters of metric as of tonal order, frequently declares open war on the metric group. It does not abolish the bar line but obstructs it and even uses it to *prevent* any group order from emerging; e.g. in Strawinsky's "Rites of Spring":

The process of group formation does not come to an end on the level of the beat. Ask the average listener to count with the melody of a Strauss waltz; more likely than not he will count "one-two-three-four." Yet this is waltz time, triple time, 3/4. The listener who counts to "four" is actually counting bars, not beats: . The bars appear as units of a higher order that in turn form the larger group. This may go on to the formation of super-groups on still higher levels. There is the difference, however, that the will of the units to join into groups, which was almost irrepressible on the level of the beat, gets progressively weaker on the higher levels; so that it does not take much for the tones to counteract it here and keep groups of higher order from forming altogether. Still, the tendency is always latent, and if the tones are willing, as for instance in Beethoven's "Hymn to Joy," this is what happens:

The corresponding phenomenon occurs on the other side of the beat, in the subdivisions. Tones that subdivide the beat are not just lined up amorphously, one after the other; they will always be heard as grouped. So it is now the individual beat that constitutes the group in relation to these subunits. E.g. in the Bach A minor fugue theme quoted before:

The following diagram gives a summary picture of the levels of metric organization (one-two grouping is assumed throughout):

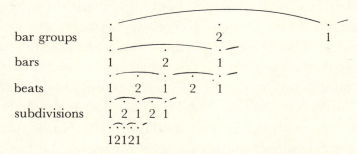

The metric organization of a piece of music, the group formation on various levels, is part of our immediate experience; when we listen we move with the music on all these levels simultaneously, and it takes but little training to recognize how a given moment is situated with respect to each of them—e.g. "one" on one level, "two" on the higher level. It is a different matter, however, to know which of these levels represents the basic beat, which the measures and higher groups, which the subdivisions. Let us imagine a simple case, with only two levels of metric organization, e.g.

```
    1       2       1       2       1
    .       .       .       .       .
1 2 3 1 2 3 1 2 3 1 2 3 1, etc.
. . . . . . . . . . . . .
```

Is this triple time with two-measure groups on the higher level, or is it duple time with each beat subdivided into three parts? No strict and fast rule can be given that would enable us to give an exact answer to a question of this kind. Very generally speaking, we can assume as a principle a certain concordance between the speed of the beat and the character of the tonal movement in terms of fast and slow. If a piece gives us the general impression of slow motion, and our counting on one of the levels seems comparatively fast, we are probably counting on the level of subdivisions: the beat will be on a higher level. If the general impression is that of a fast movement, and our counting is comparatively slow, we are probably counting on a level above the beat: the unit of our counting is then the measure, not the beat. To take a concrete example: the first two movements of Beethoven's so-called "Moonlight Sonata" (op. 27, no. 2) have the same metric organization: two levels, groups of 2 × 2 units above, groups of three units below, almost exactly as shown in the last diagram. The first movement is definitely slow; the counting on the lower level would be rather fast, so this is the level of subdivisions; the higher level represents the beat, with 2 × 2 beats to a measure, and each beat subdivided into three parts. The second movement is rather fast; the counting on the upper level is comparatively slow, so the beat is on the lower level, three beats to a measure; the unit of the higher level is the whole measure, and 2 × 2 measures form the group of higher order.

The Time Wave

The beat with its concomitant manifestations of groupings of higher and lower order constitutes what we understand as meter in music. What then is *rhythm?*

First, we must establish the distinction. Meter and rhythm

are not synonymous. We speak of duple, triple, compound meter; we would not speak of duple, triple, compound rhythm. We say of a piece that is in 2/4 time, or in 3/8 time; we would not say that it is in 2/4 rhythm, in 3/8 rhythm. We praise the rhythmic quality of a good performance; we would not praise an accomplished performer for playing in time. A beginner's playing may be metrically correct but rhythmically lifeless. What is the difference between the two things, meter and rhythm?

When we speak of meter we think, first of all, of that which *divides* the flow of time: the evenly distributed time marks, the regular beat that parcels out equal time units. The adequate visual symbol of this is the straight line with marks cutting off equal stretches: |————|———|———|———|———|———|———⟶

We now turn our attention from these marks, the point-events that make the divisions, to that which makes the *connection* from one mark to the next, the intervals between the marks. What happens there?

There seems to be only one answer: Nothing; or, to phrase it positively: time just passes.

The logical consequence of this answer is that any one interval between two consecutive marks can in no way be different from any other interval between two consecutive marks. This is expressed in the visual symbol, too: the straight line between any two consecutive marks is always the same.

This conclusion, however, is contradicted by experience. We have observed that a regular beat will under normal conditions be experienced as organized into groups. The experience becomes manifest in our counting: after counting so and so many numbers, two, three, four, as the case may be, we come up with "one" again. This shows that an element of recurrence is present in the experience; we do not only advance; in some sense we also keep returning. To consider the simplest case, duple meter: our counting, "one-two-one," expresses that the third of these beats is not experienced as just another beat but rather as *another "one";* the advance in time that this beat marks is also, and predominantly, a return. Since it is impossible to have an experience of returning without first having had an experience of leaving, the whole course from "one" to the next "one" assumes the character of "going-away-and-coming-back."

Now we know something about the "nothing," the mere passing of time in the intervals between consecutive beats: it has the character of a motion, more precisely of a motion away-from-and-back-to; it is not an advance as on a straight line, and the interval between "one" and "two" is *not* the same as the interval between "two" and "one." The two intervals are rather complementary; "two-one" takes us back to where "one-two" has taken us away from.

The most adequate visualization of these events is the wave line, with "one" marking the crests of the waves, "two" the troughs: . Whereas on the straight line the time marks separated interval from interval, on the wave line they connect, they link up phase with phase; they indicate the moment where one phase of the wave unnoticeably runs into the other.

The situation is more complex though not essentially different in triple meter. Here the descending phase is not immediately followed by the ascending; an interval intervenes and delays the return motion, "one-two" becomes "one-*and*-two" or, if the counting goes right on, "one-two-three": . The wave of compound meter might be pictured containing a subordinate crest at the midpoint (or midpoints): .

The wave line is a universal symbol for rhythmic processes in general. By shifting our attention from the discontinuity of the time marks to the continuity of the intervals between the marks, from the beats that separate the intervals to the intervals that connect the beats, we have turned from the metric to the rhythmic aspect of the phenomenon. A performance that is rhythmically alive will communicate the beat not as a series of disconnected time marks separated by empty intervals of equal duration but rather as a continuous process, the incessant beating of a time wave.

The wave symbol shows the two seemingly contradictory tendencies of rhythmic processes: the tendency to return again and again to the starting point, the tendency to go on and on endlessly. Initial and final phase of the single wave complement one another symmetrically. The descent from crest to trough is balanced by the subsequent ascent from trough to crest; and the return to the crest closes the circle, achieves balance. But the very same instant opens a new circle and upsets the balance by leading on to a new downward phase. The listener is caught and carried along by this process of continual return and continual advance; it is the ground, a moving ground indeed, on which his meeting with the tones takes place.

Musical rhythm, however, is more than just the beating of the time wave. In order to understand it we must recognize it as springing from the correlation of *two* factors of which the time wave and its recurrent accent pattern is only one; the other is the pattern, or rather the complex of patterns created by the actual motion of the tones: patterns of long and short durations, of dynamic stress, emphasis and de-emphasis, of high and low pitches, of the articulations and punctuations of phrasing. We have mentioned that each of these is a source of accent patterns in its own right, which may or may not reproduce that of the meter. Durations may simply duplicate the beat, or subdivide it regularly or irregularly, or distribute long and short values in any way they wish (within the restrictions of measured music). As the long tone as such, compared to the short, carries the greater stress, there is the choice of having the stress of the relatively longer tone coincide, or not coincide, with the strong beat of the measure. The same is true of dynamic accents; they can simply imitate the accent pattern of the bar, or run straight against it as in off-beat accents that stress the weak beats of the measure, or in syncopation that puts accents *between* the beats; or they may be distributed quite irregularly, in complete independence of the bar structure. As to pitch: Like the longer tone, the higher pitch conveys the idea of greater stress; so again the stress of the higher tone may coincide with the stress of the strong beat, may contradict it, or operate quite independently of it. The reverse is true of tones at the bottom of the tonal body, in the bass. Here it is the lower tone that carries the stress, as we could observe in the Chopin Mazurka. Finally the phrases, with their beginnings and endings, their larger and smaller context, their heavier and lighter punctuations, like sentences, clauses, word groups in a poem, can arrange themselves differently in relation to the metric structure, begin and end together or not together with the bar, extend in conformity or not in conformity with the groups of higher order, and so on.

Each one of these elements, duration, dynamic stress, pitch, and phrase, constitutes an area of freedom of tonal motion under the law of meter. On the continuous tension between the two factors rests the rhythmic life of our music. Basically, they are in agreement—they could not well be otherwise, as it is the tonal motion itself from which the beat is born. Yet they play, as it were, a game of conflict and reconciliation that ranges all the way from perfect harmony to seeming indifference and outright rebellion. The foundation is the beat. The time wave, or rather the multilayered wave complex, beats on and on, with inexorable regularity. Spread out on its surface, as it were, carried along by it, superimposing their ever changing patterns on the sameness of its pattern, are the tones. Every phase of the wave has its specific sense of direction: falling away from the crest, approaching the trough, pulling out of the trough, approaching the crest again, reaching it again. Every tone, every group of tones will be imbued with precisely the sense of direction of the part of the wave on which they fall and which carries them along. The wave is the law, there is no escape from it; but the tones have the freedom to do something with the wave: to simply string along with it, to stress it and make it a thing of great importance, to minimize and hide it, to cross its regularity with all sorts of irregularities, to put it in question, to contradict it openly, to produce all sorts of combinations of these possibilities by doing the same or different things in the different areas—all the while relying on the wave to give the proper meaning to whatever they do, measuring the value of their freedom against the validity of its law.

The Interplay of Tone and Time

A series of examples should give some concrete meaning to these explanations. We begin with the simple and typical. A minimum of tension between freedom and law is represented by the typical hymn tune, which has practically all tones except those at the end of each verse of equal duration and identical with the beat. There are no marked dynamic accents, no outstanding pitch differences, the phrases fit smoothly into the bar pattern. However, the simple duplication of the beat, even if it is just the repetition of the same sound, is still capable of a high degree of rhythmic differentiation. Compare the 𝄞 ♩♩♩♩ at the opening of Beethoven's Violin Concerto, op. 61, with the 𝄞 ♩♩♩♩ later in the same movement. The beginning requires absolute evenness of sound (very difficult to achieve), ‿‿ ; the slightest indication of the 4/4 accent pattern would make it sound ridiculous, like a dilettante conductor's counting "one-two-three-four-go!"; the tones must

119

be allowed to fall into the pattern, to generate the wave from
their own volition, as it were. The other place admits of no
differentiation of accent either: each sound is hammered out at
the peak of dynamic intensity; but here the intention seems
rather a violent contradiction of the natural pattern, a most
forceful opposition to any gradation of accent as implied in the
wave. How different again the whipping up of the wave at the beginning of the fourth movement of Bruckner's Eighth Symphony:
. Or compare again the ever so slight
indication of the *one*-two-three grouping at the beginning of the
Scherzo of Bruckner's First Symphony with the frantic
in the second movement of Beethoven's Ninth,
and both to the of the opening measures of any waltz.
In the waltz the simple reproduction of the triple-time pattern,
one-two-three-one-two-three, would be deadly. Here the phrasing does the trick; play , and the people will be on their
feet. Metrically it is the same thing, triple time; rhythmically,
it is a different world altogether. How pitch and dynamic
accent affect the rhythm in the simplest time pattern can be
observed in the first measure of the theme of Beethoven's Quartet, Opus 59, No. 1, . The breaking off of the ascending motion just on "four" of the measure and the following
downward skip on "four-*one*" directly counteracts the accent
pattern of the bar. Later, with dynamic stress thrown in, this
leads to . Here the tension of time accent and tone
accent is at a maximum, . In the difference between this
and the normal where time and tone move in accord,
, we almost touch the core of rhythm in measured music.

Continuous regular subdivision of the beat in two, three, four
parts through a whole piece occurs frequently. A few examples
chosen at random:

(Schubert)

120

(Chopin)

(Beethoven)

(Bach)

The accompaniment of Schubert's song "Nacht und Traeume" spreads its motion evenly across the intervals between the beats; the tension between meter and rhythm, the wave and the distribution of tones on the wave, seems at a minimum. (This does not mean that rhythmic life is at a minimum; it is life in harmony with the law, at peace; for the performer, much more difficult to bring out than tension and strife.) In the Chopin example (from the A flat Polonaise) the pitch pattern puts an accent, exactly the same accent, on each beat—which is, and is not, in agreement with the metric structure. In the Beethoven example (from the Appassionata Sonata, op. 57) there is a most interesting interplay between metric pattern and the up and down of the pitch pattern between beat and beat: first ∪ , then ∩ , then again ∪ , then //. Abolish this, reduce it to a uniform , and the interest is gone. That the Bach theme would be rendered lifeless by just accenting the beats has been mentioned before. Its rhythmic life lies in the tension between phrase and beat: the subphrases under the larger phrase context begin all *after* the beat, thus: . (It is clear that this cannot be expressed by simply moving the accent: ; this would make nonsense of it. The sensitive player will rather avoid all dynamic accents and trust that as long as he *feels* both meter and phrase his playing will communicate them.) It might be contended that the difference between the Schubert and Chopin and the Beethoven and Bach examples is simply one of melodic interest. Of course it is; but the point is that pitch pattern that produces melody is *as such* always also productive of rhythmic pattern. Otherwise it would not be possible to kill a melodic line by neglecting the rhythmic sense of its pitch pattern. Play the Prelude of Bach's Cello Suite in G as a straight subdivision of the beat,

 ,

and it becomes a tedious exercise; give it its full rhythmic life

by phrasing sensibly, , and it will be

experienced as a fascinating and profound tonal discourse.

There are also typical ways of subdividing the beat *un*evenly, namely, by a regular alternation of long and short tones, with the long tone always coinciding with the beat and occupying either three-fourths or two-thirds of the interval between successive beats: e.g. ♩♪♩♪ (sometimes ♪♩♪♩), or ♪♪♪♪, usually written as 6/8 time, ♩ ♪♩ ♪. The difference between the two, quantitatively insignificant, is rhythmically considerable. The first, the so-called *dotted rhythm,* with its succession of halts and sudden starts, the short note as it were always making a rush for the beat and just catching it, has the effect of sharply pointing up the moment of the beat itself; it is therefore the preferred rhythm of all marching music. Slowed down, it changes into the stately and solemn motion of funeral marches and other dignified processions. Speeded up and sustained it becomes the most excited and exciting of all rhythms: a great example of this occurs in the last movement of Beethoven's Seventh Symphony. Another remarkable instance is No. 5 of Schumann's Kreisleriana, op. 16.

The other type of uneven subdivision of the beat, ♩ ♪♩ ♪, has exactly the opposite effect, of de-emphasizing, of smoothing out the marks of the beat. It is the rhythm of music that appeases, that sets movement to rest, as in pastoral pieces or in cradle songs. (It is curious that the difference between war and peace musically reduces itself to a difference of the ratio 3:1 and 2:1

in the relative durations of two successive tones.) A beautiful example is the melody of Suzanna's aria in Mozart's *Figaro,* . Here the beat has become almost weightless, as it is cushioned by the counteraction of the pitch pattern at the beginning, the going *up* with the metrically unaccented short note. The character of this rhythm, too, varies with the speed. If it is slowed down it acquires a quality of great heaviness, of dragging motion, as for instance in the opening chorus of Bach's *St. Matthew Passion,* which is dominated by the persistence of this rhythm in the bass. In fast motion it may assume the character of an uncanny haste: so in the last movement of Schubert's D minor Quartet, "Der Tod und das Mädchen":

A combination of both types produces the pattern, the rhythm of a graceful dance called Siciliano. Its chief interest lies in the changed role of the last third of the subdivision, which in the underlying rhythm was the *short* tone but now appears as *long,* as a brief halt, in relation to the preceding sixteenth. In slow speed this produces a halting, broken kind of motion; we hear it with this character for instance in the aria "Erbarme dich" in Bach's *St. Matthew Passion:*

In fast motion it gives the impression of a controlled rush. The outstanding example of a whole piece dominated by this rhythm is the first movement of Beethoven's Seventh Symphony. Wagner in the "Ride of the Walkyries" contrasts it with the atypical of the Walkyries' call. Richard Strauss' Elektra dances her triumph to this rhythm; its peculiar impact there is due to the tension between metric pattern and pitch pattern, which has the *highest* tone fall on the critical last third of the subdivision: .

Another typical form of uneven subdivision is ♪♫♪♫. This too accentuates the beat, but not as incisively as the dotted rhythm; there is more elasticity to it, more of a padded action, so to speak. It is the dominant rhythm in the first movement of Schumann's Piano Sonata in F sharp minor, or in Brahms' Intermezzo in C sharp minor. Dynamically reinforced, as for instance at the opening of the last movement of Beethoven's Seventh Symphony, it becomes something of a lash. Similarly in Scarlatti's Sonata in G, Longo No. 286: one will not easily forget the smashing effect of the sudden ♪♫♪ breaking into the smooth motion of the running sixteenths.

The typical representation of disagreement between metric wave and tone distribution—of rhythmic dissonance, so to speak—is syncopation. A tone is syncopated when it enters precisely in the interval between two beats and extends over the movement of the next beat: that is, something happens when nothing ought to happen, and nothing happens when something ought to happen. Dynamic stress may support syncopation; but it is not a matter of dynamic accent, it is purely a matter of timing, of the *beginning* of a tone making a mark in time at a moment when there is, strictly speaking, no time for a mark. In fact, in the absence of any supporting dynamic accent the effect of syncopation can be the more disturbing and intriguing· as it seems to happen by mere chance, by a sort of continuous accident, out of pure whim, e.g. in the following example:

(from Beethoven, Piano Sonata, Opus 2, No. 3)

If the meaning of syncopation, the running counter to the order of the beat, is to be clearly understood, the beat itself must somehow be in the picture; either directly, as in the example just quoted where the lower part takes care of this, or indirectly: when a beat has persisted for a while, it can be expected to go on inside the listener without direct support from the tones. In the following measures from Beethoven's Piano Sonata, Opus 101 no tones represent the beat; there is syncopation only, one compact body of syncopated sound:

Yet the time wave that has been started previously now continues as an inner motion exclusively, whose mute but precise accents make the listener aware of the rhythmic meaning of the sounds, their coming "too soon," with the time wave always reaching the crest within the sound, thus:

Tones   – – – – –
Time wave   ᴜᴜᴜᴜ

In some instances the presence of the beat is purely ideal, as when a piece *begins* with a syncopated sound. The first measure of Schumann's "Manfred" Overture has this rhythmic pattern: ♪♫♫♫| . In a case like this, the manner of sound production is all the performer has at his disposal to communicate the sense of syncopation.

   More often than not a musical thought, a theme or melody, will go beyond the typical and produce a time pattern all its own, in which the different types of motion are freely combined. Such an individualized rhythmic profile belongs with the theme or melody most intimately and in a sense *makes* it just as much as the pitch pattern does. There is no scarcity of examples.

Chopin, Polonaise, op. 40, no. 2

Verdi, *Trovatore*

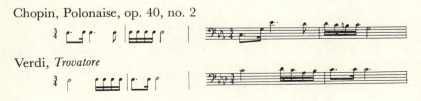

Verdi, *Traviata*

Mozart, *Figaro*

Bach, 3-part Invention

A few remarks to these examples. The personality of the Chopin theme, rhythmically speaking, shows right at the start, in the first two beats. On the one hand, the Polonaise rhythm calls for a good metric accent, "*one*-two-"; on the other hand, there are the two consecutive upward leaps of the melody, supported by a dotted rhythm: a sharp melodic and rhythmic lift occurring precisely at the moment of the rhythmic dip, . In the next measure the crowding of four short tones in the first beat, followed by a long tone stretching through the rest of the measure, also runs against the norm; the long tone "belongs" on the strong beat, the proper place of the many short tones is the last beat where they fittingly lead up to the "one" of the next measure. This is what we get in the melody from *Trovatore*. Here, however, the movement is not permitted after the effort of the rapid sixteenth notes to come to a due rest, comparatively speaking, with a long tone on "one," but is swept off the ground again by a dotted rhythm that displaces the long tone and moves it to the second beat. Change this into , and it will be flat. The peculiar rhythmic charm of the *Traviata* melody is due to the short-long rhythm at the beginning of the measure, with the long tone extending over into the second beat, (this is 6/8 time with 2 beats to the measure). The effect is of stillness filling most of the measure, with motion only at the beginning and end. If it were or the charm would be gone. (The primary source

126

of this rhythmic idea is the word "addio" to which the first three tones are sung, [♪ music notation]; but the word by no means *prescribes* the rhythm, it might just as well be, as in Mozart's "Cosi fan tutte," [♪ music notation].) In the *Figaro* march the rhythmic interest springs not only from the beginning with the *short* note of a dotted rhythm but mainly from the fact that this note is also the highest in pitch. [♪ music notation] would be trivial. A similar situation occurs in the famous minuet from Mozart's *Don Giovanni*: [♪ music notation]. Had it been [♪ music notation] instead of [♪ music notation], the piece would not have become famous. The rhythmic story of the Bach theme is this: lively motion at the beginning brought to a halt in the middle of the first measure; released again, rushing through the rest of the measure and the beginning of the next; suddenly slowed down just on the last eighth note before the third beat.

A few more examples might further illustrate the main points. *Long-short and short-long at the beginning of the measure:* the theme of Bach's Organ Fugue in A major has an interesting alternation between the normal and the abnormal: [♪ music notation] [♪ music notation]. The high-low relation is also brought into play here, in the contrast between the abnormal [♪ music notation] and the normal [♪ music notation]. *Few-many distribution of tones in the bar:* this [♪ music notation] (from Weber's *Freischuetz*) is normal; this [♪ music notation] (from Beethoven's Quartet, Opus 95) brushes sharply against the grain. *High-low in relation to metric accent:* Compare Beethoven's Piano Sonata, op. 111 [♪ music notation],

which deliberately keeps the high tones away from the strong beat, with Mozart's [♪ music notation] (from the *Magic Flute*). A combination of few-many and high-low distribution gives Wagner's "Ride of the Walkyries" its rhythmic distinction: [♪ music notation]. Move

the bar line, , and it becomes hackneyed.
High-low relation plus dynamic stress against metric accent:

(Beethoven's Seventh Symphony)

If in a piece the tones close ranks, as it were, and move as one compact body of sound, there will be only one rhythm present at a time:

(Schubert, Piano Sonata, op. 78)

However, usually the tones will split and pursue different rhythmic patterns at the same time. The uneven motion of one part may be brought into relief by the even motion of another, or several individualized patterns may be combined into one complex whole. In the Bach aria quoted before, from the *St. Matthew Passion*, the Siciliano rhythm of the melody is supported by a continuous ♪♪♪ ♪♪♪ motion of the bass. In the first chorus of this work the even ♪♪♪ ♪♪♪ motion of the upper parts contrasts with the persistent ♪ ♪♪ ♪ of the bass. When there is a distinction of melody and accompaniment the latter may stay neutral and let the rhythmic pattern of the melody stand out against a background of even motion; or it may combine a more individualized pattern of its own with that of the melody, e.g. in Chopin's A major "Polonaise":

Melody
Accompaniment

or, with brilliant effect, in Verdi's "Aida":

Melody
Accompaniment

Occasionally the parts may even differ in metric organization, as in one of Chopin's waltzes where the melody has two beats to the measure, the bass three, while a middle part moves on the neutral ground of continuous eighth notes:

In the ball scene from Mozart's *Don Giovanni* three different meters are combined, 3/4, 2/4, and 3/8, with the beat of the 3/4 acting as a common measure:

All this is still very simple and almost primitive compared to the complexities of some 20th century music and of the music of other civilizations. The following diagrams show the metric structure of two sections of Elliott Carter's String Quartet:

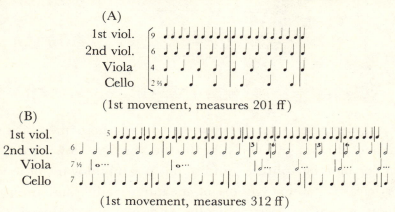

(A)

1st viol.
2nd viol.
Viola
Cello

(1st movement, measures 201 ff)

(B)

1st viol.
2nd viol.
Viola
Cello

(1st movement, measures 312 ff)

In (A), counting from the bottom up, the metric unit shrinks progressively by one-third from part to part. In other words, the metric unit of the 1st violin part is $\frac{2}{3}$ of that of the 2nd violin part, which is $\frac{2}{3}$ of that of the viola part, which is $\frac{2}{3}$ of that of the cello part. In (B) the 5 quarters of the 1st violin correspond to 3 of the cello, 4 of the cello to 6 of the 2nd violin; viola and cello have the same metric unit, but the bar lines never coincide.

Phrase

So far we have not said much about *phrase*. A phrase in music, much as in language, is a succession of sounds closely connected by a common bond of meaning—with the difference that in language the individual symbol, the single word, has already some meaning in itself, while in music meaning is created by context exclusively, by the interrelation of tones: the single tone has no meaning. In this sense phrase seems almost synonymous with melody as we tried to understand it in the first section of this book. Phrase is the more flexible term, though. We think of a melody always as a whole, while phrase applies to wholes or parts, as exemplified in Haydn's famous melody (2nd movement, String Quartet, op. 76, no. 3)—*one* melody, but three levels of phrase (indicated by appropriate symbols):

A large phrase is an articulated whole whose members are smaller phrases that may be further broken down into still smaller member phrases, and so on, possibly down to the very particles of context, atoms of meaning, individual intervals. The punctuations that define the phrases will not always, as in language, separate phrase from phrase; in music, the end of one phrase may very well also be the beginning of the next. Punctuations usually are strong and clear on the upper levels, between larger phrases; they get progressively lighter and less marked on the lower levels, and on the lowest may be quite in-

distinct and ambiguous. To take a chance example: Should the
beginning of the Bach theme quoted before be articulated this
way

or this

?

One way or the other will make quite a difference in the sense
of the movement; in one case it will be an alternation of upward and downward moves; in the other a succession of two
downward motions. If the next two measures are phrased thus:
, it is the upward fourth that talks; if thus:
, the downward fifth. We see here that phrase,
which is produced by meaning, in turn produces meaning (and
can also destroy meaning). Quite often there is more than one
way of phrasing that makes good sense. This can be compared
to different interpretations, equally valid, of one sentence, expressed by different intonations of speech. Through phrasing
every performer necessarily becomes an interpreter in the strict
sense of the word; phrasing should therefore be his chief concern. The means of expressing phrase articulation are usually
the most delicate and intangible modifications of tone and tone
duration. If it is overdone music becomes pedantic, didactic,
a bore.

Fundamentally, phrase is a rhythmic entity, not only because it is a structured course extending in time, but because
in music "extending in time" is in itself a rhythmic event. Time
in music is never a neutral background, an empty receptacle
of extension; it is itself organized, structured, the time-*wave*.
The question of how a phrase fits into the wave pattern, the
metric pattern, is therefore of greatest importance rhythmically.
The rhythmic quality of a musical phrase depends not only on
its articulation, the inner punctuations, the way it runs its

course from beginning through middle to end, on the distribution of its decisive moments, its own accents, but on all these together *in relation to the time wave* and its accent pattern. An example, to show the principle: the beautiful introductory phrase of the slow movement of Mozart's Piano Concerto in G, K. 453: [music notation]. If the rhythm of this phrase were to be expressed by a visual symbol it would not be this ⌒ but this ⌒. The rhythmic experience can only be explained in terms of the combination of both elements; complete agreement first, the phrase breathing with the time wave, as it were; then, after the halfway mark, the separation, the phrase lifting itself from the wave, way ahead of the next crest. One has only to substitute this

[music notation]

to realize the rhythmic difference.

There are three typical relations of phrase to meter, resulting from the three possibilities of *beginning: with* the bar, *on* the beat; before it, on the *upbeat;* after it, *off* the beat. The main themes of Beethoven's Fifth Symphony offer good examples: the offbeat phrase of [music notation] in the first movement, the upbeat phrases of [music notation] and [music notation] in the middle movements, and in the last movement [music notation] entering right on the beat. The phrase rhythm of a theme is usually carried on and continued in the subsequent development. As the beginning of a phrase always makes some sort of accent, the result will be, in the case of upbeat and offbeat phrasing, a constant tension between the accent patterns of phrase and bar. This tension is very often a principal source of rhythmic life; e.g. the offbeat tension in many of Bach's compositions.

In one respect complete subordination of phrase to meter is a common phenomenon. We have mentioned the tendency of bars to form groups of higher order, usually with two or four bars to the group. This indicates that the time wave is not always a simple wave either; two or four individual waves may join to form super-waves which on a larger scale repeat the structure of the single two or four beat wave. It seems that the tones love to go along with this tendency—at least they loved to do so for the first 300 years of the era of the bar line, and they still do in jazz today —fitting their phrases into this metric pattern. The result is the ubiquitous four-measure phrase, one of the principal features of tonal organization:

This chance example, from Beethoven's E flat Trio, op. 70, no. 2, is typical in other ways, too. It shows that the tones like to carry this principle of organization one step further by joining two four-measure groups into an eight measure period, and that this formal development can be given a tonal justification and meaning by having the first phrase end on a tone of unrest (in this case $\widehat{2}$), the second on $\widehat{1}$. This brings the two groups into a significant relation of balance disturbed and restored, tension set and released, "question" and "answer." If the tones are willing, this process can continue to still higher levels. In slow motion, the two-measure group replaces the four measures.

There is a crucial difference, however, between the four-measure phrase and the metric group of four units. In such a group, "four" has always the function of leading to a new "one"; and a new "one" is a new beginning: the time wave has no end. A phrase, however, must have an end; there is no endless phrase. In the four-measure phrase the fourth measure *is* the end; that is, the tones simply make an end here, as it were, against the tendency of the time wave, be it the temporary end of a subordinate punctuation or the final period.

Quite often in a four-measure phrase the distribution of long and short notes creates a characteristic time pattern that gives the phrase an almost tangible rhythmic individuality. It is a popular game among musicians to tap such a rhythm and ask to what music it belongs. Beethoven once thought such a rhythmic profile interesting enough to be stated all by itself and to act as a theme, a germ from which the following music could grow; the second movement of his Quartet, Opus 59, No. 1, begins with the cello alone: 𝄢 ♩ ♪♫ ♪♫ ♫♫♫ .

An impressive time pattern of this kind, tying two consecutive four-measure phrases into one rhythmic unit, appears at the beginning of Chopin's B flat minor Scherzo, op. 31:

The two halves of the eight-measure period are held together by the force of contrast. Particularly effective is the contrast here between the amount of *silence* in the first half and the fullness of sound in the second. We observe that rests act as elements of a time pattern just like tones: the metric wave continues to beat right through the rests exactly as it does through the tones; its course is not affected by the temporary absence of tone. The combination of sound and silence in one rhythmic context is a particularly challenging possibility. It also tests the art of the performer, who has to make the listener realize that these rests are not empty, that the void is filled with rhythmic life.

This example is interesting in another respect, too. It shows a departure from the norm of the four-measure phrase: the second of the two phrases does not end on the fourth measure but is extended so as to lead directly, without as much as a breathing spell, into the new beginning, make end and beginning coincide. A normal version, such as

or [musical notation]

would not have anything of the density, the relentless drive of the original.

It is with the four-measure phrase as with any other norm in music: each one of these limitations at the same time opens a new area of freedom. Every norm makes possible another way of departing from the norm; one could almost say that at the bottom this is what the norm exists for: to allow the going beyond, the meaningful transgression. With a good composer the departure from the norm of the four-measure phrase will always mean so much more in interest, tension, and satisfaction. It will never be experienced as something willfully and externally taken away or added to, but will come from, and be justified by, the inner necessities of tonal relations. We quote one simple and charming example, from Weber's *Freischuetz,* without much comment beyond the symbols used to explain the structure:

It is clear—the picture of the time pattern makes it even visually evident—that the high point of the whole phrase is the moment in the middle where the movement slows down to the pace of the beat itself. This coincides with the ascent to $\hat{5}$. The strong punctuation after this, in measure 12, requires at least an equally strong period at the end; but in measure 16, where the end was due, the slipping into the motion of measure 4 prevents this and necessitates an extension to make good for the missed opportunity. (Note the surprising offbeat phrase in the second half of measure 16, as if the tones were themselves surprised by their slip and hurrying to remedy it.)

In the last example the discussion of rhythm has become a discussion of form. No sharp line separating the two can be drawn. An eight-measure period that, seen from below, as it were, appears as the biggest result of the group-forming tendency of meter, seems from above the smallest member of a formal pattern, involved in the context of large-scale form. In the Schubert Impromptu, which we analyzed in an earlier chapter, the smallest section of the form was an eight-measure period that joined with another like period to form the *A* section of an *A–B–A* structure. All the way through, from the bottom to the top, the same structural forces seem at work. The symmetry of the single metric wave with its successive phases balancing and complementing each other reappears on the highest level in the symmetry of the great circle forms; the wave of two phases in the two-part forms, the wave of three beats, with the middle interval separating the complementary ascending and descending phases, in the three-part or *A–B–A* forms. Finally, the other tendency of the wave, the tendency to go on and on, to produce link after link of an endless chain, has its counterpart in the great chain forms. Thus in the last analysis the great musical forms appear as rhythmic phenomena on the largest scale, as outgrowths of the same germinal forces that shape the single time wave: smallest particle and largest whole obeying the same law.

IV ✦ Polyphony

We now turn to the discussion of the consequences of a previously noted and momentous discovery, which more than any other single factor has made Western music what it is: the discovery of "more than one tone at a time."

One might ask why such a commonplace thing should be called a discovery. The fact remains that it is commonplace among us who are used to it, but nowhere else. More significant still: in those rare instances where something like it occurs in the music of other civilizations it seems to have happened by accident; the move is not followed up, there is no grasp of what it means; the thing is not actually seen, not actually discovered.

A comparison of tone and color may help to clarify the problem. "More than one color at a time" is a commonplace phenomenon universally. If we reflect on it, we find that it rests on the simple fact that colors are located in space. We perceive different colors simultaneously because they appear at different places. The moment this prerequisite is dropped—e.g. when lights of different color are projected on the same screen—we get not different colors but one mixed color. "More than one color at a time" is possible because, and as long as, space keeps them apart.

Simultaneous tones are not separated by space. If different tones sound together we do not hear them located at different places. Every single tone is at the same place as every other tone, namely, all over the place. Reasoning from analogy with color one would conclude that "more than one tone at a time"

137

is as impossible generally as "more than one color at a time" is in the special case when the colors are not spatially separated.

Actually tones behave in a unique and unexpected way, in a way nobody could guess or reason out before the event. Two colors, red and blue, produce two color sensations if they are spatially separated and one sensation of a color somewhere between red and blue if they are not spatially separated. Two tones sounding together, c and e, produce neither two tone sensations nor one sensation of a tone somewhere between c and e, say d. They produce *one* sensation, not of tone, though, but of a new thing, a chord. The event is a necessary one; simultaneous tones cannot but unite, merge, and by merging produce the new phenomenon, the chord.

The uniqueness of the chord lies in its two-faced nature. It is one and whole, yet the component parts, the individual tones that brought it into existence, have not completely disappeared in its oneness, have not entirely given up their identity. Although it is the oneness of the phenomenon of which we are primarily aware, it takes but a little turn of the attention to distinguish the individual tones within the compound—at least in the case of simple chords. To do it with more complex chords takes training; and many a chord defies the skill of even highly trained ears. Yet *potentially* any tone of any chord can be heard as an individual; and this potentiality supports the edifice of our music.

(The frequent comparison of chords with chemical compounds is therefore only half correct. Like the merger of chemical elements, the merger of tones produces a new thing with new properties; but in the chemical compound the fusion of the elements is complete, the component parts have entirely given up their identity in the new thing that emerges from their fusion.)

Two offshoots have grown from "more than one tone at a time," answering the two faces of the phenomenon. Emphasis on "the one out of the many" leads to *harmony;* emphasis on "the many within the one" leads to *polyphony.* We shall discuss polyphony first. This corresponds to the historical sequence. It took five centuries of polyphony before harmony was discovered.

The Second Dimension

The primary interest of music is not in tones as such but in movement of tones. The really important thing for music is not "more than one tone at a time" as such, but the possibility of "more than one movement at a time."

We understand that this possibility rests on the nature of the chord, its "many in one" aspect in particular. If different tonal movements, different tone lines go on simultaneously, different tones will sound together all the time. Each one of these tones is a link in one particular linear context. If the merger of tones sounding together were complete, if the individual tones lost their identity in the fusion, the linear context would be broken, or rather no linear context could ever emerge. Represented in graphic symbols:　　　　　　　　　　　　　　—the "hori-

zontal" event is possible because the "vertical" event does not abolish the identity of its component parts.

The pre-polyphonic state of music is represented by Gregorian Chant: one single tonal line, complete and whole in itself; a one-dimensional process. The step from this to polyphony can be compared to the step in geometry from the line to the plane. The coexistence of one-dimensional lines implies the existence of the second dimension. So the coexistence of tonal lines calls into being a second dimension of tonal events.

In our discussion of polyphony we shall be mainly concerned with the question of what music has gained by becoming two-dimensional. (There is no doubt that something has been lost in the move, too. Read any account on Gregorian Chant by people steeped in it, particularly the people from the Solemnes monastery, and you will be impressed by the sense of loss, of an ideal destroyed, a perfection gone when music became polyphonic. The perfection was that of the absolute individual; the loss, as we know from the discussion of meter, was chiefly in respect to rhythm.)

For a first general experience of two-dimensional as against one-dimensional music one may listen to the beginning and subsequent sections of Schütz's *St. Matthew Passion*.[1] Here the alternation between chant-like narration and polyphonic choruses makes us strongly aware of the added dimension in the latter. The thread of the single tone line spreads to become a broad flow, contracts again into a line, spreads again, and so on. With the second dimension comes an increase in complexity, in richness of expression, in poignancy, perhaps also in significance. One might also reflect on the following extraordinary fact: When a number of people talk all at the same time, the result will necessarily be nonsense, disorder; while if these people sing rather than talk, the result may be a super-sense beyond the sense of each individual's part, a supreme manifestation of order.

With every change from a monophonic to a polyphonic section one also feels the corresponding change in rhythm: in the polyphonic sections the individual parts are subjected to the rigid rule of the meter; the monophonic sections are free from such restriction.

One also notices a marked difference of character between the tone lines in one- and two-dimensional music. The former seem not quite melodies, one might say not quite music, they are more like melodious speech. The latter are more like melodies or in any event are definitely song, music, not speech. It is as if the tones, confined to one-dimensional existence, held a

[1] See Section of Scores, p. *18*.

comparatively low opinion of their potentialities and considered themselves chiefly servants of the words; while with the advance into the two-dimensional mode of being they became aware that they might in themselves constitute a complete language, independent of the verbal languages and capable of achievements beyond the potentialities of these verbal languages. And so they came into their own, developed an idiom of their own, and gave new content to the old word "music."

On the other hand, the one-dimensional line appears self-sufficient and complete as it is; while the individual line of the two-dimensional compound clearly cannot stand alone. It is in need of some addition, of a complement; its character is manifestly that of a part of a more comprehensive whole. This reminds us that, although polyphony rests on the "many within the one" aspect of the chords, its individual strands exist for no other reason than the building up of the whole of which they are the parts, a "one out of many."

Individuality of Parts

It is not as simple an affair to listen to simultaneous tonal movements as to watch simultaneous movements of bodies. We hear the total movement of all the individual motions combined; we are not so easily aware of individual tone lines. The first chorus of the Schütz work uses what is perhaps the most effective device to make the listener aware of the presence of individual tone lines: the successive entries, to the words "wie es beschreibet," of the individual parts with the same distinct phrase. This is called *imitation*. Different movements at the same time ensue here from having the same movement at different times.

It is by no means indispensable or even desirable for the listener to be aware at all times of the individual strands of tonal motion that together make up the polyphonic whole. He

141

rather follows the lead of the tones in this respect, which show an infinite flexibility in dealing with their second dimension. Again a spatial metaphor may help to explain the point. Different lines drawn side by side across a plane are one thing; the plane itself, the uniform area between the lines is another thing. The tones have it in their power to emphasize the diversity of individual movements whose coexistence implies the second dimension, or to turn the light away from the individual lines, thereby allowing the uniform expanse *between* the lines, the second dimension, to sound forth directly. However, in space this is an either-or proposition; while in music there are innumerable stages of transition, countless combinations. In fact, the shifting from one of these stages to the other—producing anything between a slight difference of shading to a sharp contrast—is a major means of expression of our tonal language.

In the very first measures of the Schütz work the principle can be heard in operation. The music begins with one single tone, and broadens gradually. In measures 1 to 5 the light is on the intertwining of the two lines of the alto and tenor; from the second half of measure 5 on, this light is withdrawn and nothing remains but a uniform spread of sound. In measure 8 the single soprano line emerges from the sound; and from measure 10 on, the uniformity is broken, the parts appear in their individuality.

The same phenomena on a larger scale may be observed in the first Kyrie, the Christe, and the beginning of the Gloria of Palestrina's *Missa Papae Marcelli*.[2] Six parts are involved in this composition. In the Kyrie, the space fills up gradually, as it were—with four parts only contributing at the beginning, a fifth joining from measure 5 on, and the sixth in measure 9—producing a gradual increase in tonal density. Each part carries on its own movement, the whole is the combination of many

[2] See Section of Scores, p. *19*.

different tone lines. Imitation is used: all parts come in with the same motive, a skip of a fourth up (after repetition of the first tone) followed by one or more steps down. The successive entries of this motive make up the first four measures; from measure 5 on this is enriched by the addition of two independent lines (1st tenor and soprano). From measure 9 on the main thing is a sort of back and forth between 1st bass and soprano (measures 9–12), 2nd bass and soprano (measures 12–15). From measure 15 on, the 1st tenor and soprano call and answer each other; this is combined with another call-and-answer between the 1st and 2nd bass and, less distinct, between alto and 2nd tenor.

This high degree of complexity gives way, at the beginning of the Christe, to a much simpler organization. Instead of many different lines combined, one line only is held up to our attention (soprano in measures 25–26, alto in 27–28, 2nd tenor in 29–30, 2nd tenor again in 31–32) with the other parts just seconding or contributing some supporting motion, as the bass in measures 27–28, soprano and alto in 29–30, soprano in 31–32. From measure 33 on, however, we quickly return to the former complexity, the tonal compound divides again in as many distinct lines as there are parts.

The situation is different again at the beginning of the Gloria.[3] (The music begins with the second sentence of the text, the first sentence, "gloria in excelsis Deo," being sung as an introduction in the traditional Gregorian Chant.) Here the parts move more or less as one body; the individuality of the contributing lines is de-emphasized, the impression is that of one homogeneous mass of sound, with the highest part standing out and forming *the* leading melody. Yet even so, here and there a sudden light falls on some individual move of a part, other than the highest, which for a moment lifts itself above the otherwise homogeneous sound—as a reminder that this is still polyphonic music,

[3] See Section of Scores, p. *20*.

143

and that the individual parts have only temporarily given up their right of self-assertion. Examples of this: 1st bass in measure 3 (a slight touch of independence only); 2nd tenor in measure 7, 1st tenor in measure 9, 2nd tenor in measure 13; 2nd bass, alto, 1st tenor successively in measures 30–32 (this gets more and more assertive); and, with outstanding effect, 1st tenor in measures 33–34, 1st and 2nd tenors in measures 36–38. We note that the most obvious factor making for individuality of a part is rhythm. Nothing emphasizes separateness like diversity, nothing de-emphasizes it like identity, of rhythmic pattern.

The state of affairs at the beginning of the Gloria must not be confused with homophonic music. "Melody plus accompaniment" is the formula that defines homophonic music; what looks like it here is only a transient state in an ever-fluctuating organization of the tonal compound. Moreover, the relation of the supporting to the leading parts cannot in this case be properly called that of an accompaniment to a melody. Accompaniment implies *harmony:* "melody plus harmony" is another way to define homophonic music; and there is no harmony in our sense of the word in Palestrina's music. It is true, however, that in this particular type of organization polyphony comes closest to homophony and harmony.

Infinite Motion

Another remarkable consequence of music's becoming two-dimensional is the possibility of infinite motion.

Every musical phrase has a beginning, runs its course, and reaches a more or less definite conclusion. There are no infinite sentences, whether the language be verbal or tonal. One-dimensional music gives us a straight succession of such sentences. Polyphonic music has other possibilities. Even though each

individual part does consist of phrase after phrase, like monophonic music, the beginnings and particularly the endings of
simultaneous phrases need not coincide. The phrases may over-
lap, allowing the movement of the whole to continue unbroken
by the endings and new beginnings of the individual parts.

Taking the parts of the Palestrina Kyrie individually, we can
follow each one through its successive phrases with their clear
endings and beginnings. Yet, for instance, at the moment the
initial phrase of the soprano reaches its end, in measure 5, the
phrase of the 2nd tenor *begins:* in terms of the whole, that
moment is end and beginning at the same time. When that
phrase of the 2nd tenor ends, in measure 8, the 2nd bass has
still one half measure to go and the soprano one full measure,
to reach the end of their respective phrases. The soprano at this
point (measure 9) makes a rather strong conclusion; yet just a
moment before this the 2nd tenor has made a new start, with
the clear sense of beginning and end overlapping. In the following, 1st bass and soprano end their phrases together in measure
12, and again 2nd bass and soprano in measure 15; yet their
beginnings and endings are all bridged by the continuous motion of one long phrase of the 1st tenor. And so on. Only towards the end of the section, from measure 21 on, do the parts
get together; one might say they are almost forced into some
agreement, as after all they must end the section together.

Infinite motion emerging from finite movements: something
of the essence of polyphonic music is expressed in this sentence.
There is always something arbitrary about the end of a polyphonic piece: the end has to be imposed from outside, as it were.
Left to themselves, following their own impulses, the tones
would move on forever. In this sense polyphonic music is much
closer to the flow of *time* than monophonic music. The single
melodic line, with the beginnings and endings of its phrases,
fills successive intervals of time, marks finite stretches of time;

while polyphonic music, the whole of its overlapping parts, represents time itself, the unbroken and unending time flow. (Homophonic music is in this respect much closer to the one-dimensional line than to the polyphonic texture.)

There is one instance in which the statement "infinite motion emerging from finite movements" describes not an essence or idea but an actuality. This is the *canon*. In a canon all parts sing or play exactly the same thing—at different times. All parts must be under way by the time the first reaches the end of the phrase; at this moment another part may be approaching the end, another has perhaps reached the halfway mark, while still another has just gotten under way. In the midst of this activity and drive all around, the first part takes a new start, either repeating the old phrase or continuing with a new one. A diagram may clarify the process:

As can be gathered from this diagram a true canon *actually* never comes to an end; it can only be broken off. This quality finds a very tangible expression in some old prints where the canon appears written on a circular instead of a horizontal staff. Sometimes even a hub and spokes are added: a wheel appears, the wheel of time. This is perhaps the closest we come —not only in music but in any symbolic expression—to a representation and perceptive realization of "the moving image of eternity." For medieval composers the canon had a particular theological significance.

An interesting *rhythmic* possibility inherent in polyphonic organization must be mentioned in this context. One-dimensional tonal motion may be either regular or irregular rhythmically, even or uneven; two-dimensional motion has another possibility: regularity springing from irregularities superposed on each other. To take as an example the beginning of the Palestrina Kyrie, the first three notes of the successive entries of the parts in measures 1–3 combine in the following way: (Bar lines are disregarded.)

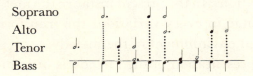

There is a tremendous difference between the normal flow of a ♩ ♩ ♩ ♩ ♩ ♩ motion carried on by one voice, and the same ♩ ♩ ♩ ♩ ♩ ♩ resulting from a combination like

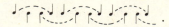

The former is, as far as rhythm is concerned, even, smooth, relaxed; the latter betrays behind a surface evenness a distinct inner tension, comparable to a state of balance resulting from counteracting forces, where the forces would remain individually discernible. (It would be misleading, therefore, to talk here about irregularities producing regularity by cancelling each other out; the irregularities do not vanish, the result is not a simple zero.)

Haydn's Emperor Quartet, 2nd Movement

For further observation of polyphony in action, and as an elementary exercise in polyphonic listening, we turn to two Haydn string quartets.

The slow movement of the so-called *Emperor* Quartet[4] is not polyphonic music in the strict sense; it is rather homophonic music with occasional excursions into polyphony. Yet the fact that one of the tonal movements that enter here into polyphonic

[4] See Section of Scores, p. *21*.

combinations is the familiar anthem tune, makes the task of polyphonic listening that much easier.

The form of the piece is "Theme and Variations." This means that a melody will be presented and then led through a series of transformations. In the present instance the melody is repeated without change in every variation; the transformation affects only the tonal environment of the melody.

The first presentation of the melody is in homophonic style, melody plus accompaniment type. With the beginning of Variation I, the accompaniment is dropped, nothing remains but the melody itself, played by the 2nd violin, and combined with it another tonal motion, carried on by the 1st violin. The contrast is marked between the preceding section, where the whole seemed to move as if it were one body, and the disparity of motion here. One should listen to this Variation twice; first, concentrating on the principal tune; then, spreading the attention and directing it towards the other movement, without, however, losing contact with the progress of the principal tune. The task is not difficult here; first, because only two tone lines are involved; and secondly, because each of the two motions follows a rhythmic pattern all its own. We have mentioned this before: Difference of rhythmic pattern makes for independence of motion; sameness of rhythmic pattern counteracts independence of motion, promotes a merger of several motions into one.

The same listening procedure should be followed in the subsequent variations. If after the playing of Variation II the question were asked, How many different motions are involved in this?—the answer would probably be: two. Actually, all four instruments take part in this section. However, only two independent motions emerge from the ensemble: the principal tune, now played by the cello, and the line of the 1st violin; the other two instruments subordinate their parts alternately to one or the other of these two leading parts. Difference of rhythmic pattern (syncopation in this case) is again a major factor signaling the independence of the line of the 1st violin; while the lack of a rhythmic pattern of their own stresses the subordinate character of the two other parts.

In Variation III, the number of parts combining polyphonically is increased to three, with a corresponding increase in the difficulty of polyphonic listening. The viola carries the tune. We notice the gradual increase in complexity from the original homophonic presentation of the principal tune through Variations I–III.

With Variation IV we seem to return to the original homophonic treatment. Closer investigation, however, shows this to be a most intricate combination of polyphony-within-homophony.[5] The tune is played by the 1st violin, as at the beginning; yet it sounds different here, has a different character than it has had heretofore. Since the tones of the tune are the same, this can only be the effect of the combination with the other parts. We need only to single out 1st violin and cello to understand what happens:

As a result of the movement of the cello the center of action (which so far has been the tone g) is temporarily shifted to e. Consequently the 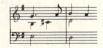 of the melody, which so far has always been heard as $\widehat{4}$–$\widehat{3}$–$\widehat{2}$–$\widehat{7}$–$\widehat{1}$, major mode, assumes now the dynamic qualities of $\widehat{6}$–$\widehat{5}$–$\widehat{4}$–$\widehat{2}$–$\widehat{3}$, minor mode. For a still more delicate shading we listen to the very first tone of the tune: the g changes its character *while it sounds,* as a consequence of the movement of the 2nd violin:

---

[5] The development of this particular type of texture was Haydn's major achievement. It became the chief distinguishing mark of the output of the triumvirate Haydn, Mozart, Beethoven, and later of Brahms. Since knowledge of harmony is necessary for its understanding, it cannot be discussed further at this point.

We conclude from this that the musical meaning of a tune is affected and may be changed by other tonal motions that go on at the same time. The musical meaning of any tone line in polyphonic music is determined not only by its own "horizontal" context but also by the "vertical" situation prevailing at any given moment.

A Lesson in Polyphony

The middle section, entitled "Alternativo," of the Minuet from the String Quartet, Opus 76, No. 6,[6] might be called a lesson in polyphony, in the form of a joke. It is as if an assignment were given: Take the most commonplace tonal motion, the movement up and down the scale; make an interesting composition of it by combining it polyphonically with other motions. We get the scale no less than thirty-two times. The repetitions are arranged in groups of four; four times down, four times up, and so on, starting either in the lowest register and gradually lifted up to the highest, or the other way round. Each group begins with a lonely presentation of the naked scale. As the scale is repeated, other lines are added, one at a time, until the number four is reached (except for the first group where we do not get beyond three parts). After this, the thing shrinks again to the single line. Eight times we thus go through the process of spreading of the tonal compound from the solitary thread to the complex flow. Each time we hear the lonely scale we are reduced to the one-dimensional state of music, more properly speaking, to a state where the second dimension is in abeyance. With the entry of a second part, the second dimension becomes an actuality; as additional parts appear, its inherent potentialities are increasingly revealed.

We observe again the role of rhythmic pattern in emphasizing

[6] See Section of Scores, p. 22.

150

individuality of tonal motion. To this is added another factor: general direction of movement. The two lines that begin on the last beat of measure 64 and extend through the second beat of measure 68 move both in the same general direction, downward. This is called *parallel motion.* The two lines that begin on the last beat of measure 80 and extend through the second beat of measure 84 move in opposite directions. This is called *contrary motion.* In measures 88–91 and in the last 5 measures, one part remains stationary while the others move up or down. This is called *oblique motion.* It is clear that difference of rhythmic pattern combined with contrary motion will make for maximum individuality of parts involved; while identity of rhythmic pattern combined with parallel motion will annihilate the individuality of the single parts, e.g. 2nd violin and viola in measures 100–104, 1st violin and viola in measures 132–136. In these cases the individual parts conjointly produce *one* movement, which, however, has more breadth, or fullness, or body than if it were carried by one part only.

Consonance and Dissonance

So far we have discussed polyphony in the general terms of simultaneity of different tonal movements. We have not yet mentioned the specific problem that musicians encountered when they ventured into the second dimension of tonal life—a problem that, while it caused them more trouble than anything else, pointed the way to new possibilities of tonal expression undreamt of in the era of one-dimensional music. That problem was the *dissonance.*

As we have seen, tones that sound together cannot help but merge into that particular sensation we have called a chord. Yet it appears that the attitude of the tones in regard to this merger is not a neutral one. They seem to like certain combinations and to dislike others; and they accompany the successive mergings with an audible running commentary of "yes" or "no." These continuous utterances of the tones' approving or disapproving the company of fellow tones they are successively asked to join we call consonance and dissonance.

The theologically minded musicians of the Middle Ages saw in the two states of consonant and dissonant sound the tonal counterpart of Good and Evil: That Which Should Be, and That Which Should Not Be. One thing the two pairs certainly have in common: the distinction as such of consonance and dissonance has been questioned as little as the distinction of good and evil; but as to the specific question of what sounds should be called consonant, what dissonant, the opinions of the ages differ just as much as they do about specific moral questions.

In this situation we shall do what seems to be most reasonable: we shall draw the line between consonance and dissonance in accordance with the generally accepted practice of music of the last 400 or so years. We shall call consonant those combinations of simultaneous tones in which—according to the idea of those who created these sounds—the merger is effected smoothly, without inner conflict, and we shall call dissonant those where the merger takes place against the will of the tones, as it were, with the result of friction and inner tension in the chord.

To demonstrate what is meant by these words we listen to all possible combinations of two simultaneous tones, beginning with pitch distance zero and running through the octave:

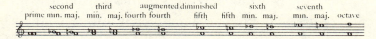

Friction, conflict, the "no" of the tones can be heard in the case of the seconds, the sevenths, and the augmented or diminished intervals; in all the other combinations the merger is comparatively smooth. We conclude:

(1) Generally speaking, consonance or dissonance is a function of the pitch distance between the tones that sound together, a function of the *intervals*. The interval, whose decisive role in tonal succession in the horizontal context we have observed, emerges in a crucial function in the vertical context, too.

(2) Seconds, sevenths, augmented and diminished intervals are dissonant; all other intervals are consonant. With one exception, the fourth, whose status changed from consonance to dissonance and back to consonance, this distinction coincides with the actual practice of almost all music that is still alive. Actually, seconds, sevenths, augmented and diminished intervals have never been considered consonant; and octave and fifth have never been considered dissonant. Thus the area subjected to changing opinions is narrowed to the fourth, mentioned before, and the third and the sixth whose status in the course of time was raised from dissonance through "imperfect" consonance to consonance without qualification.

There are of course various theories which try to explain *why* certain intervals should be judged consonant and others dissonant, thereby establishing a sort of absolute standard. The most venerable of these is the *number* theory, according to which an interval is consonant when the corresponding numerical ratio is one of small whole numbers (e.g. the consonant octave, $1:2$, or fifth, $2:3$, compared with the dissonant minor second, $15:16$). The open question in this is: When does a number cease to be small: Why should $5:6$ be consonant and $8:9$ dissonant? Also, there is disagreement with musical practice whenever the fourth $(3:4)$ is deemed dissonant. Finally, the introduction of equal temperament where all intervals except the octave involve highly complex numbers, seems irreconcilable with this theory.

Another theory tries to make feelings of pleasantness and unpleasantness the decisive criterion. This would of course make the whole distinction completely arbitrary and disqualify it as a valid element of the tonal language. No expression whose meaning changes with the subjective reactions to it can be part of any language. Moreover, after Wagner and particularly Debussy, we should know that the most pleasant sounds of music are what according to all rules must be called dissonances.

In most music textbooks we find consonance and dissonance equated with rest and unrest. The validity of this interpretation is confined to the laboratory where we test isolated sounds. We shall see presently why it becomes invalid in the musical context. Finally, the theory which explains consonance and dissonance in terms of the series of overtones cannot be properly discussed except in connection with the phenomena of harmony.

The Control of the Dissonance

What does it mean when we say that we determine consonance and dissonance *in accordance with the practice of music?*

In music to consider a sound dissonant means to acknowledge its state of inner tension and to be responsive to its *will not to be.* Music is movement of tones. Dissonance becomes a factor in music if and when it is possible to put this tension, this will, into the service of that movement. This is achieved by giving the tension of dissonance a more or less definite *direction,* thus transforming its merely negative will not to be into a *positive* desire to disappear *in favor of a certain other sound,* a less tense sound, normally a consonance. In a chance dissonance, ♯♯, we hear nothing but a formless "no!" In a musical dissonance, e.g., ♯, this force will appear definitely channeled; we hear the positive desire for a certain other sound to take its place, namely ♯. This is achieved here by combining the tension of the dissonant state with the tension of a tone $\widehat{7}$; the progression from the dissonant chord to the subsequent consonance towards which the dissonance was directed and which, as the technical term goes, acts as its *resolution,* coincides with the move $\hat{7}$–$\hat{8}$. Thus the new dynamic factor that originates in the second dimension of tonal life, dissonance tension, makes its contribution to the overall purpose of the tonal movement. This, and nothing else, is the basic musical meaning of dissonance.

It would be rash to conclude that the contribution of dissonance to the musical context must always follow the pattern of this example. Music handles dissonance about as it handles the will of the tones in general: it is always free, within limits of meaningful context, to follow or to counteract that will. Our expectation of the resolution of a dissonance may be satisfied, or it may be deceived. We may have to wait a while before we get the resolution, perhaps even a very long while; sometimes we may not get it at all. Dissonance tension may stress the dynamic quality of a tone, as it did in our example; but it may just as well contradict it, e.g. when dissonance is combined with tones of rest. Yet whatever happens, there will always be direction, plan, control, fitting of the dissonance-consonance relation into the building of an organism of tonal motion. (Although we do not understand too well at present what goes on in atonal music, there is no reason to assume that it has done more than radically modify and enhance the role of dissonance without, however, changing its essential musical meaning.)

Why should the occurrence of dissonance, as we said before, cause so much trouble to music? In order to understand the problem we must approach it via a detour through a question of probabilities: How many consonant combinations of simultaneous tones are possible?

Our former classification of consonances and dissonances according to interval can also be formulated as follows: All combinations of simultaneous tones are consonant, provided augmented and diminished intervals are avoided and no two tones that are neighbors on the scale are forced to sound together. (The latter condition covers both seconds and sevenths; e.g. the combination c–d may take the form 𝄞 or 𝄞.)

This seems very liberal. Since the seven-tone system of our music contains only one augmented and one diminished interval (e.g. f–b and b–f respectively in C major and A minor) and since less tones are scale neighbors of any tone than non-neighbors, probability seems to favor consonance over dissonance by a wide margin.

Actually the very opposite is true. The sole condition that no scale neighbors may occur together if a sound is to be consonant limits the number of possible consonances most severely. First, every combination of more than three different tones must be dissonant. Second, not more than three combination patterns of three different tones can be consonant. (Octave repetitions of a tone do not count as different tones.)

We can reduce this to a problem of points in space. Given a series of points continuously numbered through 7:

$$1 \quad 2 \quad 3 \quad 4 \quad 5 \quad 6 \quad 7 \quad 1 \quad 2 \quad 3 \quad 4 \quad 5 \quad 6 \quad 7 \quad 1$$
$$\cdot \quad \cdot \quad \cdot \quad \cdot \quad \cdot \quad \cdot \quad \cdot \quad \cdot \quad \cdot \quad \cdot \quad \cdot \quad \cdot \quad \cdot \quad \cdot \quad \cdot \quad \text{etc.,}$$

find the groups of differently numbered points that do not include two neighboring points. Beginning with 1, 2 is out, 1–3 is possible; if 1–3 is picked, 4 is out, 1–3–5 is possible; if this is chosen, 6 is out; 1–3–5–7 is not possible, because 7 and 1 are neighbors. Proceeding the same way we find 1–3–6 and 1–4–6 as other possible combinations; this is all. Whichever number we choose as starting point, the pattern of the groups will remain the same; e.g. 2–4–6, 2–4–7, 2–5–7.

Transferred to music and expressed in terms of intervals, this says: Our music knows only three consonant tone combinations; they are:

fifth $\begin{bmatrix} \cdot \\ \cdot \\ \cdot \end{bmatrix}$ third / third   sixth $\begin{bmatrix} \cdot \\ \cdot \\ \cdot \end{bmatrix}$ fourth / third   sixth $\begin{bmatrix} \cdot \\ \cdot \\ \cdot \end{bmatrix}$ third / fourth

156

Combinations of more than three different tones are always dissonant. Also, of the two thirds of the first pattern one must be major, the other minor; if both were minor, or major, the resulting fifth would be too small or too large, a diminished or augmented fifth respectively, that is, a dissonant interval.

The standard number of parts in polyphonic music was four in Bach's time; four to six in Palestrina's time and earlier. Three-part pieces are rare, two-part pieces very exceptional. Thus the probability for vertical combinations in polyphonic music to be dissonant all the time is very great indeed; the only way to avoid it, if more than three parts are involved—which is the normal situation—is to have two or more parts at any given moment use the same tone (including its octaves) and, in addition, to have all the parts all the time conform to one of the three consonant interval patterns.

Now we understand the problem. At issue is the freedom of tonal movement. If the individual parts of polyphonic music proceed together in freedom, each one on its horizontal way following its own impulse, would not chance dissonances occur all the time, whose formless "no!", whose chaotic clamor would constantly interfere with the perception and understanding of the horizontal context, thus bringing the music altogether to ruin? On the other hand, if for these reasons consonance, not dissonance, were the rule in polyphonic music, would not the rigid conditions of consonance, the need of each individual part to fit itself at every moment into one of those three vertical patterns, utterly destroy any thought of freedom of movement in the horizontal sense? And in fact, the very beginnings of polyphonic music, with the taboo on dissonance the chief concern, offer a spectacle of parts moving as in fetters and chained one to another. Compared to the wonderful freedom of movement of the solitary line of one-dimensional chant this appears like a state of abject servitude.

The task, then, was to reconcile the demands of the horizontal and vertical dimensions: to re-conquer the freedom of horizontal motion of the individual part while at the same time having the vertical situation always under control. By subjecting itself for centuries to a most severe discipline music solved the problem in a truly spectacular manner. Nothing quite like it can be found among man's mental achievements, except perhaps in the history of mathematical science. The discipline that did it is *counterpoint*.

The problem and the achievement of counterpoint can be stated in one formula: *control of the dissonance;* not just in the negative sense of shutting it out altogether or rendering it harmless if in the interest of freedom of horizontal motion it cannot be avoided, but in the positive sense discussed before of utilizing it as a contributing factor in the musical context. The "trick" consists in making each dissonance appear to the ear as a specific deviation from a consonance, the result of a departure from, and the anticipation of a return to, a specific consonance. Three elementary moves satisfy this demand, giving rise to three types of musically meaningful dissonance: *passing tone, neighboring tone,* and *suspension.* Passing tone: On the way from a tone which is part of a consonant combination, to another tone which is part of the same or another consonant combination, the movement may touch one (or more) dissonant tones: [7]. Neighboring tone: If a tone, instead of just sounding on, moves out of its pitch to the next higher (or lower) tone and back again, a dissonance may be involved in the move: . Suspension: If the move from a tone to its lower (or upper) scale neighbor is *delayed,* a dissonance may result from the delay (in consequence of the movements of the other parts); the belated taking of the move restores consonance, resolves the dissonance: . Thus every dissonance appears, if one might say so, logically bounded by consonance; and the general law of move-

---

[7] o symbolizes consonance. • dissonance.

ment in music reads: from consonance through dissonance to consonance. (In later stages of the historical development it will not be necessary to have the "framing" consonances always actually present; sometimes a presence in idea will suffice. The surer music gets of its means, the more it frees itself from the necessity to spell out every single link in the chain of its meaning.)

It so happens that the three basic types of dissonance are all neatly exhibited in the first four measures of the Schütz example.[8] The d of the tenor, which is consonant in measure 2 becomes dissonant when it is tied over ("suspended") into measure 3 where it clashes with both the e flat of the alto and the c of the bass; the dissonance is properly resolved by the belated move d–c. The d in the alto of measure 3 is a dissonant passing tone, clashing with c of both tenor and bass, on the way from the consonant e flat to the consonant c. There is another suspension dissonance at the beginning of measure 4 where the c of the tenor delays its move to b, thereby producing a clash with the d of the alto. Finally, in measure 4 we get the dissonant neighboring tone a, as a part of the *b–a–b* movement of the tenor, clashing with g of soprano and bass. (What looks superficially like the same sort of thing, 𝄞♪♪ of the alto in measures 3/4, and 𝄢♪♪ of the tenor in measures 4/5, means something different musically in each case. In the alto move the first tone, 𝄞♪, is a dissonant passing tone resolving to the consonant c; in the tenor move the first tone is consonant, the second a dissonant neighbor.) Had the moves d–c and c–b of the tenor in measures 2/3 and 3/4 *not* been delayed; had the alto in measure 3 proceeded directly from the consonant e flat to the consonant c, without touching the tone in between; had the tenor in measures 4/5 been satisfied with just holding out the b and refrained from engaging in a neighboring tone movement, there would have been no dissonance:

[8] See Section of Scores, p. *18*.

159

Soprano
Alto

Tenor

Bass

But neither would there be very much interest in the music of these measures; nor could we detect any particular significant relation of this tonal utterance to the words that go with it: Das Leiden unseres Herrn, The Passion of Our Lord.

A merely acoustical dissonance, a chance dissonance, is a disturbance that affects the sound as a whole. A musical dissonance is a disturbance that affects the sound as a whole *and* allows us to fix responsibility for the disturbance at certain points. If dissonance arises in consequence of a simple motion whose origin and destination are easily perceived, the ear will be led to place the blame where it belongs; it will know which tone of the vertical compound can be said to be out of place and what move would get it in place again. Although the tension of the dissonance spreads over the whole of the compound, the tendency to restore balance is concentrated in one tone (or in more than one tone, if more than one disturbance-creating motion is involved). For instance, if the tones c and d sound together apart from any musical context, as an isolated acoustical event, all we hear is: clash, friction. The mere question, which of the two tones was responsible for the clash, is meaningless; and the other question, what should be done to end the friction, could not be answered reasonably either, except by saying that the sound should stop altogether. On the other hand, when c and d clash and produce dissonance at the beginning of measure 3 of the Schütz example, the ear is fully aware that the suspended tone d is responsible for the disturbance and ought to get itself out of the way by moving on to c; and when the tones c and d clash again at the beginning of the next measure, there is no doubt that this time it is the tone c that is to blame, and that the way to resolve this dissonance and restore the balance of sound would be the move c–b. Thus the orderless tension of dissonance is put to work for the ordered purposes of tonal movement; a crude force of nature has been civilized.

We know the effects of conditioning on our reactions. Conditioned as we are today by the dissonances of atonal music, of modern jazz, and by the endemic noises of industrial society in general, must not the reaction of our ears to these dissonances of Schütz's music greatly differ from that of his contemporaries 300 years ago, and thereby even change the meaning of that music? There can be no doubt that whatever there is in dissonance that is determined by reaction and susceptible to conditioning will be affected that way; we observe our own changing reactions, our "getting used" to the dissonances of modern music. Yet there can be as little doubt that this is only the sensory element, the mechanically sensory element, the factor that makes for pleasantness and unpleasantness of the sensation, and not the musical element, of dissonance. If it were, if the tonal language relied in its expression on the sensory element of dissonance, most of the older music would have lost interest for us, we would have "gotten used to it." The *musical* meaning of dissonance in those Schütz measures is exactly the same for us as it was for the people of his days; we hear and understand it exactly as they did. We follow a meaningful movement through alternating states of harmony and discord; as dissonance breaks in on consonance we become fully aware of the precious nature of the concord now destroyed —but we also rest assured, by the very nature of the discord, that the lost harmony can be restored if we but want to: Disturbance of order holding out the promise of order restored; the spectacle of That Which Should Not Be controlled and dominated by That Which Should Be, presented for the greater glory of God.

The whole course of the development of our music during the last 1,000 years—and perhaps not of music only—seems reflected in the story of the mutual relation of consonance and dissonance. First, consonance is the only state of sound believed admissible in music, dissonance is banned. Gradually dissonance is admitted and brought under control, its unique contribution to the tonal language is discovered and effectively used. Consonance, however, continues to dominate the field; it is the rule, and dissonance the exception. This state culminates in Palestrina's and Lasso's music during the 16th century. Things continue to shift; dissonance develops and expands; the number of dissonances intervening between framing consonances increases. Numerically, dissonance is no longer the exception, the two states of sound appear as equal partners in building up the tonal whole. With all this, however, there is no change in the basic relation between the two; dissonance remains deviation, disturbance of the *only true* state of sound, which is consonance. This is the state of affairs in Bach's and Handel's, in Haydn's, Mozart's and Beethoven's time. After this the point of equilibrium is passed. Dissonance takes up most of the space; it becomes the rule, and consonance the exception; it allows consonance less and less chance for *actual* presence while still keeping it in view as the *ideal* goal towards which all dissonance is ultimately striving. Richard Wagner's music marks this precarious stage. Today, dissonance has become the normal state of sound. Whether or not consonance still occurs, the fundamental dynamic relation between states of sound no longer appears in the form of dissonance-consonance; it has been transformed into a relation between dissonances of higher and lower degrees of inner tension. Consonance, if admitted, is nothing but the mildest form of dissonance, so to speak, dissonance whose inner tension approaches zero.

Consonance without Rest

We still have to explain why the usual textbook equation of consonance and dissonance with rest and unrest is out of line with the realities of music.

Consonance and dissonance are a function of the intervals between the tones sounding together. In the laboratory where we test the properties of isolated sounds, the consonant and dissonant qualities of the intervals are the only possible source of rest and unrest in sounds. In the musical context, however, other factors come into play: namely, dynamic tone qualities. Their voice will be decisive in determining rest and unrest in sounds. An octave or a fifth is certainly always consonant; whether or not, in a musical context, it is also at rest will depend entirely on the dynamic quality of the tones involved. A given octave, say c–c, will be at rest if the tone c happens to be $\hat{1}$; it will betray no rest whatsoever is c happens to be $\hat{2}$ or $\hat{7}$. It will be in a semibalanced state if c is $\hat{3}$ or $\hat{5}$. The fifth c–g, will be a balanced sound if c is $\hat{1}$ and g is $\hat{5}$; it will lack balance and decidedly point beyond itself if c is $\hat{5}$ and g is $\hat{2}$ (examples anywhere). Thus a consonance, far from being always at rest, will be at rest only if no other tones than $\hat{1}$, $\hat{3}$, and $\hat{5}$ are involved, which is the same as saying that most consonances are not at rest. On the other hand, the fact that dissonances always spell unrest can be explained in terms of dynamic qualities, too: Of two tones that are scale neighbors, or that form a diminished or augmented interval, one at least must be an unbalanced tone.

Summing this up, the correct statement about consonance and dissonance in their relation to rest and unrest in music should read: All sounds in a state of rest are consonant; but not all consonances are at rest (the majority are not). All dissonances express unrest; but not all sounds that express unrest are dissonant.

Two more points might be mentioned here. (1) If a balanced and an unbalanced tone join in a consonant interval—e.g. $\widehat{1}$ and $\widehat{6}$—the result is *un*balance. The equilibrium of $\widehat{1}$ does not nullify the lack of equilibrium in $\widehat{6}$; on the contrary, the latter affects and upsets the former, it proves to be the dominating quality of the sound. (2) Dynamic quality does *not* decide which tone of a dissonant combination is "responsible"—in the sense defined above—for the event. If a balanced and an unbalanced tone are involved in a dissonance, either of them may be the culprit. For an example we turn again to Haydn's "Alternativo" and compare the dissonance e♭–f at the beginning of measure 81 and measure 120. In both instances e♭ = $\widehat{1}$; it is a clash of $\widehat{1}$ and $\widehat{2}$. In the latter case the part of the 2nd violin, instead of doing the "proper" thing and taking the $\widehat{2}$–$\widehat{1}$ step together with the $\widehat{7}$–$\widehat{1}$ of the viola, 𝄞♭ lingers on through a suspension, 𝄢♭ . So the f, $\widehat{2}$, is out of place here and ought to give way by proceeding to $\widehat{1}$—which it does. In the former case the situation is exactly the opposite. Here the lower part, the cello, instead of coordinating its move, $\widehat{1}$–$\widehat{7}$, with the viola's $\widehat{1}$–$\widehat{2}$, 𝄢 , overextends its first tone, 𝄢 . So as a result the e flat, $\widehat{1}$, becomes responsible for the dissonance and is obliged to take care of the proper resolution by moving on to $\widehat{7}$—which it does. We meet here the odd situation of a $\widehat{1}$ *tending toward* $\widehat{7}$, and of a $\widehat{1}$–$\widehat{7}$ move *in accordance with* the acting forces, indicating systems of tension working on different levels, with "$\widehat{1}$ tending toward $\widehat{7}$" belonging to the outermost surface. (It might be advisable in such a case not to talk about $\widehat{1}$ but rather about the "tone just above $\widehat{7}$.") This should give us an idea of the complexity and consequently the richness and differentiation of expression that the tonal language acquires when music expands into the second dimension.

J. S. Bach, Two-part Invention, No. 1, in C Major[9]

Bach's Two-and-Three-part Inventions, or Inventions and Symphonies, as he called them, true models, on a small scale, of polyphonic composition, offer an excellent opportunity to combine the study of certain details of polyphonic texture with that of the behavior of tones in developing and organizing the *whole* of a composition.

First a large-scale view. The piece does not move on in an unbroken flow from beginning to end; twice the movement reaches a relatively strong punctuation (beginning of measures 7 and 15), only to pick up immediately after it. Thus the whole is divided into three subsections of near equal length (6, 8, 7 measures, respectively).

The punctuations coincide with declared shifts of center. Beginning with $c = \hat{1}$, the punctuation of measure 7 gives us g as $\hat{1}$, that of measure 15, a as $\hat{1}$. These are not random movements: g is a fifth above c, that is, the move is the closest in terms of key relation; a is the relative minor. We begin to move out of the c orbit with the f sharp of measure 4, very likely to g, of which f sharp is $\hat{7}$. The explicit acknowledgement that $g = \hat{1}$ comes with measure 7. We do not stay there long, though. With the f (natural) of measure 9 we move out of g again. For a while (measures 10/11) it looks as if the movement is going to settle on d as $\hat{1}$; this, however, is disavowed in measure 12, where with g sharp we move into the orbit of $a = \hat{1}$. The new center is declared in measure 15 and relinquished again in the same measure. Approaching the end, the movement searches for a return to c, the original center. In measures 17/18 it seems to get there; yet the mark is overshot, as it were, and we are carried out of the c orbit again, towards $f = \hat{1}$, the tone a fifth below c. Measure 20 corrects the mistake, takes us definitely

[9] See Section of Scores, p. 23.

where we belong, but not without a last movement of wavering that gives a highly personal touch to the ending of the piece.

Microscopic view: The whole thing flows out of the first idea: , more strictly the first half of it (we shall see presently in what sense the second half of this idea is itself an outgrowth of the first). While the upper part is still engaged in pronouncing the second half, the lower part comes in with the first "imitation." The two halves of the idea make sense not only in succession but simultaneously, too. We observe that the phrase begins not on the beat but on the sixteenth after the beat ("offbeat" phrasing); it will be that way all through the piece. Measure 2 repeats the content of measure 1, starting a fifth higher (this is standard procedure). In measure 3, beginning on the 2nd sixteenth, the upper part tries an exact inversion of the first phrase, , likes it so well that it runs it off four times in a descending chain, spanning a whole octave (from to at the beginning of measure 5). The lower part in the same time works on the idea of the four ascending notes of the initial motif, , doubling their time value. Measure 5 has the initial motif right side up and upside down alternating in lower and higher parts. Measure 6, drawing closer to the first punctuation, seemingly free from the pattern of the leading idea, is still tied to it: the thirds of the upper part, , grow directly out of the preceding thirds of the inverted motif.

Measures 7–8 correspond to measures 1–2, with g as center, and the role of the two parts reversed. Measures 9–10 carry this further, using the inversion of the motif. (Measures 7–11 are tied together in a gradually ascending motion.) Measures 11–15 correspond to measures 3–7, with parts reversed, and the center shifting from d to a instead of from c to g. A change occurs in the middle of measure 13: here and only here in the whole piece both parts move for four beats at the same pace of sixteenths. Within the narrow range of the means employed in this composition, this has definitely the effect of climax.

166

After the climax comes the release: in measures 15–18 the two-part texture is practically suspended; in the back and forth between the two parts each brings its motion to a halt while the other talks. The result is clean dialogue. Another new element here is the change of direction of the motif from measure to measure (earlier, the direction changed only after two measures). A last trump is saved for measures 19–20, applying the chain idea of measures 3–4 in *upward* direction; moreover, the chain spells out here the full octave from ♪ to ♪ , proclaiming thereby emphatically the return to the rule of c.

There is not much to say about dissonance and consonance in this piece; dissonance is not a paramount issue in two-part music. Still in the very first measure the dissonance-consonance situation gives us a nice cue regarding the tonal meaning of the main idea and its skeleton. Appearing first all by itself, ♪ might imply the meaning ♪ ; after the second half of the measure, however, we know better. The second sixteenth note of the bass, d, is dissonant against the c of the treble; it is a passing tone between the consonant c and e. This gives, as a first reduction: ♪ . More important still, the f on the 4th beat is again dissonant (augmented fourth f–b); this disqualifies it for the prominent place attributed to it in our first tentative reading, ♪ . It rather assumes the function of a neighboring tone, thus: ♪ (reduced from ♪). Now we recognize the 2nd half of the initial idea, ♪ , as an outgrowth of the first: ♪ . The full skeleton of this measure is:

The following are other Bach Inventions suggested for similar study:

Two-part in D major, F major, F minor
Three-part in C major, G minor

167

A few random remarks concerning these pieces are given below.

Two-part in D Major

The overall structure, as defined by the movement of the center, is interesting for its regularity:

The movement of the center from a to b and back to a represents a large-scale neighboring tone move; b = $\hat{1}$ can be understood as a structural neighboring tone.

At the beginning of measure 54 the bass, instead of proceeding as expected from a to d, $\hat{5}$–$\hat{8}$, which together with the $\hat{2}$–$\hat{1}$ move of the treble might have produced the final punctuation, takes the step a to b, $\hat{5}$–$\hat{6}$; as a result, the anticipated balance is upset, the final period is deferred, the tones have to try for it again. As noted before, in the coincidence of a balanced and an unbalanced tone, like $\hat{1}$ and $\hat{6}$, it is the quality of the *un*balanced tone that dominates the sound.

Two-part in F Major

Intricate structure of the "commonplace" theme:

The background structure shows strict symmetry; in the foreground, the two halves appear different: sameness behind diversity.

Moving from $\hat{1}$ to $\hat{8}$ and back to $\hat{1}$, the theme seems to accomplish in itself a complete release of whatever tension it sets up: there is the danger that the movement, hardly begun, might come to a dead stop, right here, at measure 3. The danger is overcome by the *overlapping* of the two parts, the result of the bass' beginning when the treble is only half way through the theme.

Two-part in F Minor

Beautiful macroscopic picture:

Most of the middle section is taken up by one large passing movement spanning a whole octave from c to c, in the course of which c = $\hat{1}$ is transformed into c = $\hat{5}$. Passing movements of this type, connecting two main stations of the movement by a series of stepwise moves, are among the most important elements of tonal architecture.

Three-part in C Major

The dissonance-consonance chain (suspension-resolution) is the chief moving agent in measures 3–7, while the theme and its inversion are just repeated over and over again in the different parts.

Skeleton:

(The dissonant d in measure 4 remains hanging in the air, unresolved; its true resolution comes only with measure 7, the move d–c in measure 5 is proved premature by what follows.)

169

Three-part in G Minor

In the absence of a theme proper the broad movement along the scale, as revealed in the skeleton, emerges as the principal organizing factor.

Skeleton of measures 1–8:

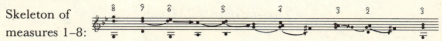

Instead of continuing $\widehat{2}$–$\widehat{1}$ and completing the scale, the movement turns around at the decisive point: $\widehat{2}$–$\widehat{3}$. The full octave is only completed with the very last measure of the piece.

Note in measures 24–28 and 57–62 the sustained tone in the bass underlying the movement of the other parts. Such a sustained tone, an element of steadiness in the midst of motion, is called *pedal point*. It is typical for the tone $\widehat{5}$ to appear in the role of pedal point, which is what happens here in both instances.

V • Harmony

We remember the earlier statement about the two ways to exploit the possibility of "more than one tone at a time." The complex sensation of different tones sounding together can be considered either as "many within one" or as "one out of many"; the first aspect produces polyphony, the second, harmony.

Historically speaking, the two ways were not pursued simultaneously. Only after polyphony, in the course of almost half a millenium, had grown to its fullest stature did the idea of the other way dawn upon the minds of the makers of music. This at least is the testimony gathered from written music and the books of the theorists. It is not unlikely, though, that unwritten music, music not dignified to be a subject for theory, the music of the people, knew and used harmony, in an elementary way, at a much earlier date. In any event, the development of harmony from the 17th century on, climaxing in the works of the great composers of the late 18th and 19th centuries, completely changed the face of music.

What then is harmony?

Palestrina may begin a composition with just one single tone held for a considerable length of time—as time lengths go in music—without anything else happening; e.g. in the motet "Dies sanctificatus" ♮. This is one way of opening the door to the tonal world, of asking the listener to enter: Just one tone! Not yet music, but the promise of music, the anticipation of music, that is—in Palestrina's sense—the anticipation of melody.

The single tone heralds the appearance of melody, and melody, a web of melodies, then flows from it.

When Haydn begins one of his symphonies thus ,

it is a different story. One tone again, but one tone resounding through all the octaves, echoing from all the corners of the tonal expanse. Again not yet music; anticipation, announcement of music, but not of melody. We do not expect a melody to flow from this tone, and none flows from it. The event stands by itself, is self-sufficient; something other than melodic line makes its appearance here. Metaphorically speaking, the sound throws open a wide gate, not just a door. Through the tone we sense the presence of a new dimension of tonal life, a dimension that transcends the linear: spatial expansion, depth.

This is the beginning of Bruckner's Fourth Symphony:

Here we have not one tone, but still one thing for the ear, one sound; it is more complex than the single tone, but no less unified. Once more, not yet music, mere promise of music, though in a somewhat different way. No anticipation, no announcement; rather like a stage, still empty, and waiting for something to happen on it.

When this does happen

we distinguish clearly the two elements: the melody, and that which is not melody, that which is spread out behind and below the melody, that on which the melody floats: tonal depth actualized in sound. The single tone of the Haydn example let the ear infer the existence of a new tonal dimension; the event here, the chord, *harmony,* spells it out in actual sound.

The Chord

In order to take a closer look at harmony we must artificially separate the two elements, melody and harmony, whose intrinsic unity makes, whose separation unmakes, music. We have no other choice. There is much music that is melody, or melodies, only and that gives us the opportunity to study melody in the living object; but there is no music that is harmony only—except for brief moments. One of these brief moments we are now taking under observation.

This is more than one tone and more than one complex sound; it is a sequence of sounds. Still we realize that it is not yet music in the full sense, not the real thing. It may lead up to the real thing, in the way of a preparation, or introduction. It actually is an introduction, the introduction to Schubert's "Serenade." Taken by itself it does not make complete sense; but neither is it nonsense. It makes *some* sense. What sense?

We listen carefully and describe what we hear. The succession of sounds does not seem arbitrary; it has connection; it has direction; it gets somewhere, seems to reach a destination. A closer look confirms that beginning and end of the sequence are the same. We recognize the familiar pattern of "away-from-and-back-to." The sequence we hear is a movement.

This movement is harmony.

Melody moves by successive steps; so, as we hear, does harmony. How many such successive steps, or moves, do we distinguish in our example?

The answer, provided by listening, is: four.[1]

Every tonal move leads from one sound to another. In the case of melody, these sounds are individual tones; and in this sense we understand melody as movement of tones. We do not know what the corresponding sounds are in the case of harmony; but we do know that in our example, since it contains four moves, there must be five of them. These sounds—whatever they are—of which we count five in our example, we shall call *chords*. Chord is to harmony as tone is to melody. We shall understand harmony as movement of chords.

(Current usage makes no precise distinction between the terms chord and harmony; it rather lumps them together as representing the *vertical* aspect of music in contrast to the *horizontal* aspect represented by melody. The terms are suggested by our system of notation, in which successive tones are written side by side, simultaneous tones above and below one another. One should not be misled by these terms, though. Since the horizontal line only, not the vertical, is customarily used as a visual symbol of movement, the implication seems to be that movement in music is carried by melody only, not by harmony. There is no doubt that traditional musical theory has itself been caught in this implication, with corresponding effect on its ability to understand harmony. To us, harmony is tonal movement just as melody is—movement of a different type, under a different law. It is precisely the mutual relation, the synthesis of the two types of movement, that has given the music of the 18th and 19th centuries its distinctive mark.)

We do not know yet what a chord is; but we can ask a pre-

[1] This result can easily be misinterpreted as due to the movement of the bass. The result, however, is the same if the right hand only is played (with rests properly filled).

liminary question. How long does the first chord of our example last? Clearly up to the point when we experience the first move of harmony—that is, the first move of the type of which there are altogether four in the sequence. This happens exactly at the beginning of the second measure. The first chord, then, lasts for the whole of the first measure. The second, as we find out, for the whole of the second measure, and so on. In this example, very conveniently, each chord lasts for exactly one measure.

If the first harmonic move occurs at the beginning of the second measure, what about the things that go on *within* the first measure. Clearly something does go on there. If this were melody we would perhaps describe it as a pendulum-like motion. In the perspective of harmony it seems to be no motion at all. The same is true for every subsequent measure. In the context of the movement of harmony the motion within each measure counts for nothing, is as good as a standstill: no movement is experienced. The term perspective was used deliberately. We are reminded of certain phenomena of visual perspective, e.g. of a movement back and forth in a straight line that does not appear as a movement if observed in the direction of the line: $\xrightarrow{\quad}$ $\overset{A \qquad B}{\longleftrightarrow}$. It seems that harmony can be looked at as rooted in a kind of auditory perspective.

With this we can approach the question: What is a chord?

A chord is that which remains one and the same, stationary, unchanged within each measure of our example, and changes with each measure. The only thing that remains unchanged in every measure and changes from measure to measure is the tonal supply, the selection of tones that feed the events of each measure. In measure 1 we hear only the tones d, f, and a, in various combinations and arrangements; in measure 2, the tones b flat, d, and f; in measure 3, e, g, b flat, and d; in measure 4, a, c sharp, and e; in measure 5, d, f, and a—this is the same as in measure 1. (The reason why the tones of each measure are listed in this particular succession will become clear later.)

A chord, then, is the result of a combination, a coming to-gether of a number of different tones—three or four, according to our example; a form of coexistence of these tones, not a *sum* of tones, no *mixture,* no *tone* at all: a tonal event *sui generis,* an auditory experience of another order than tone. Again we are reminded of a phenomenon of visual perspective: the experience of depth that arises from certain arrangements of lines in a plane. The chord is not *in* the tones but somehow above or be-hind or about them, a radiation, an aura, one further step removed from materiality.

The first essential characteristic of the chord is its oneness. The chord in harmony is *one*—one thing, one experience—just as the tone in melody is. We have mentioned this before: the oneness results from the merger of simultaneously sounding tones into one auditory sensation. The individual tones that make up the compound do not disappear in the merger, do not give up their identity altogether; they remain recognizable as individual components and in simple cases can be distinguished even by the untrained ear.

The second essential characteristic of the chord is its inner organization. By playing the chord on the piano and stressing the individual tones, ♭, or by letting the ear pick them out and singing them in succession, , that organiza-tion is made explicit to the hearing. What we hear is not three tones of different pitch, or three tones combined in a pleasant sound, but three tones definitely, audibly related to each other: dynamically related in a familiar way. If we analyze in this manner, for instance, the first chord of our example we hear the tone d as $\widehat{1}$, f as $\widehat{3}$, a as $\widehat{5}$. Thus the chord exhibits a com-plete dynamic structure within itself, with one tone acting as the dynamic center and the other two depending on it in the way of a $\widehat{3}$ and a $\widehat{5}$. The same analysis applied to the chords of

measures 2 and 4 gives the same result: in measure 2 we hear
b flat = $\widehat{1}$, d = $\widehat{3}$, f = $\widehat{5}$; in measure 4 it is a = $\widehat{1}$, c sharp = $\widehat{3}$,
e = $\widehat{5}$.

We restrict our observation for the time being to these three-
tone chords, leaving aside the four-tone chord of which measure 3 of our example shows an instance. In each case, then, the
three-tone chord appears as a well-balanced, self-sufficient
sound, a small dynamic system in a state of equilibrium, with
its sun, tone $\widehat{1}$, and its planets, tones $\widehat{3}$ and $\widehat{5}$: a closed and unified whole produced by three tones in this specific dynamic
relation. This chord is the *triad*—the holy chord of our music,
to some purists its only chord, certainly the most important,
the fundamental phenomenon of harmony. The tone that functions as the dynamic center of the triad is called its *root;* the
other two are referred to as the *third* and the *fifth* of the triad. If
we understand harmony as the third dimension of tonal life,
the triad is the elementary form of three-dimensional tonal
existence. A tone manifests itself as a three-dimensional being
by becoming the root of a triad. In this sense the root can be
considered as the *representative* of the whole triad. The triads of
our example are accordingly referred to as D-triad, B flat-triad,
and A-triad.

The third essential characteristic of the chord can be demonstrated in the following way. We reduce the harmonic sequence
of our example to its bare essentials, the flat statement of the
five chords:

Now we substitute for the last measure

this } or this or this :

in the sense of the movement, which is the sense of harmony, it makes no difference. Harmonically, it is always the same thing. As long as the tones that build up the chord are the same, the chord is the same, no matter where, in which octave, in which arrangement the tones sound. *The chord is indifferent to the distribution of its component tones in the tonal expanse.* What difference there exists is one of sonority—an important one in other respects, but not in the specific context of harmony.

This property of the chord follows logically from our understanding of the triad as the unified whole of dynamically related tones.

$$\text{Take the triad } \begin{aligned} a &= \hat{5} \\ f &= \hat{3} \\ d &= \hat{1} \end{aligned} \; .$$

The tonal expanse contains a number of d's, f's, and a's, one in every octave. Yet to question which of these d's is the root of the triad is obviously pointless. $D = \hat{1}$ means, any $d = \hat{1}$. The same is true of the other two tones: any $f = \hat{3}$, any a is $\hat{5}$. Consequently, it cannot make any difference to the triad as the system $\hat{5}, \hat{3}, \hat{1}$ which of the d's, f's, and a's actually sound. The chord remains the same in any case.

This statement needs to be qualified. Let us substitute for the last measure of our example

the component tones are the same as before, d, f, a; their respective dynamic qualities are the same, $\hat{1}, \hat{3}, \hat{5}$; so the chord is the same. Yet the feeling is different. Something has happened to the equilibrium of the sound. The ear still accepts it as the destination towards which our little sequence was moving; but its balance seems disturbed. A comparison with the former examples reveals the cause of the disturbance. There, the lowest tone of the chord was always d, its root; here it is f, the third, or a, the fifth. We conclude that the chord is fully balanced only when its root sounds also as its lowest tone.

The earlier statement has to be qualified accordingly. At one point, the lowest point, its acoustical basis, the chord is *not indifferent* to distribution or arrangement of tones. If the chord is to appear in its normal sound state, as it were, the root must occupy that place (technical term: chord in *root position*); otherwise, that is, with the third or the fifth of the chord at the bottom, its sound state will be markedly upset (these other positions are called *first* and *second inversions*). Clearly the possibility of presenting the same chord in different states of sound, and vice versa, of having different states of sound represented by the same chord, makes for a high degree of differentiation of the harmonic language.

Triads, Seventh Chords, Deviations.

We take a look at the acoustical structure of the triad. Since the chords of measures 1, 2, and 4 of our example were all triads, this sameness should be reflected in the structure. We write each chord in the order suggested by its dynamic organization: root at the bottom, third above root, fifth above third: . The similarity of structure is apparent in the interval pattern: in each instance three tones arranged by thirds. However, the thirds are not arranged the same way in all three cases. In the first chord, the third between the lowest and the middle tone is minor, the other major; in the other chords it is the reverse, the lower third is major, the upper minor. We recognize a corresponding difference in sound: the first triad has the minor mode sound, the others, the major mode sound.

179

This establishes the general distinction of major and minor triads. The first of the three chords is the D minor triad, the other two are the B♭ major and A major triads. The exact pitch pattern of these two types of triads is this:

	TRIAD		MAJOR	MINOR
fifth	⎡ · ⎤	third	minor	major
	⎣ · ⎦	third	major	minor

We remember the pattern: it is one of the three possible consonance patterns of our music. *The triad in this position, in root position, is a consonance.*

What happens if the thirds of this pattern are both either minor or major? The result is this:

minor third	⎡ · ⎤		major third	⎡ · ⎤	
minor third	⎣ · ⎦	diminished fifth	major third	⎣ · ⎦	augmented fifth

As the fifth is no longer perfect, the sound has become dissonant. The dynamic structure is obscured; the ear fails to recognize root, third, and fifth; the distinction of the root position is abolished. Accordingly these two sounds, the *diminished* and *augmented triads,* should rather be considered triads by name only. (It seems that irregularity of pitch pattern is a precondition of dynamic organization. It was the same in the case of the diatonic and chromatic scales. When irregularity in the pitch distribution is replaced by regularity, the dynamic structure vanishes.)

What about the *inversions* of the major and minor triad? The D minor and B flat major triads, for instance, in first inversion (with the third at the bottom) would look like this: 𝄞 ; for the second inversion (fifth at the bottom) of the same chords the picture would be this: 𝄞. Pitch patterns:

180

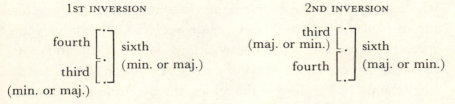

We recognize the remaining two of the three possible consonance patterns of our tonal system. That is to say not only that the triad, major and minor, is consonant in every position; but—since it contains in itself all possible consonance patterns—that it is the *only* consonance of our music.

As to the four-tone chord of which we find an instance in measure 3 of our example (component tones e, g, b♭, d), we restrict ourselves at this point to the barest statement of fact. The pitch pattern of the four-tone chord, in the most general terms, is this:

third ⌐ ¬
third │ │ seventh
third └ ┘

The structural principle is the same as in the triad, but it is carried one step further: one more third is piled on top of the other two. This makes for the interval of a seventh between the root and the fourth tone. We call the fourth tone the *seventh* of the chord, and the whole chord, the *seventh chord*. As it contains four different tones, the seventh chord is necessarily dissonant; its sound state is always tension, not, as in the triad, balance. Consequently the essential properties of the chord that we observed in the triad—oneness, dynamic organization, root as representative of the chord, indifference to distribution of component tones with the exception of the lowest tone—will appear in the seventh chord in a more or less modified way.

These two chords, triad and seventh chord, constitute the

181

whole of the material of harmony. Incredible though it seems, the immensely rich and resourceful world of harmonic events spread out in the great compositions of the 18th and 19th centuries grew from the discovery and exploitation of two chords, from the understanding of the forces, the dynamic potentialities contained in them. That is not to say that in all 18th and 19th century music we hear nothing but triads and seventh chords. We may hear any combination of tones. But if what we hear is not a triad or a seventh chord, the sound will definitely *be related,* *audibly* related to such a chord. It will be understood by the ear as a *deviation* from a triad or a seventh chord; we shall hear in the sound the tendency to resolve itself into the particular triad or seventh chord from which it deviates. The meaning of the sound is always clear from the context. For instance, the sound ♮ is not a triad; its component tones do not fit the triad pattern. Yet in the context ♮, that sound is unmistakably heard as a deviation from the triad which follows: the tone c is out of place, belongs to the next lower pitch: ♮. The sound ♮ is not a seventh chord, its four tones cannot be arranged in the proper pattern. In the context ♮, it is heard as a deviation from the ♮ triad.

The deviation may go so far as to produce sounds that on paper look like triads or seventh chords and also sound that way if heard by themselves, yet in the context of harmonic motion assume an entirely different meaning. ♮ looks like an inversion of the E minor triad, and heard by itself sounds like it, too. In the following context ♮, it is no longer that triad but a deviation from the G major triad, produced by the tone e, which went out of its way, as it were. ♮ looks and sounds like an inversion of the C major triad; if we hear it in the context ♮, the strong tendency of the sound towards the chord that follows reveals it to the ear as a deviation from that sound, the G major triad, produced by *two* tones

being out of place: e and c, which "should" be d and b: ♪♪♪ .
(As these matters involve problems of harmonic context they
lie somewhat beyond the present scope of the discussion. They
will be more fully clarified later.)

Most harmony textbooks list a third chord besides triad and
seventh chord, the so-called chord of the ninth, a sound in
which *five* tones are joined at intervals of thirds:

$$\left.\begin{array}{l} \text{third} \\ \text{third} \\ \text{third} \\ \text{third} \end{array}\right\} \text{ninth}$$

We are more in line with logic and experience if we consider
this a deviation from the seventh chord rather than a chord in
the strict sense; the tone that produces the ninth is an exagger-
ated octave, so to speak; it tends to the octave, it belongs there,
e.g. ♪♪ . Also the sound is not indifferent to the distribution
of component tones. Who would hear ♪ and ♪ as the
same chord?

In the course of the 20th century revolution of the tonal
language, harmony has moved away from the strict notion of
chord. Sounds appear in which tones combine in all sorts of
ways; and these sounds are no longer deviations from triads
and seventh chords: they are, and are heard to be, meaningful
in themselves. We may call them chords in a wider, unqualified
sense; they possess the property of oneness; but they lack dynamic organization, they have no root, and the principle of
inversion does not apply. We shall see later how as a consequence of this development the *motor* function of harmony was
diminished and its *color* function enhanced.

Unfolding of Chords

We return once more to the strict notion of the chord. The chord is indifferent not only to the disposition of its component tones in the tonal expanse but also to their distribution in time. A chord may *unfold in time*. This was implied when we substituted the compact form 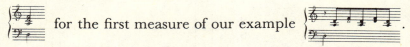 for the first measure of our example .

Harmonically, there is no difference; it is the same thing in either case, the D minor triad. *There is no limit to the number of ways that unfolding may choose.*

are all different appearances of the same chord. Thus harmony faces a problem, and an opportunity, that could not arise in melody. A tone can only sound—louder or softer, to be sure, played or sung, by this or that voice, this or that instrument— but that is all. A chord, however, can come into being in innumerable different ways of presentation, each one having its peculiar character and correspondingly influencing the total musical experience.

Where is that which all these different presentations have in common, where is the chord? If the chord is togetherness, a meeting of tones, where do they meet? Certainly not in the actual sound of the tones: in some of the examples there is not even any sounding together of tones, only succession. We have said it before: the chord is not *in* the tones but, in a sense, above them, more immaterial than the tones themselves. As that which is the same in all those different appearances it is something like an *idea*—an idea to be heard, an idea for the ear, an audible idea. Hearing harmony implies far more than a mere responding of the sense organ to tonal stimuli. The ear that hears the sequence of our example and recognizes that the content of the first measure is one chord, that of the second one other chord, and so on, has an awareness of ideas; it performs acts of integration and differentiation; it brings together what belongs together and keeps apart what should be separated; it understands succession as meaning simultaneity; it forms sums and knows when one summing operation comes to an end and the next should begin. These are acts of thought that must be attributed not to the intellect but to the sense organ. We had occasion earlier, in connection with the understanding of melody, to recognize the capacity of the ear to think. In the case of harmony this capacity manifests itself in an ever more elementary, incontestable way. In fact, without the power of the ear to think, common to all people—although, like all thinking power, present in different individuals in different degrees—music could be neither composed nor understood.

The freedom of presentation includes the possibility of presenting a chord incomplete, with one or more of its tones left out. We could for instance play the last measure of our example thus:

relying on the capacity of the ear to supply in thought the missing tone a and to take the sound for what it is meant, the D minor chord. (Supply in thought, not imagination: one does not *imagine* the missing tone; one hears what sounds, $\frac{f}{d}$, and one knows, one's ear knows, that this means $\frac{f}{d}$.) On the other hand, the unfolding in time of a chord can carry in its way tones that do not belong to the chord.

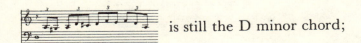 is still the D minor chord;

the foreign tones do not destroy the chord, they are rather absorbed by its superior power, and the ear understands them for what they are, mere surface modifications. The following accompaniment (from a Mozart aria)

is an elaborate and expressive presentation of the chord sequence:

Here we reach the borderline of harmonic and melodic motion; the transition, as we see, is gradual, there is no sharp dividing line in the body of music.

Harmonic Degrees

Melodic motion arises from a difference in the dynamic quality of tones, from their different states of balance and unbalance. What does harmonic motion arise from? Or, to put the question in another, more specific way: How is it possible for triads to become involved in motion?

Every triad forms a closed dynamic system, perfectly balanced about its center, the root. Its sound is the very image of tonal stability. How can a succession of such images of stability constitute movement?

We hear the A major triad, [musical notation]. It is hard to imagine how this sound could convey an experience of movement. With its constituent tones bound into one compact whole by the action of the tonal forces it is firmly at rest within itself.

Next, we listen again to the sequence of our original example and stop at measure 4:

This is the same A major triad; but the balance of the sound is gone. Rest has given way to acute unrest, self-reliance to an urgent demand for continuation. The closed sound is all open, as it were, and calling to be closed. What has happened?

The root of this triad is the tone a. We know that in music there is no tone which is simply a, nothing but a; there is always a tone a *with a certain dynamic quality*. What is the dynamic quality of the tone a, the root of that triad, in the context of our example?

The key of the sequence is D minor: $d = \hat{1}$. Consequently, $a = \hat{5}$. In the musical context of the example the root of the A major triad has the dynamic quality $\hat{5}$.

As long as a triad is considered by itself, in the vertical context only, its root is always $\hat{1}$. When the triad appears as an element in a musical sequence the horizontal context takes precedence over the vertical. Acting through the root, tonal forces from outside invade, so to speak, the triad. Since in music the root of a triad is always at the same time a tone in a given seven tone order, and subject to the action of the forces of that order, the whole triad can be lifted from its solid foundation, and its balance upset. Then, instead of rest, its sound expresses unrest, instead of balance, tension. The chord as a whole acquires a distinct dynamic quality that is the equivalent, in the harmonic dimension, of the dynamic qualities of single tones in melody. These dynamic qualities of chords give rise to harmonic motion in the same way that dynamic tone qualities bring about melodic motion.

Chords as elements of harmonic motion, with their dynamic qualities determined by the position of the root in the given seven tone order, are called *harmonic degrees*. We identify them by Roman numerals. The chord of the first degree, or I, has the tone $\hat{1}$ of a seven tone order as its root. (It is obvious that this is the only triad at rest in a musical context.) The chord of the second degree, II, has the tone $\widehat{2}$ as its root; and so on, through VII.

Considering for the moment triads only, we could say that the harmonic degrees originate when each of the seven tones of the system expands into the third dimension of tonal life, asserts itself as a three-dimensional being. This it accomplishes by calling forth and tying to itself those other two tones of the system that are related to it, like a $\widehat{3}$ and a $\widehat{5}$ to a $\widehat{1}$, and that together with it form the triad pattern. In C major, for instance, the tone c, to become a triad, would call forth the tones e and g, the tone d would enlist the tones f and a, and so on. The complete file of the seven harmonic degrees, in C major, would look like this: [musical notation: I II III IV V VI VII] . It appears that of these seven triads three are major—namely, I, IV, and V—three minor—II, III, and VI—and one, VII, diminished. This is of course true for every major key. In the minor keys the picture is more complex, due to the choice of two possible pitches of the tones $\widehat{6}$ and $\widehat{7}$; also the distribution of major and minor triads among the seven degrees is different. II in minor is normally a diminished triad.

Next, we spell out in terms of harmonic degrees the chord sequence of our original example. To this end, we must first identify the root of each chord, either by ear or by imagining the component tones arranged in the proper pattern. The roots are: d, b♭, e, a, d. With d = $\widehat{1}$, this gives us the following series of harmonic degrees: I–VI–II–V–I.

This series of Roman numerals stands for a particular harmonic motion just as, for instance, $\widehat{1}$–$\widehat{3}$–$\widehat{2}$–$\widehat{1}$ would stand for a particular melodic motion; though in a different sense. The latter series symbolizes an actual tone-to-tone movement; the former does not. The Roman numerals symbolize a chord-to-chord progression, a movement, that is, that occurs in a different dimension altogether from that of tone-to-tone motion. It

188

cannot even be maintained that the series of Roman numerals symbolizes a movement of *roots*. As the root represents the chord, so the succession of roots merely *represents* the movement of chords. Strictly speaking, there is no movement of roots. What should it be? Take, for instance, the root of our first chord, the tone d. Which d is it, this one, 𝄢, or this 𝄢, or this 𝄞? Any one, all of them; the question is pointless. The root of the chord is not any particular d, it is that which all tones d have in common, it is d-ness, so to speak. The same is true of the root of the next chord, b flat. What sort of move would that be, from d-ness to b flat-ness?

With this in mind we can settle a question that may easily be a source of confusion. Chord-to-chord moves, chord progressions, are classified according to the interval between the roots of successive chords. I–VI, for instance, is a *third-progression,* because the interval between the two roots—in our case d–b♭—is a third. We understand now that this term does not imply an actual tone-to-tone move spanning the interval of a third. It may happen that way—as for instance in our example where the bass moves actually a third down, from d to b flat—but it is by no means essential.

Consider the following situation: 𝄢. This too is I–VI; yet no actual move of a third occurs in the progress from the first chord to the next, and in fact no tone-to-tone move at all. The actual behavior of the tones in the progression from one chord to another is of no more significance to the harmonic sense of the move than the actual behavior of tones in presenting a chord is to the harmonic meaning of that chord. The term *interval,* then, if applied to the relation between two roots, has a different, more abstract meaning; it is not simply a pitch distance between two tones. The interval between the *tones* d and b♭ is either this 𝄞, a third, or this 𝄞, a sixth; the interval between the *roots* d and b♭, that is, between any d and any b♭, must be pictured somewhat like this:

Is this a third or a sixth?

The question is again pointless; it could be called either. In actual practice it is always called a third. A succession whose roots are a third apart is called a *third-progression;* downward, as for instance in I–VI, , upward as in I–III, .

The last move in our example is V–I, A-chord to D-chord. The interval between the *tones* a and d is either a fourth up, , or a fifth down, .

Is the interval between *roots* a and d,

a fourth or a fifth? Another moot question. Again, according to common usage, whenever the interval between the roots of two successive chords leaves us a choice of calling it either a fourth or a fifth, we *always* refer to the move as a *fifth-progression.* Consequently, there is no need in harmony for the term fourth-progression. IV–I is a fifth, too, though an upward fifth, e.g. , while V–I is a downward fifth, . Again, the direction of actual tone-to-tone moves does not affect this terminology. In the last two measures of our example the move a–d appears, in the bass, as an upward fourth; the chord progression will still be referred to as a fifth down. IV–I is always a fifth up, although the bass may be doing this: .

There is another kind of chord progression of which our example shows no instance: the succession of two chords the roots of which are scale neighbors: e.g. I–II. This is called *second-progression.* (Melodically the two tones could form either a second or a seventh.)

This completes the list of harmonic intervals: Progressions by seconds, by thirds, by fifths, upward or downward; there are no others. The fourth is absorbed by the fifth, the sixth by the third, the seventh by the second; and the octave constitutes no harmonic interval, as two chords with roots an octave apart are identical.

A Scale of Harmonic Degrees

We go back to our series of Roman numerals, I–VI–II–V–I, representing the root progression D–B flat–E–A–D. First observation: Only the first of these four moves is *not* a fifth.

Next, we observe and describe what we hear in each of the successive moves. When VI follows upon I the experience is simply one of having been set in motion, of a movement having begun. The sound of VI makes the ear sense that the chord is not in a state of balance, that we are not where we ought to be, and that we have to go on to something else. However, the sound gives no indication of any definite *direction* where the movement should proceed.

When II is reached, the realization both of having gone away from somewhere and of having to go on to somewhere is further strengthened and clarified. At this point the dissonance is an important contributing factor. (That it is not the essential factor can be demonstrated by substituting the tone g for e.) Yet there is still no clear indication of the direction in which the chord would desire the movement to proceed.

The moment V sounds, the picture changes. Not only is the will to go on more sharpened, more outspoken than in the earlier chords (by the way, without the chord being dissonant); in addition, there emerges a clear indication of a direction which the movement ought now to follow. This is confirmed by the entry of I, which the ear understands as the sound toward which V was tending or pointing and which thus clearly emerges as the goal the little sequence had set out to reach.

In order to demonstrate the directional quality of V one could experiment with the example and go on to chords other than I after V. There will be a clear response of "rejection" as distinguished from the "acceptance" of I. This rejection and acceptance has nothing to do with "beauty" or "interest" or "feeling"; it is not a matter of "aesthetics"; it is simply an acknowledgment of facts: This is what the chord wants, this is not what it wants. The ear in making these judgments registers its awareness and understanding of the action of tonal forces. Of course there may be more beauty, more feeling, greater aesthetic interest in chords other than I following upon V; in fact, there would be no music, and consequently no musical aesthetics, if tones would do only what the tonal forces want them to do. The lack of directional quality in the other chords, particularly II, can be similarly demonstrated by the *absence* in our immediate response of a clear-cut "yes-no" distinction when instead of V other chords follow upon II. When later on in the song from which our example is taken (Schubert's "Serenade") a chord which is *not* V follows upon II, as occurs in measure 12/13, the listener will not register any rejection; he will simply take it as just another possible continuation—possible in the sense of not running noticeably counter to a will of the tonal forces.

A major difference in the dynamic aspect of tones in melody and chords in harmony is apparent in this description. In the dynamic state of individual tones other than $\hat{1}$ there is always audible not only a certain tension but together with it also the direction in which the tension points for its resolution. In the harmonic degrees other than I we hear tension, but no direction —with the sole exception of V in which both tension *and* direction are audible. (In our example we met with only four of the seven harmonic degrees; inclusion of the rest would not have changed the result.) It seems that in the case of the harmonic degrees the influence of the center of the seven tone order is in general strong enough to upset the balance of the chord as a whole, but not strong enough to turn the whole chord around, as it were, and make it point in the direction of I. Only in the case of V, that is, of the chord whose root lies a fifth above the tone $\hat{1}$, is that action strong enough to produce both unrest and pointing.

We remember that among the seven tones of the diatonic system the striving towards $\hat{1}$ was strongest in $\hat{2}$ and $\hat{7}$ ("raised $\hat{7}$" in the case of minor), that is, in the two tones situated closest to $\hat{1}$, just one step removed from it. Reasoning by analogy, one can conclude that, if V points more markedly than any other harmonic degree to I, it must lie closest to I, be just one step removed from it. If this is granted, "one step" in harmony means "a fifth"; the fifth is the *minimum* move, the unit move; and two chords are nearest to each other when their roots are a fifth apart. This seems to indicate a sort of polar relation between melody and harmony: we remember that in the scale the tone $\hat{5}$ marked the dynamic turning point and in this sense the *maximum* distance from $\hat{1}$. Again we found the fifth defining closeness of relation among *keys:* those keys appear closest to each other whose centers lie a fifth apart. Also in the series of numerical ratios the first ratio that produces a new tone, $2:3$, corresponds to the fifth; or, expressed in acoustical terms, the first overtone apart from the octave (which is not a new tone) is the fifth.

All this gives special significance to an earlier remark, namely, that in the sequence I–VI–II–V–I only one move was not a fifth-progression. Our example is quite typical in this respect; the more harmonic sequences we observe, the clearer it will become that the most common, the normal way for harmony to move is by fifths—just as the most common, the normal way for melody to move is by seconds. Both observations, the unique dynamic relation between V and I, and the frequency of the fifth as an interval of harmonic motion, point to the same conclusion: The fifth is the equivalent in the dimension of harmony of the second in the dimension of melody; it is the *norm* of motion, the standard interval.

Taking the fifth as the unit, we can build *a scale of harmonic degrees:*

I–V–II–VI–III–VII–IV–I

In the melodic scale the first and the last tone, $\hat{1}$ and $\hat{8}$, were in a sense the same, in another sense not. We tried to do justice to this situation by visualizing the scale in the image of a wave-like curve. In the harmonic scale the I at the beginning and the I at the end are absolutely identical. Accordingly, the proper visual symbol would be a figure that runs back into itself. We choose the circle.

Just as in the melodic scale the steps are not all the same but are either major or minor seconds, so in this scale the fifths are not all alike, all perfect; at one place, between IV and VII, we get a diminished fifth. We also note that the three major triads, I, V, and IV, are all together on one side, the three minor chords, II, VI, and III, on the other; the diminished triad, VII, lies between them.

If one listens to the full sequence of the scale, from I to I, in either direction, clockwise and counterclockwise one will notice a striking difference. Whereas in the melodic scale the overall sense of the motion, "away-from-and-back-to $\hat{1}$," emerged unambiguously in either ascending or descending direction, in the harmonic scale this is clearly not the case. Only in clockwise direction, that is, by descending fifths, does the sequence reach I as its goal, does it convey the sense of "back-to I"; counterclockwise movement, by ascending fifths, does not produce this effect: the concluding I lacks all sense of finality.

We understand why this must be so. In the melodic scale $\hat{1}$ can be reached either from above, by $\hat{2}$–$\hat{1}$, or from below, by $\hat{7}$–$\hat{8}$, with a sense of finality because the pointing towards $\hat{1}$ is equally strong and clear in $\hat{2}$ and $\hat{7}$. In the harmonic scale, however, only the chord "above" I, namely V, has this quality; consequently I can be approached and reached as a goal only from above, through V, not from below, through IV. Incidentally, both tones $\hat{7}$ and $\hat{2}$ are component parts of the V triad, $\frac{\hat{2}}{\frac{7}{5}}$.

The unique property of the melodic scale—that continued motion in the same pitch direction brings about a reversal in dynamic direction so that upward in pitch can mean both "away-from" and "back-to," and downward in pitch the same —this property is lacking in the harmonic scale. A clear directional quality is apparent only in the relation of V to I; I–V says "away-from," V–I, "back-to." From this the direction of the progression derives its fixed meaning; moving upward by fifths means "going-away-from I"; moving downward by fifths, "approaching I." Clockwise motion is motion with the acting forces; counterclockwise, against them. This creates a problem for the move IV–I; it will be discussed later.

The Dominant Chord

The technical term for I is *tonic chord,* for V, *dominant chord.* Superficially the terms seem ill chosen. After all, it is I that dominates the events, not V. Yet how can I manifest itself as the dominating power if not through its action on other chords? Since V is the only chord audibly directed towards I, it is by virtue of V only that I can effectively establish itself as the center of action. Any harmonic motion, in order to express the rule of I, must be ultimately channeled through V. In this role, then, as the chord that dominates the *access* to I as I, and on which I depends for the manifestation of its power, V seems quite appropriately called the dominant chord.

Because V–I possesses that unique quality of a terminal move it became the preferred means for setting punctuations in the flow of harmonic motion. Susceptible of infinite shadings of emphasis it is equally capable of marking semicolons, periods, the ends of paragraphs, chapters, the whole work. V–I in any of these various terminal functions is called the *dominant cadence.*

What gives the dominant cadence, the move V–I, its unique position? Two triads in succession, roots a fifth apart, direction downward: this event can be duplicated at other places of the scale, e.g. between II and V. Accordingly, II–V should sound like a dominant cadence.

However, when we hear it, e.g. ,

we find no cadence quality, no sense of finality in the second chord. Why?

II–V and V–I are different in one respect only: II is a minor triad, V is major. In fact, we need only to change in , and the cadence quality will immediately appear. We conclude that for the succession of two triads to have the effect of a dominant cadence not only must the root progression be a fifth down, but the first of the two chords must be major.

We see easily that all along the harmonic scale this condition is fulfilled nowhere except between V and I. II, VI, and III are minor chords; VII is the diminished triad. In the case of IV–VII the first chord is a major triad; but the dissonant VII cannot possibly function as a goal. Only between I and IV are the con-

196

ditions of V–I exactly duplicated. Yet it would seem that things would have to be turned upside down if I–IV should be understood as a move *toward* the center.

This will also help us to understand the particular problem of V in minor. Of the three tones of the V triad, $\widehat{5}$, $\widehat{7}$, and $\widehat{2}$, the tone $\widehat{7}$ is available in minor in two pitch positions, diatonic and raised. If the diatonic position is used, V becomes a minor triad; for instance, in A minor ♭♯ ; no cadence effect will result from this V–I, ♭♯ . Only with $\widehat{7}$ in raised position will V be a major triad, ♯ , and V–I a cadence, ♭♯ . (This corresponds to the "borrowing" of $\widehat{7}$ from major in the ascending minor scale for the purpose of giving the move $\widehat{7}$–$\widehat{8}$ the quality of a conclusion.)

With all this the full story of the unique position of V is not yet told. So far we have considered the chords of the I–V–I sequence as represented by triads. In this case each sound taken by itself, in its vertical context, is a consonance. This need not be so; on the contrary, the sense of the horizontal context, balance-disturbed-restored, will be made much more telling if it is paralleled in the vertical context by a sequence of consonance-dissonance-consonance; that is, if V triad is replaced by V seventh chord. In symbols: I–V_7–I.

It is in V_7, the *dominant seventh chord,* that the extraordinary virtue of the Vth degree is fully revealed. V_7 is the only sound in music capable of establishing with one stroke a dynamic center. One single tone has not yet any definite dynamic quality; one single triad may be almost any degree. Yet we need only to hear ♭♯ and we know immediately where we are: we hear the direction of the sound; its point of destination is the C triad; so its root, the tone g, must be $\widehat{5}$. Thus a completely defined dynamic field comes into being the moment the chord sounds. The center is not pronounced directly—music has no

197

way of accomplishing this—but indirectly, by the sound's audibly pointing at it.

The component tones of V_7 are $\hat{5}$, $\hat{7}$, $\hat{2}$, $\hat{4}$; pitch pattern:

minor third

minor third

major third

At one place only of the diatonic order can the particular pitch pattern be realized:

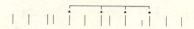

Uniqueness of position corresponds to uniqueness of function. We also observe that the triad of the seventh degree (in the case of the minor mode the raised seventh degree) is quite literally contained in the dominant seventh chord. Being a diminished triad, that is, a sound that does not stand very solidly on its own feet, it is taken over, so to speak, by the stronger chord to the extent that it can act as its delegate and, if need be, substitute for it: I–VII–I is a kind of more fleeting version of I–V_7–I. The power of substitution extends even to the VII_7 chord, and particularly to its minor mode form ♯, a pile of three minor thirds adding up to the interval of a diminished seventh and called the *diminished seventh chord*.

We have briefly referred before to the paradoxical situation that exists between I and IV. The symbols I–IV–I clearly indicate a move away from and back to the center. On the other hand, I–IV, "away-from I," is a fifth *down:* a clockwise progression that in the order of the harmonic scale normally expresses motion *towards* I; and IV–I, "back-to I," is a fifth *up,* a counterclockwise progression that normally means *away-from* I. Consequently, a progression like ♯ can be heard either as

198

I–IV–I or, with the reverse sense, as V–I–V. The situation is somewhat reminiscent of certain drawings that can be seen either jutting out from the surface of the paper or in the contrary sense, pointing inward. Here then we have a possible conflict of meaning—an interesting opportunity to introduce ambiguity, suspense, surprise, but also another and different way for I to prove its power, namely, by actually reversing the sense of the moves and making them say the opposite of what they would normally say. Introduced in the course of a sequence, I–IV–I gives the impression that I is testing itself: after going the normal way, a try in the opposite direction. A typical example, from Schubert's song "Fruehlingstraum" (No. 11 in the *Winterreise*), measure 5–12:

The full impact of the move, however, is felt when it comes at the very end of a piece, when the position of I can no longer be challenged, as a sort of last word: e.g. ♯. We recognize here the familiar sound of the "Amen" that concludes many pieces of church music. IV–I in this particular function is called *plagal* or *subdominant cadence* (the term plagal is taken from the medieval modes; subdominant is the technical term for the chord of the IVth degree)

It is interesting to compare the two cadence formulas, I–V–I and I–IV–I, in their relation to the tone $\hat{1}$. In the course of I–V–I the tone $\hat{1}$ is lost and recovered, ; but $\hat{1}$ persists through all of I–IV–I, . In I–V–I, something happens to $\hat{1}$ from the outside, so to speak; it is momentarily pushed out of the picture; its reappearance is the point of the story. In I–IV–I the whole story occurs inside $\hat{1}$, as it were; we hear the tone $\hat{1}$ itself go through a process of changing and restoring its original state (from root of the chord I to fifth in the chord IV

199

and back to root of I). As nothing happens horizontally in respect to $\hat{1}$, the character of the event as a move in depth only, in the depth of the tone $\hat{1}$, stands out naked.

The I · · · V–I Pattern

Harmonic motion, although it follows its own ways, is not different from melodic motion in the respect that it derives its meaning from the active presence of a dynamic center. With the power to proclaim that presence vested in the dominant chord, tonal harmony in the last analysis will always appear on the way to a dominant cadence and contained in the formula I · · · V–I: the dots that represent the "away-from" phase of the motion stand for anything from one straight move to the most roundabout detours, involving all sorts of retardation and suspense.

The example quoted before shows a typical way of filling in the dots. The move away from I goes beyond the minimum I–V by reaching one step further back on the harmonic scale to II, or two steps, to VI; the return is accomplished clockwise along the scale. Resulting progressions: I–II–V–I, I–VI–II–V–I. (The latter, with II in the form of a seventh chord, is also the progression of our very first example, from the "Serenade.") The move away from I can also be taken in the other direction, to IV; retracing the steps and circling I, as it were, the movement returns by way of V: I–IV–V–I. Diagram of these progressions:

In minor the III chord, the relative major chord, is often touched on the way from I to V: I–III–V. Altogether these progressions represent a kind of basic vocabulary of harmony. The actual movement of chords may simply duplicate them; if it does not, they still act as the regulating and organizing force from the background that guarantees meaningful cohesion, very much as the melodic skeleton does in the movement of tones.

A very different interpretation of the dashes in the I . . . V–I formula appears in the accompaniment of the refrain phrase 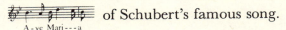 of Schubert's famous song.

It is at the same time a small but very fine example of harmonic motion departing from the norm and still regulated by it.

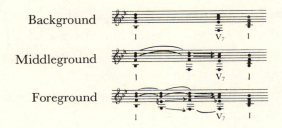

Of the three "planes" of the above sketch the last represents the actual music, the "foreground"; the other two, "middleground" and "background," are theoretical and explanatory. The background shows the straight I–V_7–I progression; in the middleground the entry of V_7 is retarded by an intervening sound that we understand as a deviation from, and tending toward, V. (This particular sound, with two of its tones out of place, has been discussed before.) In the foreground still another sound is interposed before the one that appeared in the middleground, a deviation from the deviation, creating additional suspense. The effect is quite complex: the first sound after the initial I creates an expectation that is fulfilled by another sound full of a definite tension that is resolved in V_7, which is the chord of most acute unrest. As a result of all this the re-arrival at I after only three moves has the character of a return from an extended journey.

The sequence just quoted occurs in measures 13/14 of the song, when the refrain tone appears for the second time. At its first appearance, in measures 3/4, the harmony runs like this: . (The arrangement of tones in the last two chords is a little different in the original; the change has been made for the sake of an easier comparison). Up to the next to last chord, V_7, the progression is the same in either case; but here the chord that follows V_7 is not the tonic.

A definite expectation of I is caused by the sound of V_7. In this instance, however, the tones choose in their next move *not* to fulfill, rather to deceive this expectation. Such a move is properly called a *deceptive cadence;* and the use of VI to work the deception is quite typical. (We observed an analogous event in Bach's D major 2-part Invention when a $\frac{2-1}{5-6}$ move of the two voices occurred instead of a $\frac{2-1}{5-8}$ that was due and that would have made a punctuation.)

The deceptive cadence is an undisguised manifestation of the freedom of tones to move against the will of the acting forces. It shows equally clearly that this is freedom under a law, meaningful freedom. The tones may choose to do or not to do what the tonal forces would direct them to do; but what they cannot choose, what they have no freedom to change, is the *meaning* of the move they have chosen. The meaning is determined by law, the law of the dynamic field. In our case it is deception. This deception is in itself meaningful: it serves the purpose of extending the scope, widening the sweep of the movement. The expectation caused by V_7 has not vanished, its fulfillment has merely been deferred. If the first try has miscarried, the continuation may succeed. The complete sequence, measures 3–5, is this:

V_7 VI   II V_7 I

The movement accepts the fact, so to speak, that it has been carried to VI instead of I and from there seeks the return on the normal road.

Functional Levels

So far it would seem that V–I is always the same cadential step setting the same punctuation. Nothing could be further removed from the facts. We have briefly alluded to the gradations of emphasis of which that move is capable. On one extreme we may find I–V–I moves so light as to preclude a feeling of cadence or punctuation. Repeated over and over again, devoid of any particular significance, like the barely noticeable swinging of a pendulum, the move has then no other function than to remind the ear of the presence of harmony as a dynamically active dimension. When the story of the music is to be told by melody alone, with harmony acting merely as the discrete supporting force, I–V–I will often appear in this role. It is incredible what long stretches of music can be filled harmonically with nothing (or almost nothing) but I–V–I, without the ear ever getting tired of it. We quote the harmonic sequence of the first song of Schubert's cycle "Die schoene Muellerin" (it does not matter that a few of the symbols used have not yet been explained):

$$
\underbrace{\text{to be repeated four times}}
$$

I–V₇–I–V₇–I; I—ᵛI–V₇–I–V₇–I—ᵛI–V₇–I–V₇–I–V of –VI–V of –V–V₇–I–V₇–I–V₇–I–V₇–I; I–V₇–I–V₇–I.

And the same chord, V, which appears here as the most insignificant and commonplace sound, will at the other extreme show itself capable of supporting the most explosive accumulation of forces and will supply the main power for the great climactic moments of a Beethoven, Schubert, or Bruckner symphony!

Between these extremes there lie innumerable intermediate

stages. The attentive listener, when he hears the sequence of the last example in the context of the song as a whole, will discover that these dominant chords are not all alike in emphasis: the swing of the pendulum varies in width, as it were, producing ever so delicate gradations of weight; and the weightier ones of the V–I moves do have a light cadential feeling. We quote another example in which these *functional differences* are more outspoken and easier to grasp; it occurs in the first part of the song "Der Mueller und der Bach," No. 19, from "Die schoene Muellerin."[2] (For the moment we are interested in this one aspect of the excerpt only; there will be more to say about it later.)

We distinguish three functional levels. The I–V–I motion of one level counts for one station on the next higher level (lower on the page means higher functionally). The V chord of the first level, measures 4 and 21, is a mere appendix of I; the chord has not even disentangled itself completely from the tonic: the tone $\hat{1}$ sounds on in the bass. (This is represented by the symbol I⁻ᵛ⁻I.) On the second level, in measures 9 and 26, V acts as a cadential chord: here V–I sets a slight punctuation. Finally, on the third level, V functions as the focal point of the whole development; everything preceding that moment is collected in it as in an emphatic question mark, and everything

[2] See Section of Scores, p. *24.*

that follows will appear as the answer. A graphic representation of these relationships may look somewhat like this:

The crucial dominant coincides with the crucial point of the formal structure, namely, in an A–B–A pattern, the moment immediately preceding the return of A. (Apparently these circumstances have forced the extension of this chord, in measures 18/19, to twice its normal length: occurring on the 4th measure of a four-measure phrase, in the accompaniment of a melody that maintains a strict four-measure phrase structure throughout, it "should" not have lasted for more than one measure. As it is, it produces the "abnormality" of a five-measure phrase, thus lifting the chord above the others and holding it up to our hearing as the moment of greatest suspense. Incidentally, the way the picture is shifted in the third part of the song so as to make this moment of the tonal story coincide with the one question mark of the poem is as simple as it is ingenious.)

Change of Center

As we know, the concept of tonality, defined as the manifestation of a dynamic center, includes the possibility that the center itself may change place, and the central position pass from one tone to another. In this connection too the dominant will prove itself all-important. The chord that has the power to make a ruler has also the power to unmake it—and to remake it.

The following example is taken from Schubert's song "Heidenröslein."[3] In order to have as clear a picture as possible, the

---

[3] See Section of Scores, p. 25.

arrangement of tones in the chords, particularly the bass line, is not exactly the same as in the original. This makes no difference to the chord progression.

The first four measures show the familiar course of events: I–II–V–I (the chord of the 2nd measure is a–c–e–g, the seventh chord of II, with the seventh in the bass; the chord of measure 3 is the dominant seventh chord with the third in the bass). The surprising event occurs in measure 6. In the chord —root position —we recognize the sound of a dominant seventh chord. This means that its root, the tone a, is now $\widehat{5}$. The key of the beginning was G major, in which a is $\widehat{2}$, not $\widehat{5}$. Accordingly, the center must have shifted: a $= \widehat{5}$ makes d $= \widehat{1}$. The change has been effected with one stroke, by the mere sound of the chord. The change is visualized by the accidental c sharp. As one dominant seventh chord only is at home in any given seven tone set, a dominant seventh chord that brings about a shift of center must contain chromatic tones (with one exception to be mentioned presently).

What follows, measures 7–10, sounds again familiar: I–II–V–VI–I–II–V–I; but now referring to the new center, d. In measure 10 we get the full dominant cadence, with the D chord as tonic. But with the next chord the spell is broken. The tone c is added to the D major triad (in the bass), transforming it into a dominant seventh chord with root d. If d $= \widehat{5}$, g $= \widehat{1}$: the center has returned to its original position. This goes hand in hand with the reappearance of the diatonic c natural in the place of the chromatic c sharp. The rest is normal: I–IV–V–I. (The third chord from the end is the deviation from V we have encountered before; the deviation and the chord from which it deviates can together be comprised under the same symbol, V.)

The difference between this example and the one from "Der Mueller und der Bach" is evident. In the former case, the chord-to-chord movement divided itself into groups that were distinguished by the same dominant chord in different functions; there was no movement from group to group. In the present case, beside the movement from chord to chord we get a movement from group to group. Seen from a distance, as it were, so that one whole group can be taken as a unit and represented by its center, the group movement of our example would be G–D–G, ♮. The pattern of chord movement reappears on the level of group movement; and V asserts itself in a new role.

In the last example the shift of center was sudden, the effect intended was a slight shock. This does not have to be so. The change can be quite smooth, by the way of an even transition rather than a skip, as for instance in the following sequence from Schubert's song "Der Wanderer,"[4] measures 23–30 (the bracketed chord can be left out for the moment):

Two four-measure phrases, each one ending with a full dominant cadence; but the chord that has the tonic quality is the c sharp minor triad at the end of the first phrase, the E major triad at the end of the second. Yet nowhere during the second phrase in which the shift must have occurred do we have a feeling of shock or surprise; the transition is so smooth that we become aware of it only after it has taken place.

A close look at the symbols will explain how this is achieved. In the example from "Heidenröslein" there was no chord that

[4] See Section of Scores, p. 26.

figured in both rows, that of center G and that of center D, at the same time. The present example takes advantage of the fact that one and the same chord may belong to different dynamic centers; or, to put it the other way around, that different centers may have certain chords in common. Here it is the F sharp minor triad that appears in this position: it belongs to both C sharp minor, as IV, and E major, as II. Accordingly, the harmonic movement can enter this station on the C sharp minor track, as it were, and leave it on the E major track, which is what happens in the last two measures of our example. The change is particularly smooth here, as only four measures before we have heard that same movement enter *and* leave this same chord on the C sharp minor track. When the F sharp minor triad sounds in measure 29 there is no indication that it is anything else here than what it was before, namely IV; and only what follows makes us realize that this time the chord was not IV but II. This sort of retroactive reinterpretation is a very common process in the hearing of harmony.

The absence of accidentals in the dominant seventh chord that effects the shift of center from c sharp to e (measure 30) exemplifies the one instance, referred to before, in which such a change may occur without chromatic tones being introduced; namely, when it is a change from minor to the relative major. In the minor mode the dominant seventh chord of the relative major is a diatonic chord. This explains why in minor keys the change to the relative major, shifting the center to the tone $\widehat{3}$, occurs so frequently and easily. In major, the center moves most easily to $\widehat{5}$.

We turn now to the bracketed chord of the last example:

When we hear this chord, ,

there is no doubt but that it is a dominant seventh chord. Its

root is c sharp; the chord to which it is in V–I relation is the
f sharp triad—the chord that actually follows. Up to this moment
the center has been c sharp; now a V–I move occurs, which is
directed at f sharp: it seems that a change of center to f sharp
must have taken place at this point. Do we hear it?

It does not seem so. From the previous analysis we know that
a change of center does take place in this sequence, but to e,
not to F sharp. In spite of the fact that it is preceded by a dominant seventh chord that is related to it as V is to I, the F sharp
triad does not emerge as a new goal of the movement; it remains a station through which the movement merely passes on
its way from C sharp to E. Had the movement at this point
taken another course,

for instance, 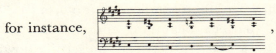 ,

the story would have been different, and f sharp would have
been confirmed as the new center.

We conclude from this that a single dominant seventh chord
does not automatically bring about a change of center. Some
additional confirmation is needed to achieve this result. When
such confirmation is lacking, as is the case in our example, the
V_7 chord has no other effect than to put added stress on the
chord to which it has the dominant-tonic relation; it throws a
strong light on it,[5] *without otherwise affecting its status as a harmonic
degree in the given context.* In our example the F sharp triad, although it is preceded by its own dominant, still functions as IV
of C sharp, II of E. The chord remains what it would have been
without the preceding V_7.

Dominant chords directed at degrees other than I, which
leave the harmonic status of their respective "tonics" unaffected,

---

[5] Note that the chord coincides with the climax of the melody and the decisive
word of the poem, "Fremdling," "stranger."

are called *secondary dominants*. The symbol most frequently used to mark them is "V of . . . ." In our example the bracketed chord would have to be marked "V of IV."

We quote another example to clarify these things further. This is the chord progression, again simplified as to arrangement of tones, in the introduction of the song "Mein!", No. 11, from the "Schoene Muellerin"[6]:

(V of –IV is the abbreviation for V of IV–IV.)

Here we have an unbroken flow of music, of the "away-from-and-back-to" pattern, beginning and ending on the D major triad; no resting place in between, no setting down on a new center; the two "foreign" V_7 chords, marked by accidentals, cannot be anything but secondary dominants. They cannot alter the meaning that their respective "tonics" have in the context of the D major tonality, namely, IV and II; but they can put emphasis on these chords, give them increased weight. That way they heighten the impact of the whole motion: the greater the weight it carries, the greater must be its power.

The logic of the sequence is more apparent in the large scale picture of the root progression:

In this diagram the I–V moves of measures 1 and 2 are summed up in one symbol, I. At the beginning of measure 3 the addition of the chromatic c natural to the D major triad transforms I into V_7 of IV.

[6] See Section of Scores, p. *26.*

210

The New Image of Tonality

Change of center on the one hand, secondary dominants on the other: this implies a black-white picture; either the center changes, unambiguously, or it does not change, equally unambiguously. Harmony, however, is not a black-white language. Here again it has all the intermediate stages at its command, all the degrees of half-certainty and half-doubt regarding the dynamic position of a chord, and it exploits these possibilities to the full. The very drama of harmony in tonal music evolves around the theme of doubt and certainty as to the holder of the real power. As an example, again on a very small scale, demonstrating what is meant by these words, turn once more to the sequence from "Der Mueller und der Bach," quoted before.

First, a remark on the symbol flat II, lowered IInd degree. The key here is G minor; we know that II in minor is a diminished triad. In some instances a consonant form of the II chord may be desirable; it can be gotten by chromatically lowering the root of the chord, in our case the tone a, $\hat{2}$ in G minor, making it a flat. The result is the chord 𝄞, the A flat major triad. Technically, this is called the Phrygian IInd degree, because the Phrygian mode has a half tone between $\hat{1}$ and $\hat{2}$ (in our case g–a flat).

The section of measures 11–19 is in need of further interpretation. The mere labeling of the chords, as done in the diagram, cannot do justice to the actual events. The V_7 chord of measure 11 root g is clearly a secondary dominant: nothing happens to confirm the following C triad in central position. But with the

V_7 chord of measure 13, things are different. This is the dominant seventh of the relative major, B flat, which would not need much support to emerge as a new center; and some support it does get from other sides, melody and meter. A slight punctuation of the melody falls on the B flat major chord of measure 14; and that chord also coincides with the ending of a four-measure phrase. In addition, the whole sequence of measures 11–14 seems now to sum up to a V of II–II–V–I progression, with B flat as I. So for one moment we have the feeling that the central power may have passed from g to b flat.

The next chord disavows this feeling: it is the G minor triad again. So the original center seems still in power. But now the motion almost inadvertently glides into the chord of measure 17, . This is the dimished seventh chord, which substitutes for the dominant seventh of D. Are we on the way to center D? Is the D major triad, which follows, a tonic or still the dominant of G? The question rises from the very sound of the chord; and as nothing happens in measure 19, when a new move was due, to resolve the uncertainty one way or the other, the chord remains pending, on the edge between being a tonic or a dominant. The G triad of measure 20 finally settles the question in favor of the original tonic.

Neither our conventional symbols nor our conventional terminology can adequately express these shades of meaning, which, after all, are the very life of music. The symbols identify either secondary dominants or new centers, nothing in between. So do the technical terms. Technically, a change of center is called *modulation*. The term should be used with extreme caution as it tends to force a black-white pattern on the interpretation, while everything in music is averse to being pressed in such a schema. It seems to require Yes or No answers to questions such as we met in the last example, where any Yes or No answer must miss the point. Does the center change in measures 11–14? Yes *and*

No! Is the D major triad in measure 18/19 a tonic or a dominant? It is neither, and it has something of both! The gradations are far too delicate, the situations too complex to be
approached with a set of fixed terms.

In the following sketch an attempt is made to give a more
adequate symbolic picture of the events of this example. The
bass line only is shown; the different metric values indicate
relative significance.

First, the movement asserts I (measures 1–10); next (measures
11–14) it turns to III; then (measures 15–19) it takes us to V;
finally (20–28) it reasserts I. A large-scale pattern emerges:
I–III–V–I; it manifests that I has been the directing power all
along.

In its limited way this example gives an idea of the new content the notion of tonality acquires through the extension of the
musical language into the dimension of harmony. Music is tonal:
this means no longer simply the existence of a dynamic center,
including the possibility that the center may change place and
even be temporarily suspended by the intrusion of chromatic
tones. Tonality means now the wielding of central power in the
face of a perpetual challenge. Harmony puts means at the disposal of music that are capable of overthrowing a center and
establishing a new one on a moment's notice. With this the position of the tone at the center has become permanently unsafe.
And the tonic meets the challenge and truly asserts its power
by actually giving it away, letting other tones take possession of
it, withdrawing from the foreground of events, but then, in the
decisive moments, proving itself strong enough to regain the

central place and force the movement back into its, the original tonic's, orbit. The musical language has relinquished the solid basis of well-defined, stable dynamic fields and established itself on fluid ground. We have mentioned the element of drama that all this has brought into music. In a sense, the notion of tonality is at stake every time; the issue must be decided every time anew. Will the original center succeed or fail to reassert itself? In some instances, notably in Richard Wagner's works, it fails, or rather no effort is put up in its behalf, and tonality is in jeopardy. On the other hand, what happens in every great composition of Beethoven, Schubert, Brahms, and Bruckner, expressed in one formula, is the ultimate triumph of tonality. We observe the central power pass from tone to tone, new centers establish themselves for apparently unlimited stretches of time, the original tonic is completely lost sight of; but if we watch the path traveled by the center itself, there emerges from the detours and meanderings of an often seemingly erratic motion a clear pattern, which betrays the action of a force behind the scenes: it is the original center—which had merely withdrawn into the background and from there had secretly controlled the course of events, leading them to a point where it could finally come out again into the open and take over— revealing itself as the supreme power in the play, the center of centers.

In order to give some concrete content to these words, we trace the motion of the center in one of Schubert's larger songs, the "Erlkoenig."[7] It is a comparatively simple but very telling example. We omit all details and concentrate on the essential points.

The key is G minor. The first movement of the center follows the normal trend to III, the relative major (measure 23). It is not really a change: eight measures later we have again returned, through V, to I. The moves that take us away from the tonic after this, from measure 39 on, carry much greater weight. The goal is again B flat, the relative major; but this time the new center establishes itself quite firmly and for a fairly long period (measures 52–70). From measure 70 on we are again on the move. For a few measures one might believe that we are once more on the way back to G, but this time things turn out quite differently. The new destination, which emerges in measure 79, is B minor! This station, however, we pass quickly. In measure 91 we arrive at center C, which, like B flat before, maintains itself in power for some time. From measure 94 the motion goes on, through C sharp (measure 103—this corresponds to B natural of measure 79) to D (measure 106), and for one brief moment even beyond D to E flat (measure 114). After quickly recapturing the movement (measure 120) D gets transformed into the dominant of G, and with measure 128 the original tonic returns to stay in force to the end.

The following sketch represents in barest outline the movement of the center:

So the movement that begins in measure 70 does carry us, after all, from III through V to I. The pattern of the whole duplicates on the large scale that of the first moves, measures 1–31. But only the first part of the large-scale course is traveled on the normal road. From III on, the motion leaves the beaten track, carrying the center chromatically upwards, exploiting every half-tone step between $\hat{3}$ and $\hat{5}$, and even going one half-tone step too far, which produces a kind of harmonic equivalent to a neighboring tone (symbol NT): D–E-flat–D. After this prolonged accumulation of tension, the return to G is effected with dramatic abruptness. (The perfect integration of this musical pattern with the events and developments of the poem is a minor miracle in itself.)

Finally, we cannot fail to recognize a kinship between the line drawn by the movement of the center and the line of the very first motif of the accompaniment, , which in this context appears as an epigrammatic anticipation of the course of the whole piece.

The question may be asked: Does the composer know all this? In a sense, he does; not in the conventional sense of knowing, though. One thing is certain: no good piece of music is ever done backwards, as it were, from the background to the foreground, beginning with the construction of some interesting abstract pattern and then filling in the music. This would be comparable to building up a living organism by finishing the skeleton first, then putting in the organs, muscles, ligaments, etc. Composing is not different from other creative intellectual activities in that it relies primarily on a spontaneous sequence of ideas. Good composers are those in whose minds the basic patterns are inborn so that they can give free vent to their spontaneity without ever going astray. A pattern itself is of no interest to anybody; what is of interest is the functioning of the pattern in a living musical organism. When Schubert wrote this song he was eighteen years old. It is very unlikely that he gave much theoretical thought to it; he probably read the poem and wrote the song in a matter of hours, as was his habit. But let us make the foolish assumption that he started with the abstract musical structure; the perfect synthesis of music and words would have been impossible for him to achieve. Of the relationship between the initial motif of the accompaniment and the ground plan of the whole song he was certainly unaware. Such things are generated, not made. We can understand them as the results of growth; not as products of conscious construction.

To sum up and conclude: How do we understand harmony?

We do *not* understand it as chords to be identified and assigned to certain centers.

We do understand it as *movement* of chords. Chords in themselves are vertical events; harmony, like melody, is a horizontal event.

We recognize certain *basic patterns* that fix the norm and lay down the law for harmonic motion—a normative law. These patterns appear not only in the chord-to-chord motion of the foreground, but equally in the motion of chord groups, subgroups, supergroups, on every plane of an often multilayered picture, testifying to the oneness of dynamic action through the whole structure.

We realize that the *freedom* of harmonic motion is freedom under that law. Harmony, insofar as it does not literally follow the pattern, and mostly it does not, still remains intelligibly related to the pattern. To make this relation explicit, to discover the threads by which every particular instance of freedom is tied to the law: this is the task. In so doing we grasp the meaning of harmony, since in harmony, as in melody, the meaning of the movement springs from the relation of its freedom to its law.

VI • Melody and Harmony

When we hear a piece of music of the "melody-plus-harmony" type, we do not experience two movements going on side by side, one of single tones, melody, the other of chords, harmony; we experience one integrated tonal motion. Neither does the composer think in terms of two separate strands of motion that he has to combine; music occurs to him all in one. Even in the special case where he has to supply harmony to an already existing melody, he will not simply add chords to it; he will absorb the melody and try to reinvent, rethink it as an event extending into a new dimension. The body of music will always be one and whole. If at any moment we take a cut through it, as it were, it will show not only the melody tone related to other tones of the melodic context, and the chord related to other chords of the harmonic context, but over and above this, melody tone and chord intimately related to each other. We cannot conclude this study without considering in some detail this third relationship, a vital factor in the functioning of the tonal organism and the source of extraordinary tonal events.

The first thing to note is relative pace: melody and harmony can move at the same pace, one chord to every tone of the melody; they can move at a different pace, harmony slower than melody, with one chord extending unchanged while the melody moves on through different tones, or melody slower than harmony, with one tone of the melody extending through successive chords. Represented schematically:

218

	Type I	Type II	Type III
Tones (melody)	. . . . .	. . . . .	. .
Chords (harmony)	. . . . .	. .	. . . . .

Examples:

Type I   (Bach)

Type II   (Verdi)

Type III   (Schubert)

In general a piece of music will not stick to any one of these types throughout but will change from one to the other according to the demands of the moment. This does not mean, though, that these three types of motion are equivalent. A distinction of normal and abnormal can be made, with type II representing the normal way; as chords have greater mass, so to speak, than single tones, their natural rate of motion is slower than that of single tones in melodies. Movement of type I is heavy, solemn, hesitant. Type III represents decidedly the abnormal, the extraordinary: stress, suspense.

Observing the three examples we may notice another fundamental difference. In the example of type I all the tones of the melody are also tones of the chords with which they sound together; they belong to these chords. The same is true of some, but not of all of the melody tones of the type II example. The melody begins on a chord tone, but with the very first move, ⬚, it breaks away from the chord and touches a tone that does not belong to the chord, a *non-harmonic* tone as it is called. The next step, ⬚, brings it back into the chord again, and there it remains for the next two moves, ⬚, only to move out

219

again and back again with . With the , the chord changes, and the rest of the melody remains within the chord. In the example of type III the extended melody tone belongs to each of the successive chords; of course, it has a different function in each one: it is third in the F sharp minor triad, root in the A seventh chord, fifth in the D triad, and third in the F major triad.

The principles that make it possible for melody and harmony to proceed together as one unified motion can best be demonstrated when both move at the same pace and when every tone of the melody belongs to the chord with which it coincides. The following discussion will therefore be based on music of type I.

Any given tone can be either the root, or the third, or the fifth of a triad and the same plus the seventh of a seventh chord. Thus there are three triads, four seventh chords, to which any tone can belong. The following table shows the possible coordinations for all of the seven tones of the diatonic system (in order to reduce the matter to its simplest terms, only triads and the dominant seventh chord are considered):

$\hat{1}$	$\hat{2}$	$\hat{3}$	$\hat{4}$	$\hat{5}$	$\hat{6}$	$\hat{7}$
I	II	III	IV	V	VI	VII
VI	VII	I	II	III	IV	V
IV	V	VI	VII	I	II	III
			V_7			

It is obvious that a unified motion of melody and harmony will not result if chords chosen merely at random from this table sound together with the corresponding melody tones. Harmony must select the chords in such a way that their succession makes sense in itself as well as in relation to the melody. We know that to make sense, in the most general terms, means the same thing in melody as in harmony: namely to convey the idea of a movement in reference to a dynamic center. It is easy to find equivalent moves, that is, melodic and harmonic moves that in their respective languages express the same dynamic idea. For instance, the meaning of the melodic move $\hat{7}$–$\hat{8}$ (sharp $\hat{7}$–$\hat{8}$ in minor) is expressed in harmony by the move V–I. Since $\hat{7}$ is the third of the V chord, and $\hat{8}$ of the I chord, the two moves combine naturally: . Similarly for $\hat{2}$–$\hat{1}$, as $\hat{2}$ is the fifth of the V chord: . $\hat{4}$–$\hat{3}$ can be paralleled either by IV–I, , or, as $\hat{4}$ is the seventh of the V$_7$ chord, by V$_7$–I, . In the latter case the dissonance of the seventh chord will sharply enhance the push of the tone $\hat{4}$ toward $\hat{3}$, while in the former case the fact that $\hat{4}$ is a root, a center of dynamic organization in its own right, will counteract (though not overcome) the unbalance of the tone in the melodic context. $\hat{6}$ returning to $\hat{5}$ has a parallel chord move in IV–I, , while $\hat{6}$ pressing on through $\hat{7}$ to $\hat{8}$ finds its harmonic equivalent in IV–V–I or II–V–I:

In the same manner we can construct elementary melodic progressions together with what might be called their natural extension into the dimension of harmony. A few examples (the larger notes represent the melody, the small ones indicate the chords):

The same principle of melody-harmony coordination can be applied to actual tunes, e.g. the following hymn tune:

Hymns, or chorales, traditionally move according to the pattern of type I, one chord to every tone of the melody. The first two tones, $\widehat{3}$–$\widehat{1}$, would agree either with a repetition of the I chord or with the move I–IV, which would logically be continued with V–I: ♪. The second half of the phrase, $\widehat{5}$–$\widehat{4}$–$\widehat{4}$–$\widehat{3}$,

I IV V I

suggests again ♪. In the next phrase we get: ♪.

I IV V₇ I   I IV II V I

The subsequent circling of the melody about $\widehat{2}$ can be paralleled harmonically by a circling about V: ♪. Finally, the

V V V I V I V V

last phrase: ♪.

V I V I VI IV I II V I

Further experimentation and observation would confirm what these examples suggest: the most elementary chord progressions suffice for harmony to move along with any simple diatonic melody. Of course, this is the barest minimum of chord motion; still there is nothing wrong with it, with the same moves being repeated over and over again. Innumerable instances can be found of harmony restricting its movement to just such a minimum. The very restriction serves a definite purpose: namely, that of focussing the attention on the melody while at the same time keeping the listener aware of the presence of the added dimension, harmony, tonal depth. Variety of a secondary order can always be provided by the different positions of a chord, by substituting VII for V, seventh chords for triads, etc. In fact, when Bach introduced the tune of our last example in one of his Cantatas—he was the supreme master in the art of chorale harmonization—he kept the harmony within the minimum suggested above, with the exception of one major change, which we shall discuss presently.

Harmony Interprets Melody

In these examples, the combination of melody and harmony was actual coordination: both did or said the same thing to-

gether, each one in its own way. This seemed natural and
normal, and rightly so; but it is by no means necessary. As
always in music, there is a norm, and there is the freedom to
depart from the norm. The chords may move in such a way as
simply to duplicate on their side the melodic moves; or they
may choose with their moves to go beyond, to interfere with, to
contradict the sense of the melodic motion. Of course, this freedom does not imply that any move can be chosen—this would
be license and would destroy the tonal whole; it must be a
meaningful transgression, a meaningful contradiction. When it is,
melody and harmony together remain a unified movement in
spite of transgression and contradiction. In fact, the true story
of the melody-harmony relation begins to unfold only at the
point where the two separate, where the relation becomes
strained and proves itself under strain.

The possibility of harmony going beyond melody is implied
in the arrangement of the table of tone-chord coordinations,
which assigned several chords to each tone. Already the most
elementary instances of combined motion showed that more
than one chord can be connected meaningfully with one tone;
thus, $\hat{4}$–$\hat{3}$ can be paralleled harmonically either by V_7–I or by
IV–I, with the effect of either emphasizing or de-emphasizing
the tendency of the tone $\hat{4}$ to move on to $\hat{3}$. The tone $\hat{4}$ can only
sound its dynamic meaning; the chord is capable of revealing
different shades of this meaning. In a later example, ,
harmony seems almost to reverse the dynamic meaning of one
of the melody tones, the first $\hat{1}$; but it does so in agreement with
the melody taken as a whole. It is clearly not the intention of
the melody that this tone should be understood as expressing
complete rest; the movement goes on beyond this point. Yet
there is not much the melody can do about it; $\hat{1}$ will always
sound $\hat{1}$, and so one has to turn to the force of the metric and
rhythmic pattern, that is, ultimately to a non-tonal force, to

provide added impulse. Harmony, however, by involving the tone in a sound which is clearly heard as a deviation from V, tending toward V, makes it unmistakably plain to the ear that this tone $\hat{1}$ does not yet mean rest, and that the movement is to go on. The chord does not destroy the dynamic meaning of the tone as such, but for the moment that meaning is moved to the background as it is overshadowed by another layer of meaning interposed by the chord. We have observed comparable phenomena in polyphony, particularly in connection with the consonance-dissonance relation, and in general when the tone of one part changed its quality as a result of the action of another part. There is no doubt that these relations of parts in polyphony are the germ from which developed the melody-harmony relations we are discussing. We shall see that the polyphonic aspect is never entirely lost, even in music of the pure "melody-plus-harmony" type.

The simplest instance of an open contradiction of melody and harmony contained in one move is the combination of $\hat{7}$–$\hat{8}$ or $\hat{2}$–$\hat{1}$ with the deceptive cadence V–VI ($\hat{1}$ is the third of the VI chord). In the following melody,

the $\hat{7}$–$\hat{8}$ step occurs twice, at the halfway mark and at the end of the phrase. Nothing would be wrong if harmony concurred at both points with V–I, . If it did, however, it would forego the chance to achieve what it alone can achieve, namely, a clear distinction between the two different functions of the same $\hat{7}$–$\hat{8}$ step, first as a semicolon, so to speak, then as a period. By substituting a deceptive cadence for the dominant cadence at the midway point, , harmony nullifies the concluding effect of the $\hat{7}$–$\hat{8}$ step and transforms release into tension. At the very moment when the melodic motion by itself comes to a temporary halt, a new movement is instigated, which runs its normal course in the second half of the phrase:

While melody divides the whole of this phrase into two halves, harmony binds the two halves tightly into one whole.

Bach, in one of his settings of this hymn tune, goes beyond the simple deceptive cadence at the point in question and instead of V–VI combines the chord move V of VI–VI with the $\hat{7}$–$\hat{8}$ step of the melody ($\hat{7}$ is the fifth of the V of VI chord):

Strictly speaking, this is no longer a deceptive cadence, as VI after V of VI, the secondary dominant, is the expected rather than the unexpected chord. The effect is much stronger than that of the V–VI move, since the secondary dominant gives VI the momentary appearance of a tonic chord, and the suspense of a possible change of center is added to the tension of the VI chord.

We have mentioned the comparative ease with which harmony shifts center, thereby providing a constant challenge to tonality, to the permanence of one center for any length of time. In combination with melody, harmony will not merely duplicate and reinforce changes of center that the melodic motion itself brings about; it will suggest changes of center where no indication of such an event is given in the melody. For instance, the beginning of the "Morning Star" hymn, ♯ , by itself can hardly be heard otherwise than as $\hat{1}$–$\hat{5}$–$\hat{3}$–$\hat{1}$–$\hat{5}$–$\hat{6}$–$\hat{6}$–$\hat{5}$—there is not the slightest hint here of a change of center. Harmony, however, can do this to it:

225

—this is Bach's preferred interpretation of the tune. The flexibility in regard to the dynamic center, which harmony introduces into the tonal compound, has profound effects on melody, enriching it with new shades of meaning and, in general, opening a new area of tonal expression. When we discussed what chords would normally go with the tune

(see page 222), we found that in the phrase  , harmony could get along with V and I; it would be the minimum, but it would be enough; harmony would be validly represented. Bach, however, at this point has the chords do this:

The center *a* is momentarily pushed into the background, and f sharp comes to the fore as a contender for the central position. This deviation from the normal is possible because the melody tones $\widehat{1}$–$\widehat{2}$–$\widehat{7}$–$\widehat{1}$ in A, can also be interpreted as $\widehat{3}$–$\widehat{4}$–$\widehat{2}$–$\widehat{3}$, center f sharp, minor mode, and combined with I–II–V–I of this center. The result is a momentary change in the dynamic sense of the melody. The return to center *a,* which follows immediately, comes as a relief after the brief disturbance and gives added significance to the step of the melody, which leads us out of the orbit of the pretended and back to the true center.

Consider the tune we quoted in an earlier chapter:

226

Heard as it stands here, this appears as a clear movement in the field of the tone d. The hold on $\hat{5}$ in the 2nd measure, on $\hat{1}$ in the 4th, unequivocally establishes the center. In measures $\hat{5}$–$\hat{8}$ the motion descends through $\hat{1}$ to $\hat{7}$, then rises again and comes to a halt on $\hat{3}$. Harmony could simply go along with this:

I V I V I I V I IV I V I V I I I V I V I V I V I I V₇ I

When this tune appears at a decisive moment in Bach's *Saint John Passion,* the following happens:

With the entry of the ♯ chord in measure 5

the clear sense of direction gets veiled; the movement seems to veer towards other centers—is it e? is it b?—even the original d appears as a momentary possibility, like a recollection, and is lost again (measure 7). The situation is too fluid to be pinned down in terms of well defined centers. Are the two chords of measure 8 I–V of E, or IV–I of B? The consequences of all this for the melody are obvious. ♯ is no longer the clear expression of $\hat{3}$–$\hat{5}$–$\hat{4}$–$\hat{3}$; instead it hovers between $\hat{2}$–$\hat{4}$–$\hat{3}$–$\hat{2}$ (center e) and $\hat{5}$–$\hat{7}$–$\hat{6}$–$\hat{5}$ (center b). In the melody by itself, the end of this phrase, ♯ , said $\hat{4}$–$\hat{3}$; now one can not decide whether what it says here is $\hat{6}$–$\hat{5}$ or $\hat{3}$–$\hat{2}$. In this case harmony, by going beyond the norm, accomplishes what amounts to a complete reinterpretation of the dynamic meaning of the melody, a reinterpretation that tends not to clarify but rather to obscure, to cast doubt, to create a problematic situation where no problem was present before. All this disappears, however, when from measure 9 on, the first center D takes over again and restores the original order. As this is a hymn, one might look at the words to find the motive behind these extraordinary developments. The lines of measures 5–8 say: "In the ultimate anxiety of death I have nowhere to turn," and go on in measures 9–10: "except to Thee who will redeem me." The conventional antithesis of the text is absorbed by the tonal movement and restated in its terms, transformed, ennobled, and perfected.

A still more striking instance of harmony interpreting melody occurs in measure 2 of this hymn, more striking because it attaches itself to one single tone, the tone 𝄞♮, on which the first line ends. In the context (center D) this is $\hat{5}$, and the chord on which the harmonic motion alights at this moment *is* a D chord; but not the D triad. It is the dominant seventh chord on d, V of IV. Thus the sound of comparative repose—comparative only because of the $\hat{5}$ of the melody—is turned into a sound of acute suspense. The friction of the dissonance, the directed tension of the secondary dominant, the added sharpness of the first inversion, all this permeates the chord and goes over from the chord into the melody tone, filling it with a quality that eludes verbal characterization. In order to grasp the full significance of the move, one ought to hear the normal and the abnormal side by side:

Again the abnormal move is not unrelated to the words; the word on which this sound falls is "tot," "dead"—referring to the dead Christ on the cross. The first word of the next line is "livest." To discover the possibility of such an interpretation and to realize it with a minimum of effort—in this case, by the mere addition of the tone c to the sound—remains, of course, the privilege of genius.

Another way for harmony to go beyond melody, one which requires no genius, a conventional transgression, so to speak, is shown in measure 4 of this hymn. The minimum of chord motion to go with of the melody would be a simple V–I. Up to this moment melody and chords have proceeded together at a regular quarter tone pace. If now the melody applies a brake and extends the tone $\widehat{2}$ through twice that duration, there is no need for harmony to do the same. The chords may still continue at the former pace, so that two successive chords will sound while the melody tone lasts. This makes it possible to combine the fuller cadence II–V–I with the step $\widehat{2}$–$\widehat{1}$:

II V I.

As a consequence the tone $\widehat{2}$ will undergo a certain development while it sounds: it begins as the root of a chord, it ends as the fifth of a chord.

One of the chorale tunes that Bach introduced both in the *St. Matthew* and *St. John Passions* begins with the following phrase: . The threefold repetition of the first tone and the possibility of different harmonic interpretations of that tone, and consequently of the whole phrase, seem to have challenged Bach's mind, and he answered the challenge with some of his most original and unique thoughts. We quote the three versions of this chorale that appear in the *Passions*. For the sake of easier comparison, we transpose them to the same key and simplify a few non-essential details (non-essential for our present purpose):

First version:

I   I   I   V   V   I   V   I   I   IV   –   V   V   I

Here the repetitions of $\widehat{1}$ at the outset, , are taken at their face value, as it were, and confirmed harmonically by a threefold statement of I: the strongest affirmation possible (the inversion of the 3rd chord introduces the first element of motion). The following moves do not get farther away than V and, in measure 3, IV. In this measure the normal IV–I–V, to $\hat{4}$–$\hat{3}$–$\hat{2}$ of the melody, is avoided and the IV chord extended through the tone $\hat{3}$. This gives a broader basis for the subsequent V–I move; suppressing I in measure 3 means strengthening its appearance in measure 4.

Second version:

I   IV₇ II₇   V   V   I   V   I   I   #VII   I   V   V   I

The first chord is again I, but this time we hear it only once, on the upbeat. With the downbeat I disappears, the harmony drops to the dark and dissonant chord of IV_7, moves on to II_7; the persistent melody tone reflects in its sound the changes of the harmonic environment that transform it from the root of the I triad to the fifth of IV_7, then to the seventh of II_7. Only after this, when the melody draws away from $\hat{1}$ and back to it, $\hat{7}$–$\hat{5}$–$\hat{1}$, the chords join in with V–I, so that on the downbeat of the next measure $\hat{1}$ and I meet again. The rest, after this strange aberration, is all normal, all V–I; no IV here, as in the first version. (The diminished seventh chord at the beginning of measure 3 substitutes for V.)

Third version:

V of -IV   IV V of V   V   V   IV   V   I   I   #VII   I   V   V   I

This is the great surprise. The chord that sounds with the first g of the melody *is* a G chord, but not a G triad; it is the dominant seventh chord on g, which will turn out to be a secondary dominant, V of IV. IV follows and is in turn followed by a diminished seventh chord, which substitutes for another secondary dominant, V of V. Again the chords take the melody tone through a series of transformations, this time an even more adventurous one. Not for one moment is the tone allowed to assert itself as what it is meant to be, namely 1̂. At its first appearance we hear it as the root of a dominant seventh chord, that is, as a tone 5̂; then as the fifth of a triad; finally as a tone belonging to a diminished seventh chord with a strong dissonance tension towards f sharp, 7̂ in the overall context. And on top of all this, when the melody returns to g at the beginning of measure 2 and one would expect harmony with a V–I move to let the tone emerge at long last in its proper meaning, as 1̂, the chords slip away again and once more succeed in circumventing the open declaration of center. Instead of I, IV sounds, the triad of which the tone g is the fifth; and it sounds as a *major* triad, not in its normal form of a minor triad. This is a startling moment, startling in the manner of an unexpected ray of light. Only after this does harmony consent to make the long overdue V–I move, which settles the question of center; but by then the melody has moved on through 2̂ to 3̂. The coincidence of 1̂ and I will not occur until the very last tone of the hymn.

We compare the three harmonic interpretations of the beginning of the tune and measure them against the I–V–I standard:

Melody		1̂	1̂	1̂	7̂ 5̂	1̂	2̂	3̂
	(1)	I	I	I	V	I	V	I
Harmony	(2) ·	I	IV$_7$	II$_7$	V	I	V	I
		I			V	I	V	I
	(3)	V of IV	IV	V of V	V	IV	V	I
		....			.V....................			I

In the first version, melody and harmony move together in the closest conjunction; in the second, melody and harmony separate after the first sound, harmony moves away from melody, as it were, and returns after a brief excursion. In the third version, one cannot even talk of separation as there is no togetherness to begin with; harmony comes out of nowhere, approaches the melody in stages, joins its movement at the end. Expressed in graphic symbols:

Melody
Harmony

To the melody the three harmonic interpretations mean a change from the straight assertion of version 1 to what one might call the qualified assertion of 2 and finally the searching character of version 3, which even begins on a note of questioning. It cannot be denied that the different interpretations are in some way related to the different stanzas of the hymn to which they are sung. The words that go with version 1 address God as the Great King; those of version 2 speak of Christ's love as manifested through the Passion; those of version 3 refer to the mystery of the Good Shepherd suffering for the transgression of the flock. The key choice also is of interest: version 1 holds the middle range (A minor); 2 is low (G minor); 3 is high (B minor).

When Bach's settings of hymn tunes are used as material for the study of the melody-harmony relation, they are obviously considered representatives of the "melody-plus-harmony" type, of homophonic music. However, if one wanted to consider them as representatives of polyphonic music, that would be equally possible and equally satisfactory. In order to understand this one needs only to forget for a while about the chords and concentrate on the bass voice of the last three examples and its combination with the treble, which carries the melody:

It appears that these bass voices are not simply a succession of tones dictated by the special concern of harmony for the lowest tones of the chords. Each one of them makes good sense as a linear movement in its own right; and in combination with the melody they all produce equally satisfactory two-part textures. More than that: the harmony of the three versions seems implicitly contained in the bass lines; in conjunction with the melody these bass lines seem almost to prescribe the ways of the chords. This is particularly true of the third version where the chromatic steps of the bass strongly imply the secondary dominants:

$$b \to c \qquad c\sharp \to d$$
$$V \text{ of} \to IV \qquad V \text{ of} \to V \ .$$

Even the striking IV major triad of measure 2 appears merely as the unavoidable consequence of the tone e natural, which the bass passes on its way from d to g. Thus one may legitimately ask: What is the primary element here? Does the composer think in terms of chord progressions, and do the successive chords yield these particular bass lines; or does he think in terms of a polyphonic combination of parts and do the chords follow as a secondary consequence from the interweaving of the parts? The fact that either assumption is equally tenable testifies to the nature of the musical whole: its constituent elements are interdependent to the degree that each appears as the consequence of the other. The new element, harmony, did not replace the older, polyphony; it came as an organic extension of that which already existed. Only at the surface does it seem as if polyphony were lost when harmony appears, only in a superficial sense is homophonic music summed up in the formula "melody-plus-harmony." A sound polyphonic texture is hidden in every valid chord progression. There is no good harmony which, together with the melody, is not also good polyphony —if not in the foreground, so in the background.

233

Non-harmonic Tones

Chorales, as noted before, represent a special case in that they keep melody and harmony moving at the same pace throughout: one chord to one tone. The principles of melody-harmony coordination, however, which we recognized in chorales, are valid beyond the limits of the special case. They apply quite generally, whether the rate of motion in melody and harmony is the same or different.

(from Weber's *Oberon*)

This is the normal situation: harmony moving at a slower pace than melody; one move of the chords to more than one move of the tones. Compared to the chorales, the co-ordination is different only in so far as here the single chord is related not to a single tone of the melody but to a group of tones: group and chord, rather than tone and chord, belong together. By defining these groups the chords go beyond their main function of making the dimension of harmony an active presence; they become a delicate means of structural articulation. In our example, which is very simple, the melodic groups defined by the chords coincide, on the whole, with the metric groups of the bars; still the comparative crowding of chord moves in the latter part has its effect. In the following example, from Mozart's last Piano Concerto, K. 595,

the chords underline a long-short structure, which without them would have remained hidden in the melody. Apart from the substitution of group for tone, the melody-harmony co-ordination is the same in music of this type as in chorales. Both examples show harmony keeping to the minimum of duplicating in the simplest possible way the sense of the melodic movement —with the possible exception of measure 9 of the Weber example where the tone e, just heard as root of I, is turned with marked effect into the fifth of IV. It is not difficult to imagine, though, that here just as in chorales harmony could go beyond the minimum, depart from the norm, contradict the sense of the melodic motion, interpret melodic groups in different ways, and so on.

In addition to all this, one more factor of major significance comes into consideration in these examples: namely, the distinction of harmonic and non-harmonic tones. We have already defined non-harmonic tones as tones of the melody that are not also a part of the chord with which they sound together. For instance, in the first measure of the Weber tune, with ♪♪♪ the melody moves out of the chord (the E major triad), touches a tone (c sharp) which does not belong to that triad, and returns again to the chord. It is easy to see why such tones are bound to occur when the melody moves while the same chord sounds on. As we know, the normal way for melody to move is by steps, from tone to neighboring tone on the scale; on the other hand, no two neighboring tones, with the sole exception of the root and the seventh of a seventh chord, belong to the same chord. Thus the very norm of melodic motion means conflict with the chord—a highly fruitful conflict. In the Mozart melody of the last example the first two moves, ♪♪♪ , stay within the chord, in fact, they outline the chord, the B flat major triad; as soon as the stepwise motion starts, every other tone lies outside the chord, is non-harmonic. Every time the melody moves out of the chord a small disturbance is created, there is friction, disagreement between tone and chord, the tone is not where it ought to be, and this "ought not" becomes audible in the tone as a pull in the direction of the next chord tone. Every time the melody finds its way back into the fold of the chord a disturbance is eliminated, order is restored, things are what they ought to be. Thus the progress of the melody from tone to tone is at the same time an alternation, an oscillation between opposite states: order disturbed and order restored. Remotely comparable to the distribution of light and shade on a visual form, the distribution of harmonic and non-harmonic tones is perhaps the most conspicuous single element *shaping* a melody. It is here that the distinction, or lack of distinction, of a melodic idea will most readily show. Nowhere is the master's hand more clearly recognizable than in non-harmonic tones.

The tendency of a non-harmonic tone towards a harmonic tone has nothing to do with the dynamic quality of the tone in the melodic context; in fact, at the surface it supersedes that quality. In the following example, also from a Mozart Piano Concerto, the non-harmonic tones (x) are, from measure to measure, $\widehat{2}, \widehat{3}, \widehat{1}, \widehat{2}$:

In the context of the tone-chord relation, non-harmonic $\widehat{3}$ tends to $\widehat{2}$, non-harmonic $\widehat{1}$ tends to $\widehat{7}$, just as non-harmonic $\widehat{2}$ tends to $\widehat{1}$. In the conflict of tone and chord the greater weight of the chord will always assert itself; it is always the chord which attracts, the tone which is attracted, and never the other way round (not even in a case like

236

where the melody tone is represented by a full chord, and the chord by one single tone).

Stepwise motion generates two types of non-harmonic tones; one in the course of a move away from a chord tone and back to it, ♪♪; the other on the way from one chord tone to another, ♪♪ . Measures 3 and 4 of the Weber tune show both, ♪♪ ; similarly, in the Mozart tune,

The relative significance of these non-harmonic tones varies greatly with their place in the metric pattern. When they occur between beats, at metrically inconspicuous points, they will hardly be recognized for what they are; when they fall on a beat the metric accent will light up the discord. In the 2nd and 3rd measure of the Mozart B flat melody, all beats except the first coincide with non-harmonic tones. Each one of these tones gets a little lift from the beat. Change this to

the sparkle will be gone. The conflict of tone and chord is most outspoken when it is intensified by the full weight of a strong metric accent:

Schubert, Winterreise,
"Der Lindenbaum"

V   I   V

and especially when, in addition, the non-harmonic tone coincides with the entry of a new chord:

Mozart, Clarinet
Quintet, K. 581

I   IV

There is a third type of non-harmonic tone, which originates not from a stepwise motion, but rather from a failure to make the step when it ought to be made, due to a change of chord. For instance:

(from Mozart's *Figaro*).

Had the melody made the move when the harmony moved from I to V, and the move or when V returned to I, it would have remained within the chord. As it defers the move and lingers on, first on e flat, then on f, it separates from harmony; the chord moves away from it, leaving the tone out in the open, a non-harmonic tone. Here again the conflict is the more emphatic as it occurs in the full light of a strong metric accent. The conflict is resolved as the delayed step takes the melody back into the chord.

The three types of non-harmonic tones have their strict parallel in the three types of dissonances arising from the combination of voices in polyphony: neighboring tone, passing tone, suspension. There is the difference, however, that dissonance in polyphony results from a conflict among individuals of the same class, as it were; while in the non-harmonic tone the conflict occurs between representatives of different classes, one of which, the chord, is necessarily the stronger. Yet this very fact engendered a degree of freedom of movement with respect to non-harmonic tones that could not be attained in respect to dissonance in polyphony. Not only do the types freely combine and produce forms that partake of all of them, but the very foundation of the non-harmonic tone as an event between harmonic tones is handled in a very loose fashion; the harmonic tones that supply the frame of reference, as it were, are anticipated, delayed, replaced by substitutes and suppressed altogether, reduced to a merely mental presence. Consider the melody from Verdi's *Aida* quoted earlier:

The extravagant skips into non-harmonic tones, , the jump from one non-harmonic tone to another, , seem the very opposite of the stepwise motion from which the non-harmonic tones are supposed to originate. Yet all this is obviously a free departure from a normal . The melody relies on the power of the chord to provide the binding force which guarantees coherence and meaning to these far-flung moves. Or take a seemingly insignificant detail in the tune of the famous march from the same opera:

The moment in question is : from the harmonic tone c the melody moves to the non-harmonic d flat; it fails to return to c, though, and instead jumps off to another harmonic tone, a flat, leaving the d flat unresolved in the air. Only after this sidestep does it comply with the norm and touch c. But now the move comes too late; the chord has changed from I to V, c has itself become a non-harmonic tone. Substitute for this the innocent : no fame would have attached itself to the tune.

There is of course one way for melody to keep clear of friction with the chords: namely, by limiting itself to movement among chord tones. Stepwise motion will then be practically excluded, the intervals will be such as can be formed by the chord tones. An example (from Weber's *Oberon*):

239

From a purely melodic viewpoint the individual moves of these phrases must be judged anything but normal: skips up and down; even a diminished fifth occurs, ♪♪. The fact that this sounds perfectly normal as we hear it indicates that the purely melodic viewpoint is out of order here. The norm against which such melodies measure their moves is not the scale but the chord. A phrase like ♪♪♪ sounds normal because each tone *is* followed by its next neighbor; to be sure, neighbor not in the scale but in the chord: ♪♪♪ . The diminished fifth sounds normal because both tones of the interval belong to the chord: ♪♪ . It does not seem correct in cases of this type to speak of a co-ordination of melody and harmony: harmony is the thing here, the primary factor; harmony releases melody, the melody is the offspring of the chord.

It is not usual for a melody to restrict itself to chord intervals for any length of time; rather, phrases of chord intervals normally alternate with phrases of stepwise motion involving non-harmonic tones, with the two types tending to balance each other. One instance of the widely followed pattern:

I   V   I

(from Mozart's Piano Concerto in C, K. 467)

We close this chapter with a telling example of the unity of melodic-harmonic thought in a great composer. The melody is sheer triviality; no student would dare to present this to his teacher: ♪♪♪♪♪♪♪ . For fully $5\frac{1}{2}$ measures the tune simply moves up and down the intervals of a triad, ♪♪♪♪ , apparently the tonic triad; this is followed by a brief chromatic passing motion, leading to ♪♪ , outlining the V chord. The harmonic progression is equally trivial: I–V–I–IV–V–I. One fails to see how anything worthwhile and interesting could possibly be achieved by *combining* these two elements. Neither of them could be called a thought. Yet as *one* thing they are indeed a thought, and a most striking and original one, worthy of the genius of the man in whose mind it arose, Verdi:

For the first 3 measures the harmony stays on I, keeping the whole to a minimum of motion. When the melody comes down the second time to a flat, , V sounds: we are set in motion. The next measure brings I again, to the of the melody, but in the 1st inversion, keeping up the tension. Now comes the great surprise: where no one expects it, at the moment when the melody repeats the old chord tone a flat, , the harmony drops away from it: we hear IV, and this leaves the a flat— which was so well embedded in the chord immediately preced- ing—way out in the open territory of non-harmonic tones, a complete stranger to the chord, and in the most acute and unexpected tension against it. What follows shows the composer in complete command of the situation. He does *not* release the tension in a step but instead takes the a flat chromatically to g natural. The melody defies the chord, discourages the idea that importance should be attached to that g flat, passes this tone quickly on the way to e flat of the next measure, $\widehat{2}$ dynam- ically (with chord V), and ultimately to $\widehat{1}$ (I). The bass voice, too, can claim a part in these events. From its perspective it would appear that the surprise IV of measure 6 is merely the consequence of the inexorable logic of the bass progression from $\widehat{1}$ to $\widehat{5}$, , which happens to arrive at g flat just at the right moment: further testimony to the organic interrelation of the parts of the tonal whole.

Epilogue

At the end of a long and not altogether easy road one may well look back and ask oneself: What has been gained in the effort? To what extent have the hopes held out at the beginning been justified? The reader was asked to take part in a search, the search for a listener's knowledge of music. What has been found? In what sense can the knowledge acquired in the process claim to satisfy specifically a listener's—as distinguished from a composer's or a scholar's—desire to know?

As a professional musician I desire to know the *how* of the making of music, the techniques and skills by which a work of the tonal art is brought into being. As a scholar I desire to know the *why*, the reasons, mostly historical reasons, for music's having become what it has become. As a listener who desires to know I am not indifferent to these questions; but they are not central to my interest. For the listener music is not, as for the composer, a thing to be made, nor is it, as for the scholar, a thing that has been made; for him music simply *is*, a naked presence. And in the face of the naked presence one question only remains appropriate: *what* is it? Whether or not he be aware of it, whether or not he articulates the question, what the listener desires to know is ultimately this one thing: What is music? His particular problem turns out to be the most universal. Only knowledge which in some way, explicit or not, falls in line with this trend of questioning can strictly be called a listener's knowledge. And since composers and scholars are listeners, too, must be listeners before becoming makers or students of music, that knowledge cannot be meaningless to them either.

243

Today many people would probably shy away from ever putting such a question. To ask blankly what music is seems to indicate an infantile and obsolete mode of thinking. Has not modern science amply demonstrated the futility of questions of the 'What is . .' type? Physicists, biologists no longer try to tell us *what* matter is, *what* life is; they observe and report on the behavior of material bodies, of living things, under various given or chosen conditions: this sums up their task as they see it. It is true that the advance of modern science coincides with this change of attitude; but it is equally true that the scientific account has helped us to understand better than ever before not only the nature of things but also the meaning of our own questions about them. The 'What is . .' question, the essential question has not been invalidated; it has been transformed. What has been invalidated is merely the search for so-called absolutes, for pat answers to big questions, as if the universe were a riddle for man to crack.

In the most general sense the present book in its limited scope has tried to follow the direction given by modern science. It reports on the behavior of tones under varying conditions of musical context, as observed by an ear capable of grasping musical contexts. However, inasmuch as its subject matter, the musical phenomenon, has no objective existence as science understands it—dynamic tone qualities do not register on any instrument—this is a thoroughly unscientific account; verification by objective means of its statements is out of the question. Still a rational account, an 'objective' description proved possible: a description of music, and of tones in music, as of things existing by themselves, independent of outside factors, doing this and doing that, moving here and moving there, attracting and repelling, developing into this and into that, behaving altogether not like artifacts, the man-made things that after all they are, but rather like things of nature, grown things, living things, with parts and whole interrelated in the way we see it in organisms, strictly subjected to the laws of an all-embracing order, at the same time exhibiting an almost unlimited degree of freedom under these laws, in fact existing by the constant interaction between their freedom and their law—a mode of existence strangely reminiscent of that of man himself. As this description emerged from one source only, the naked presence of music, the knowledge it produces ought to fall in line with the direction of questioning evoked in the listener by that presence. However elementary, restricted, smallish the results of the search may appear if measured against the vastness of the listener's wonder, they should somehow prove not incommensurable with it—as a very small number may be commensurable with a very big one. This at least is what the author hopes to have accomplished.

And where, in all this, is there a place for *emotion,* which so many believe constitutes the very essence of music—so much so, in fact, that music is quite commonly referred to as the language of emotions?

There just is no place for emotion in the context of the essential question. Not because music can be divorced from emotion; it never can, there is no musical experience without emotion, that is to say, there is no way of grasping a musical context, the motion of tones, otherwise than by partaking in it, by inwardly moving with it—and such inward motion we experience as emotion. But the inward motion of the man is one thing, the motion of the tones is quite another; and the latter is the cause of the former, not the other way around. To say that the essential nature of music is emotional is like telling a person who wonders and inquires about fire that it is that which warms him—when it was precisely the fact that it did warm him which moved him to wonder and inquire. This applies to the composer's situation as it does to the listener's: the composer's emotions, too, are the effect, not the cause, of tonal motions, in this instance of the tonal motions which arise in his own mind. Great music is written to realize as yet unrealized inner experiences, not to express those already realized. Richard Wagner in saving himself at the lowest state of disenchantment and dejection by discovering the music of the Meistersinger Prelude may be called here as a highly appropriate witness.

It is obvious that a problem as complex and ramified as that of music and emotion cannot be disposed of in a few cursory sentences of an epilogue. Yet for us to understand the relation of our search to the essential question it is necessary to draw the lines clarifying what belongs where. The very separation of the musical phenomenon from its psychological consequences makes it possible for the essential question to come into proper focus. What is this thing we have been describing, movement of tones in dynamic fields, that it can move man in such a way? Who is man that this almost-nothing, this 'nothing but tones' could become one of his most significant experiences? In a famous line at the end of *Faust* Goethe expressed the thought that all transitory things have the character of metaphor, that is, point beyond themselves, have meaning. Could it be that tone, because it is the most transitory of all things, is therefore the most meaningful? These are clearly no longer musical problems; they are problems of a theory of meaning, problems of philosophy. They cannot be approached, however, except on the basis of an understanding of the elementary nature of musical phenomena such as this book undertook to convey.

It seems that all we can claim to have achieved is the exchange of one question for another, or even less than that, the exchange of a dim to a less obscure form of the same question. The only comfort lies in the suspicion that this is perhaps what the truly wondrous things want us to do: not chase for answers but understand the questions and, implicitly, the questioner.

246

Index*

hymns, 119, 221-22, 234; "Allelujah," 13, 16, 21, 37, 38-40; "Eternity," 24, 37; "Morning Star," 225-26; D major (in St. John Passion), 23, 45, 226-27; E flat major, 63-64; G minor, 62-63

imitation, 141
interplay of tone and time, 119-30; continuous regular subdivision of beat, 120-22; simple duplication of beat, 119-20; uneven subdivision of beat, 122-24
intervals, 64-69; augmented, 66; consonant, 153; defined, 64, 77; described, 65; diminished, 66; dissonant, 153; fourth as consonance or dissonance, 153; harmonic, 189-91; inversion of, 65; major and minor, 66; meaning of, 77-79; natural position of, 79; octave, 25, 26-27; octave complements, 65; perfect, 66, 67; prime, 65f.; ratio of, 67-69, 70 (diagrams, 68, 73); sixth as consonance or dissonance, 153; third as consonance or dissonance, 153; unison, see (intervals), prime

key, defined, 51; fifth defines relationship, 193; movement in a piece, 54-55
key relations, 56-59; importance of fifth, 59; law of, 59; shift of 4 and 7 in minor, 57-58 (diagram, 58); shift of 6 and 2 in minor, 59
key signatures, 52, 54, 58-59 (diagram, 59)

language and music, 17, 18
Lasso, Orlando di, 162

madrigal, 95
Maelzel, Johann, 106
major, 31-34, 36; function of 3, 31; function of 6 and 7, 32; parallel major and minor, 56-57; relative major, 56; triad, 179-81
"Marseillaise," 78
melodic motion, origin of, 186
melody, 11-79, 218-41; change of dynamic center, 44-48; character defined, 64-65; creation of, 38-40; defined, 21, 36; ending of a, 11-12, 19, 20; and harmony, see following entry; relationship between tones, 17; in relation to phrase, 130; skeleton of, 42-43; structure of, 83; as succession of intervals, 64; use of non-harmonic tones, 236
melody and harmony, 172-73, 218-41; elementary progressions, 221-22 (diagram, 221); harmony interprets melody, 222-23, 227-28; polyphonic aspect of, 224; relative pace of, 218-20

Mendelssohn, Felix, 40
meter, 98-136; beat, 99-104, 119-24; beat defined, 100; compound, 116, defined, 100, 115; duple, 104-105, 115-16; group formation, 108-14; group formation, obstruction of, 110-12; organization of, 113-14 (diagram, 113); relations to phrase, 132; triple, 105, 116
metronome, 106-107
Middle Ages, moral concept of consonance and dissonance, 152
minor, 31-34, 34-36; ambiguity of 7-8, 34; ambiguity of 6 and 7, 34-36; change to relative major, 208; elements from major, 35-36; function of 6 and 7, 32; function of 3, 31; parallel major and minor, 56-57; problem of dominant triad, 197; relative minor, 56; triad, 179-81; use of III, 200
mode, 24, 30; Aeolian, 34; Dorian, 33; Ionian, 34; Lydian, 33; medieval, 33-34; Mixolydian, 33; Phrygian, see Phrygian
modulation, see tonality, change of center
monophony, 81-82, 140
motet, 95
motion, contrary, 151; expressed in time wave, 116; harmonic, 200; infinite, 144-47; oblique, 151; parallel, 151; stepwise, 64f.
Mozart, Wolfgang Amadeus, 53, 82, 149n, 162; Cosi fan tutte, 127; Don Giovanni, 127, 129; Figaro, 123, 126, 127, 238; Haffner Symphony, 61; Magic Flute, 137; Piano Concerto in C, 236, 240; Piano Concerto in G, 132; Piano Concerto in B flat, 234-35, 237; Piano Fantasy in C minor, 96; String Quartet in E flat, 62; String Quartet in G, 61; unspecified musical examples, 186, 237
music, atonal, 55-56; beginning of academic study of in America, 6-7; as concept, 17; and contemporary audience, 3; development through consonance-dissonance relationship, 162; as historical discipline, 5-6; and knowledge, conflict of, 5, 7, 8; in relation to emotions, 245-46; repetition in, 87; role of professionals, 8, 9, 243; as theoretical discipline, 5-6
music appreciation, vi

non-harmonic tones, 234-41; defined, 219, 235; parallel to dissonance in polyphony, 238; types of, 237-38
notation of time values, 101-104
number, law of, 69; theory of consonance, 153; and tone, 67-69

Scores

Tape recordings of these scores, at $12.50 per three-reel set, may be ordered from Princeton University Press.

From Schubert, Impromptu, op. 142, No. 3 (cf. text p. 84)

J. S. Bach, Twelve Little Preludes No. 3 in C minor (cf. text p. 84)

Schubert, Impromptu, op. 142, No. 2 (cf. text p. 85)

Schubert, Moment Musical, No. 2 (cf. text p. 88)

From Beethoven, Piano Sonata, op. 13 (cf. text p. 89)

J. S. Bach, Prelude and Fugue in C minor,
The Well-Tempered Clavichord, I (cf. text p. 92)

Fugue

From Chopin, Mazurka, op. 7, No. 1 (cf. text p. 99)

From Schütz, St. Matthew Passion (cf. text pp. 140, 159)*

* See below, p. 33.

From Palestrina, Missa Papae Marcelli (cf. text pp. 142-143)

Kyrie

Gloria

From Haydn, String Quartet, op. 76, No. 3
(cf. text p. 147)

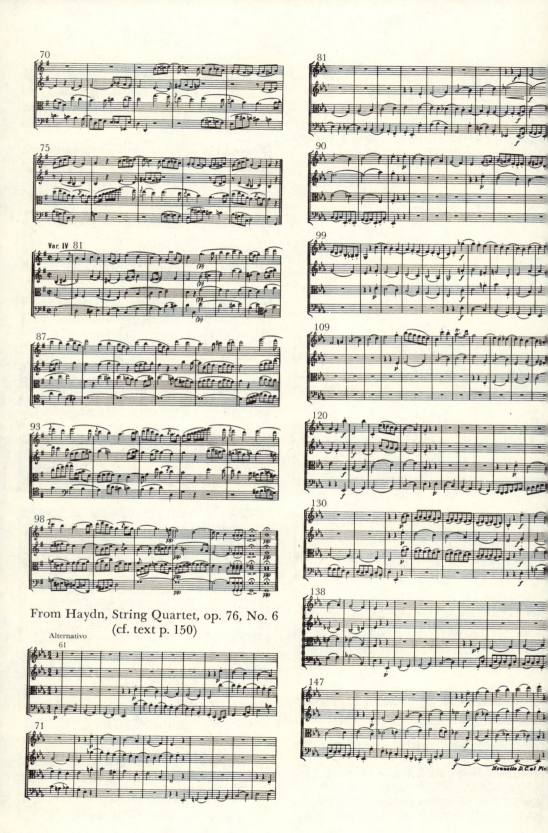

From Haydn, String Quartet, op. 76, No. 6
(cf. text p. 150)

J. S. Bach, Two-part Invention, No. 1 (cf. text p. 165)

From Schubert, Der Mueller und der Bach (cf. text p. 204)*

* See below, p. 34.

* See below, p. 34.

From Schubert, Der Wanderer*
(cf. text p. 207)

Die Son - ne dünkt mich hier so kalt, die
Blü - the welk, das Le - ben alt, und was sie re - den lee - rer Schall, ich bin ein Fremdling
ü - berall.

* See below, p. 34.

From Schubert, Mein! (cf. text p. 210)

Mässig geschwind.

Schubert, Erlkoenig (cf. text p. 214)*

* See below, p. 35.

23   Kind;   er hat   den Kna _ ben   wohl in dem Arm,   er

fz p   *fz p*

28   fasst   ihn si_cher, er hält ihn   warm.

34   Mein Sohn,   was birgst du   so bang dein Ge_sicht?   Siehst,

pp

40   Va _ ter, du   den Erl _ kö _ nig nicht?   den

45   Er _ len _ kö _ nig mit Kron'   und Schweif?   Mein Sohn, es

Vater, mein Vater, und hö - rest du nicht, was Er - len - könig mir lei - se ver -

spricht?   Sei   ruhig,   bleibe ruhig, mein Kind;   in dürren Blättern säuselt der

Wind.   „Willst, fei - ner_ Kna - be, du   mit   mir gehn? mei - ne Töch - ter sol - len dich

war - ten schön; meine Töch - ter_ füh - ren den nächt - lichen Reihn, und   wie - gen und tan - zen und

sin - gen dich ein,   sie   wie - gen und tan - zen und   sin - gen dich ein.‟

Mein

95
Va - ter, mein Va - ter, und siehst du nicht dort Erl - kö - nigs Töchter am dü - stern

101
Ort? Mein Sohn, mein Sohn, ich seh' es ge - nau; es

107
scheinen die al - ten Wei - den so grau.

113
Ich lie - be dich, mich reizt deine schöne Ge - stalt; und bist du nicht wil - lig, so

119
brauch' ich Ge - walt. Mein Va - ter, mein Va - ter, jetzt fasst er mich an!

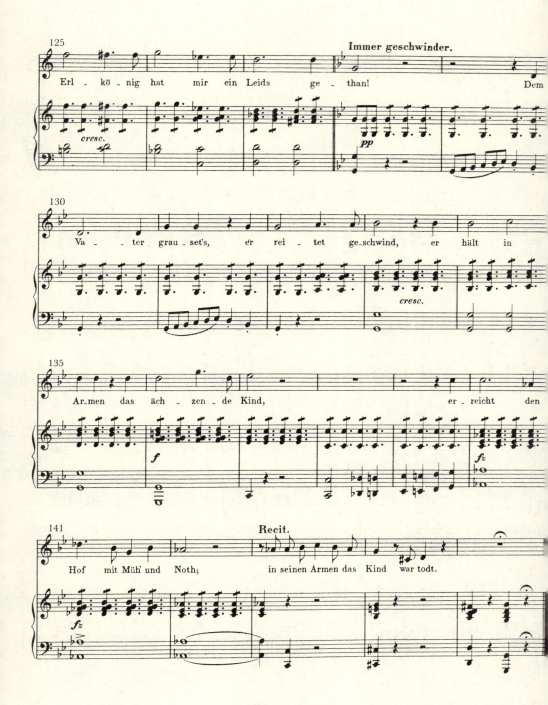

From Schütz, St. Matthew Passion
(Section of Scores, p. 18)

Introitus

Das Leiden unsers Herren Jesu Christi,
wie es beschreibet der heilige
   Evangeliste Matthaeus.

The life of our Lord Jesus Christ,
as told by the holy evangelist Matthew.

Evangelista

Und es begab sich,
da Jesus alle diese Rede vollendet
   hatte,
sprach er zu seinen Jüngern:

And it came to pass,
when Jesus had finished all these
   sayings,
he said to his disciples:

Jesus

Ihr wisset, dass nach zweien Tagen
   Ostern wird,
und des Menschen Sohn wird
   überantwortet werden,
dass er gekreuziget werde.

You know that after two days the
   Passover is coming,
and the Son of man will be delivered
   up
to be crucified.

Evangelista

Da versammleten sich die
   Hohenpriester und Schriftgelehrten,
und die Ältesten im Volk,
in dem Palast des Hohenpriesters,
der da hiess Caiphas,
und hielten Rat,
wie sie Jesum mit Listengriffen und
   töteten.
Sie sprachen aber:

Then the chief priests and the elders of
   the people and the scribes
gathered in the palace of the high
   priest,
who was called Caiaphas,
and took counsel together
in order to arrest Jesus by stealth
and kill him.
But they said:

Hohepriester und Schriftgelehrte

Ja nicht, nicht auf das Fest,
auf dass nicht ein Aufruhr werde
   im Volk.

Not during the feast,
lest there be a tumult among the
   people.

Evangelista

Da nun Jesus war zu Bethanien,
im Hause Simonis, des Aussätzigen,
trat zu ihm ein Weib,
das hatte ein Glas mit köstlichem
   Wasser
und goss es auf sein Haupt,
da er zu Tische sass.
Da das seine Jünger sahen,
wurden sie unwillig und sprachen:

Now when Jesus was at Bethany
in the house of Simon the leper
a woman came up to him with an
   alabaster jar of very expensive
   ointment,
and she poured it on his head,
as he sat at table.
But when the disciples saw it
they were indignant, saying:

Die Jünger Jesu

Wozu dienet dieser Unrat?
Dieses Wasser hätte mocht teuer
   verkauft
und den Armen gegeben werden. . .

Why this waste?
For this ointment might have been sold
   for a large sum,
and given to the poor. . .

From Schubert, Der Mueller und der Bach (The Miller and the Brook)
(Section of Scores, p. 24), translated by Henry S. Drinker

Wo ein treues Herze in Liebe vergeht,
da welken die Lilien auf jedem Beet;
da muss in die Wolken der Vollmund
geh'n,
damit seine Thränen die Menschen
nicht seh'n;
da halten die Englein die Augen sich
zu,
und schluchzen und singen
die Seele zur Ruh'.

When a heart is faithful and dies ever
true,
the lilies all wither, the roses too;
the moon high in heaven no more
appears,
but hides in the cloudbanks that none
see its tears;
the angels are silent, their carolings
cease,
they sob in their sorrow:
"Now rest ye in peace."

From Schubert, Heidenröslein (Heath Rose)
(Section of Scores, p. 25), translated by Henry S. Drinker

Sah ein Knab' ein Röslein steh'n,
Röslein auf der Heiden;
war so jung und morgenschön,
lief er schnell, es nah' zu sehn,
sah's mit vielen Freuden.

On a bush a rosebud grew,
rosebud on the heather;
young and fresh with ruby hue,
wet with early morning dew,
in the glad spring weather.

Röslein, Röslein, Röslein rot,
Röslein auf der Heiden.

Rosebud, rosebud, rosebud red,
rosebud on the heather.

Knabe sprach: Ich breche dich,
Röslein auf der Heiden.
Röslein sprach: Ich steche dich,
dass du ewig denkst an mich,
und ich will's nicht leiden!

Said the lad: I must pick you,
rosebud on the heather.
Said the rose: And if you do,
I will prick you, so we two,
suffer both together!

Und der wilde Knabe brach,
's Röslein auf der Heiden;
Röslein wehrte sich und stach
half ihr doch kein Weh und Ach,
musst' es eben leiden.

But the boy tried once again,
plucked it from the heather;
rosebud pricked his hand in vain,
useless all her woe and pain,
useless altogether.

From Schubert, Der Wanderer (The Wanderer)
(Section of Scores, p. 26), translated by Henry S. Drinker

Die Sonne dünkt mich hier so kalt,
die Blüthe welk, das Leben alt,
und was sie reden, leerer Schall,
ich bin ein Fremdling, überall.

The sun that shines here seems so cold,
the blossoms dry, and life so old;
their speech is alien, empty air,
and I a stranger, everywhere.

From Schubert, Erlkoenig (Erlking)
(Section of Scores, p. 27), translated by Henry S. Drinker

Wer reitet so spät durch Nacht und Wind?	Who rides in the night so late and wild?
Es ist der Vater mit seinem Kind;	It is the father with his young child;
Er hat den Knaben wohl in dem Arm,	The boy lies snug and tight in his arm,
er fasst ihn sicher, er hält ihm warm.	he holds him safely, he keeps him warm.
Mein Sohn, was birgst du so bang' dein Gesicht?	My son, why hide you your face so in fright?
Siehst, Vater, du den Erlkönig nicht?	The erlking, father, there in the night!
den Erllenkönig, mit Kron' und Schweif?	the fearful erlking, with crown and tail!
Mein Sohn, es ist ein Nebelstreif.	My son, 'tis but a vaportrail.
"Du liebes Kind, komm' geh' mit mir,	"You darling child, come go with me,
gar schöne Spiele spiel' ich mit dir,	the flow'rs are fairest there by the sea;
manch' bunte Blumen sind an dem Strand,	so many games you and I will play,
meine Mutter hat manch' gülden Gewand."	and your clothes will all be golden and gay."
Mein Vater, mein Vater, und hörest du nicht,	My father, my father, and did you not hear,
was Erllenkönig mir leise verspricht?	what erlking whispered so soft in my ear?
Sie ruhig, bleibe ruhig, mein Kind;	Now fear not, lie there quiet, and still,
in dürren Blättern säuselt der Wind.	the night wind stirs the trees on the hill.
"Willst, feiner Knabe, du mit mir geh'n?	"O, come, dear boy, come you home with me,
meine Töchter sollen, dich warten schön;	where my daughter waits you, a fair maid she,
meine Töchter führen den nächtlichen Reihn,	with her sisters dancing the whole night long,
und wiegen und tanzen und singen dich ein."	they'll rock you to sleep with their dancing and song."
Mein Vater, mein Vater, und siehst du nicht dort,	My father, my father, O now see you not,
Erlkönig's Töchter am dustern Ort?	the erlking's daughters in that dark spot?
Mein Sohn, mein Sohn, ich seh' es genau,	My son, my son, it is as I say;
es scheinen die alten Weiden so grau.	'tis only the willows, olden and gray.
"Ich liebe dich, mich reigt deine schöne Gestalt,	"I love you so, and want you to go there with me,
und bist du nicht willig, so brauch' ich Gewalt."	and go you not willing, by force let it be."
Mein Vater, mein Vater, jetzt fasst er mich an,	My father, my father, he gave me a blow;
Erlkönig hat mir ein Leids gethan!	Erlking has hurt me and bids me go!
Dem Vater grauset's, er reitet geschwind,	The father shudders, he rides fast and wild,
er hält in Armen das ächzende Kind,	he holds yet tighter his weak moaning child;
erreicht den Hof mit Müd und Noth;	he reaches home in fear and dread;
in seinen Armen das Kind war todt!	and in his arms there the child is dead!

Victor Zuckerkandl

VICTOR ZUCKERKANDL was born in Vienna on July 2, 1896. He studied music theory and piano in Vienna, conducted operas and concerts there and in other cities, and received his Ph.D. in 1927 at Vienna University. From 1927 to 1933 he was music critic for newspapers in Berlin and taught music theory and appreciation in Vienna during the years 1934 to 1938. Dr. Zuckerkandl came to the United States in 1940, and for two years was a member of the music department at Wellesley College. In 1942–44 he worked as a machinist in a Boston defense plant. He was on the faculty of the New School, in New York, teaching courses on music theory, during 1946–48. Under a grant-in-aid from the American Philosophical Society, Dr. Zuckerkandl developed a music course especially for the liberal arts student. Instead of being a technical, survey, or appreciation course, it dealt with the nature, structure, and significance of the tonal language which had been used by great composers of the past. After he joined the music department of St. John's College (Annapolis, Maryland) in 1948, the course was adopted as requisite for liberal arts students at the College. Dr. Zuckerkandl's book *The Sense of Music* (Princeton, 1959), presented this approach to a larger audience.

Dr. Zuckerkandl twice held a three-year Bollingen Fellowship. The first award enabled him to write another work, *Sound and Symbol: Music and the External World,* first published in 1956. A second volume, *Sound and Symbol: Man the Musician,* which he finished before his death, will be published subsequently in Bollingen Series. Under the second Bollingen Fellowship, Dr. Zuckerkandl worked on a study of the creative process in music as exemplified in the Notebooks of Beethoven. His other publications included contributions to the *Harvard Dictionary of Music;* a book, *Vom musikalischen Denken* (Zurich, 1964); and articles in British, German, and Swiss journals.

Beginning in 1960, Dr. Zuckerkandl was an annual lecturer at the Eranos Conference held each August in Ascona, Switzerland, and his papers appeared in the *Eranos Jahrbücher* (Zurich). From 1964, when he retired from St. John's College, until his death on April 24, 1965, he resided in Ascona and lectured at the C. G. Jung Institute in Zurich.